The Musical Artistry of Rap

The Musical Artistry of Rap

MARTIN E. CONNOR

Foreword by KYLE ADAMS
Afterword by ILAN ZECHORY

McFarland & Company, Inc., Publishers
Jefferson, North Carolina

LIBRARY OF CONGRESS CATALOGUING-IN-PUBLICATION DATA

Names: Connor, Martin E., 1990– author.
Title: The musical artistry of rap / Martin E. Connor ; foreword by Kyle Adams ; afterword by Ilan Zechory.
Description: Jefferson, North Carolina : McFarland & Company, Inc., Publishers, 2018. | Includes bibliographical references and index.
Identifiers: LCCN 2017055843 | ISBN 9780786498987 (softcover : acid free paper) ∞
Subjects: LCSH: Rap (Music)—Analysis, appreciation. | Rap (Music)—History and criticism.
Classification: LCC ML3531 .C663 2018 | DDC 782.421649—dc23
LC record available at https://lccn.loc.gov/2017055843

BRITISH LIBRARY CATALOGUING DATA ARE AVAILABLE

ISBN (print) 978-0-7864-9898-7
ISBN (ebook) 978-1-4766-3043-4

© 2018 Martin Connor. All rights reserved

No part of this book may be reproduced or transmitted in any form or by any means, electronic or mechanical, including photocopying or recording, or by any information storage and retrieval system, without permission in writing from the publisher.

Front cover images © 2018 apartment/jepard/iStock

Printed in the United States of America

McFarland & Company, Inc., Publishers
 Box 611, Jefferson, North Carolina 28640
 www.mcfarlandpub.com

To everyone, everywhere,
for everything they ever did for me

Acknowledgments

To Kanye, Sheila, Bill, Will, Joe, Molly, Harry, Kate, Satori, Jean, Karen, Kate, Sally, John, Jack, Stacy, Bette, Justin, Kyle, CJ, Sohaib, Will, Dan, Kevin, Jim, Matt, Guthrie, Harry, Yu-Hui, Danya, Tom, Matt, Allan, Kevin, Bo, Meg, Erin, Terry, PJ, Dan, Tom, Pat, Ann, Anthony, Shah, Liz, Anthony, Mikhail, Chris, Adam, Diran, Jean, Sabrina, Akash, Talib, Jon, Chris, Tupac, Marshall, Harry (again!), Karen, Tim, Rivers, Franklin, Liam, Lauryn, Wyclef, Prakazrel, Cedric, Omar, Tariq, Calvin, Reuben, Katrina, Justin, Omar, Corey, Dennis, Robert, Tony, Harry, Austin, Niko, Marvel, LE, Elsa, Claude, Samuel, Johann Sebastian, George, John, Paul, Rose Marie, Dewey, Richard, Eric, Karen, Bertrand, Arvo, Nasir, Kendrick, André, Trevor, Wayne, Jayceon, Curtis, Andre, Yasiin, God, and Adam: thank you!

Table of Contents

Acknowledgments vi
Foreword by Kyle Adams 1
Introduction 3

1. Rhythm 11
2. Melody 64
3. Motivic Development 78
4. Structure and Performance Practice 108
5. Texture and Orchestration 144
6. Instrumentalism 166
7. Masters of the Form 176

Epilogue 195
Afterword by Ilan Zechory 197
Appendix: Songs Analyzed 199
Chapter Notes 202
Bibliography 205
Index 209

Foreword
by Kyle Adams

In the past fifteen years, scholarship on rap music has grown exponentially. Musicologists, music theorists, ethnomusicologists, and scholars from a variety of non-musical disciplines have all found rap to be fertile ground for research. This is hardly surprising; rap is one of the few truly new art forms to have emerged in the past half-century, and attempting to understand its musical structure is exciting, challenging, and rewarding for the generation of scholars who grew up listening to it.

Martin Connor is one such scholar, and his work promises to address the challenges of hip-hop analysis head on. His enthusiasm for the music is limitless, and he clearly knows a wide variety of songs from different artists and different time periods. Moreover, his work celebrates the differences inherent in rappers' approaches: Connor's goal in analyzing rap music is not to smooth out stylistic differences but to explore them; to dig deep and understand how and why rappers craft their unique sounds.

Along the way, Connor has hit upon a unique approach to the vexing problem of rap transcription. In his view, transcription serves to archive rap performances, not necessarily to make them reproducible. While his system of noctuplet notation might at first seem a bit cumbersome to read, it nevertheless proves to be an effective way to transmit and compare the nuances of hip-hop rhythm and articulation. His idiosyncratic system allows him to highlight rhythmic correspondences and differences between individual verses and individual artists in novel and thought-provoking ways.

The Musical Artistry of Rap offers a multi-faceted look at hip-hop music. Connor explores rap many angles, discussing rhythm (naturally), melody, motive, articulation, and more. He also does not shy away from experimenting with all sorts of different methodologies. He has assimilated and drawn from much of the existing scholarship on rap, and thus approaches rap music from a number of analytical perspectives, each time explaining why he feels a given approach is relevant for a given topic and demonstrating what sorts of analytical conclusions he feels are possible.

This book was written with a deep love and respect for rap music. I imagine that those who share this love and respect—music theorists, scholars, even rappers and producers—will approach it just as eagerly as I did.

Kyle Adams (Ph.D. CUNY) is a professor at the Jacobs School of Music, Indiana University Bloomington, and chair of the Department of Music Theory. His research is on 16th century and hip-hop music. His "On the Metrical Techniques of Flow in Rap Music" (Music Theory Online, 2009) is frequently cited.

Introduction

This musicological study is a wide-ranging, corpus-based empirical survey of 135 individual songs by 56 different rap artists, using compiled music transcriptions, that analyzes these performers' oeuvres with a diverse array of pre-existing analytical techniques, applied by musicologists for the understanding of other musics for centuries.[1] In this way, it builds the empirical argument that the modern rapping idiom, when considered as a vocal genre, constitutes a highly-developed synthesis of radically complicated rhythms, intonational systems, motivic developments, song structures, performance practices, textures, orchestrations, and instrumentalism.[2] These adjectives are not meant as affirmative or positive value judgments of the worth of rap, but only as comparisons by which rap can be better understood within a wider context of all vocalizing styles, such as the singing style of common practice period classical music, or the sprechstimme of Arnold Schoenberg. The final chapter is a capstone on those first six chapters that summarizes the earlier discussion by assembling the previous quantitative pieces of evidence into broad, qualitative takeaways about the individual oeuvres of critically-acclaimed and popularly-acclaimed rappers, such as Kanye West.

As a result, it is a direct response to the wonderful body of work supplied by Dr. Kyle Adams, currently of Indiana University. While Dr. Adams posits Adam Krims as the rap analyzer pioneer in his own 2016 article "The musical analysis of hip-hop,"[3] this author would, in turn, assign that position to the adjudicator himself. Since it is of a kind with much of the work to come in the ensuing chapters, Dr. Adams' nuanced, bottom-up empirical approach has been more fruitful for the generation of my own work, rather than Krims' top-down, taxonomic approach. I am also greatly indebted into the motivation and inspiration I have received from my readings of and interactions with Dr. Guthrie Ramsey, one of the few other scholars who has approached the music of rap with the same level of appreciation, understanding, and enthusiasm as Dr. Adams.

Besides Adams' own parsing of rap studies into categories "Krims" and "other," I would posit my own dichotomy, dividing rap studies into the "novel" and the "traditional." The novel category of rap studies generates new methods of analysis for understanding rap musicologically, creating new techniques and approaches with each subsequent article or book. Studies within this category include much of Krims' 2000 title "Rap music and the poetics of identity," where the author relies on a subgeneric, qualitative taxonomy for rap melodies, in the manner of *creatio ex nihilo*. Another example is the utilization of statistical and linguistic methodologies for the analysis of flow in Kendrick Lamar's 2015 track "Momma" by Dr. Mitchell Ohriner, conducted in a 2016 presentation to the Society of Music Theory Pop Music Interest Group.

Traditional rap studies, however, attempt to apply the same methodologies that musicologists have used for centuries to understand music, such as rhythmic transcription, instrumental classification, and even voice-leading graphs. Studies in the latter category includes Adams' own 2008 article, "On the Metrical Techniques of Flow in Rap Music," as well as the excellent work of Paul Edwards' and his transcribed diagrams from studies like 2009's "How to Rap." Within this category, this present work at hand can also be found. As a result, traditional technical terms and phraseology as diverse as passagio, tessitura, triplet, augmentation, diminution, polyrhythm, additive rhythm, metric modulation, homophony, cover, remix, standard, rondo, freestyle, and more can all be found in the pages to come. Thus, the general hypothesis I herein attempt to falsify or verify through specific proof is that the nature of rap contains a minimum of dissimilarity to previous musics, and a maximum of similarity.

This posited dichotomy reveals that the epistemological point from which all musicological studies on rap depart is an assumption that rap is either fundamentally similar to previous musics, or that rap is fundamentally unlike previous musics. Because he summarizes the competing modes of historical thinking that led to this clash, and because his eloquently-stated aims dovetail so well with my own, the 2016 article by Dr. Mitchell Ohriner, "Metric Ambiguity and Flow in Rap Music," may now be quoted at length:

> ... [W]hen music theorists first began publishing studies of popular music, scholars from other disciplines ... took issue with music theory's primary focus on structures of melody and harmony (McClary & Walser, 1990; Shepherd, 1991; Covach, 1999).... [I]mporting methods of analysis designed for older genres, music theorists

allegedly both missed the point of the music and furthered colonialist agendas (Middleton, 1990, p. 105; Frith, 1987, p. 145).... Even at that time music theory was not as myopic as its detractors maintained.... Because scholars ... have addressed the digital representation of pitch, both as low-level audio features and symbolic chord structures ... it is unsurprising that the first corpus analyses of popular music would start by addressing those features.

Of course, the novel and traditional approaches are frequently combined across the work of the same scholar, and sometimes, even, within the very same article, as in the case of Dr. Kyle Adams work. Additionally, neither of these two categories is in itself better, or even more helpful, than the other, it must be noted. However, the places to which such separate characterizations of rap have historically been taken by observers certainly do have quite different consequences in the wider discourse. Accordingly, they constitute the reasons for why I have consciously decided to take an extremely traditional approach to rap music here.

The assimilation of a new musical genre into specific demographic, socioeconomic, and classist positions within society has played out repeatedly in the past, and is always ongoing. Most relevant to rap's case, this process played out in a particularly explosive manner at the advent of jazz music in the late 1800s. Just like rap, jazz was codified and systemized by members of the United States' African-American community. Coming as it did from a lower socioeconomic class, the musical establishment of the time, made up of its schools, institutions, and concert halls, was predisposed to look askance at it.

This is established by many scholarly investigations that have been conducted in the decades since. In a monograph that goes on to argue the opposite conclusion of his referents, James Lincoln Collier summarizes the prevalent scholarly thinking at his time, in 1988, on the early reception of jazz by the White American mainstream:

> Neil Leonard, in his highly regarded *Jazz and White Americans*, says, "at first almost all the statements reported in the press condemned jazz." Sidney Finkelstein, in one of the best books on jazz from the 1940s, says, "It was a social, communal people's music, and it was a ghetto music." Whitney Balliett says that jazz had been "ignored or misunderstood for its forty-year life" in the United States.[4]

It seems that many commentators in the early 20th century were everywhere ready to lament jazz as not only bad music, but as a harbinger of immorality as well, in rhetoric that's reminiscent of the modern world's culture wars over rap.

That cold reception of a marginalized community's unique art form into society at-large historically echoes the shock waves that have been sent throughout society over the past few decades. Indeed, a similar wave of apocalyptic reactions have likewise greeted the genre of rap since its arrival in the 1970s. Without the serious defense of rap by a scholarly community that promoted this idiom as constituting a highly-developed synthesis of incredibly diverse approaches to all aspects of music, the sounds of rap music were denigrated by societal commentators with large media platforms. Any onlooker who truly loves this music, such as this author, could never stand by and abide such putdowns, while simultaneously conceiving a possible solution: an empirical investigation of rap along purposefully-traditional lines.

Accordingly, it was the complicit silence of a majority of the musical community outside of rap artists and fans, made up of performers, composers, and scholars, that enabled the perpetuation of an unchallenged characterization of rap as alien, foreign, and, thus, bad. This scholarly dismissal of rap enabled the resultant material damage to this inherently-constructive music, whether through the racist censorship and temporary outright ban on 2 Live Crew's 1989 album *As Nasty as They Wanna Be* in 1990, or through the indictment of artists like N.W.A. in the court of public opinion by means of misrepresentative missals from police authorities like the F.B.I.[5] These views have even been espoused by rap artists themselves, such on The Roots' 1999 song "Act Won (Things Fall Apart)," from their album *Things Fall Apart*, or their 1996 song "Intro," from their album *Illadelph Halflife*. On both of these tracks, a lack of appreciation for rap records as being either valuable commercial phenomena or valuable artistic phenomena is decried by rap luminaries like Harry Allen.

These negative outcomes are, indeed, directly related to the lack of a scholarly defense of rap in the face of societal reactions to what are, at the root of it, musical techniques that remain largely impenetrable to everyday laypeople. A lack of discussion about the positive musical value of rap was a direct contributor to the kind of societal resistance to an art form that, un-coincidentally, first sprang from the minority communities of America in the 1970s.[6] For all of these reasons, a book that thoroughly explores the view that rap is essentially like previous kinds of music in its technical aspects is not just desirable, but necessary. Certain writers, like Bertrand Russell, in his critique of pragmatism in the final chapter of his 1945 title "A History of Western Philosophy," are understandably uneasy about allowing us to judge our ascertainment of truth by its social consequences. However, such a justifiable wariness of preconceived bias towards certain findings can be tempered by forthrightness and openness about individual philosophies that might lead to such bias, and accordingly create more societal good than might happen through isolated analysis. This societal contribution would be enhance by not just generating new knowledge for new knowledge's own sake, but by generating truly useful, life-affirming knowledge, which is the responsible scholar's task.[7] By making the personal reasons for an initial assumption clear, and basing evidence on a standard of proof that would be the same for any other empirical study, responsible musicology can therefore not just increase the public body of knowledge on the rap genre, but also work to fill in the void of anxiety and depression in many people's life that is currently restructuring the modern world at a frightening pace. In fact, empirical psychological studies have documented rap and hip-hop's ability to help cure depression, according to a study by a group of Cambridge psychologists that was recently published in The Lancet Psychiatry.[8]

This is not the identification of a Marxist bogeyman. Although it would eventually grow to become the single most widely consumed genre of music, a deep-seated cultural resistance to the rap genre can even still be viewed in certain media channels.[9] A 2013 article in *The Wall Street Journal* by Juan Williams decries the supposed differences between African-American music made at the time of Martin Luther King, Jr.'s 1963 "I Have a Dream" speech in Washington, D.C., and the alleged messages of the music made by African-Americans today. As he says, "The emotional uplift of the monumental march is a universe of time away from today's degrading rap music—filled with the n-word, bitches, and 'hoes' [sic]—that confuses and depresses race relations in America now." While focusing on one 2013 song from a rapper he criticizes by name, Jay-Z, Williams ignores other empowering songs by the same artist, such as "Minority Report," which attempted to bring attention and awareness to the ongoing plight of New Orleans citizens, even more than a year after the devastation of Hurricane Katrina was thought to have receded in the minds of many middle Americans.

Another disheartening results of this scholarly blind spot came from no less a transgressor than our nation's judicial system. In the *New York Times* article "Seeking Clues to Gangs and Crime, Detectives Monitor Internet Rap Videos," the authors detail how New York City police departments have been following rap music videos online for evidence in order to catch criminals. Yet this policing tactic, which misreads and misinterprets conventions of the rap genre, has never been instituted for other kinds of music, like rock or country. The fact that this civil critique from police departments came as late as 2014 is no salve for the burns of rap genre's adherents who feel slighted. In another troubling move, judges and courts have been found to admit rap lyrics, hypothetical artistic creations, as concrete evidence, as in the 2014 Louisiana trial of Torence "Lil Boosie" Hatch or New Jersey's Vonte Skinner.

President Barack Obama himself was involved in his own rap-related controversy when First Lady Michelle Obama invited Chicago rapper Common to perform at the White House in 2011. The administration was attacked by critics and the right-wing media for supporting Common, a supposedly "controversial" and "vile" rapper. But Common's real message at the small concert was specifically against violence, as he performed such lyrics that called for outreach and support for victims of gun violence. The outcry against Common showed that some news outlets were skeptical of the genre as a whole when they lumped this particular rapper, renowned in the rap community for his politically conscious messages, into a supposedly uniform group of gangsters and thugs. There was little similar protest against past White House guests like musician James Brown in 2001, who, unlike Common, has been convicted of multiple crimes that involved drugs, weapons, and domestic violence.

Coupled with this dereliction, though, is the unavoidable certainty that, as a new type of music, rap seems to have recently assumed a position of arbiter alongside the musical establishment's other gatekeepers. New York rapper Jay-Z performed at Carnegie Hall in 2012, the hallowed venue of world premieres by an illustrious list of classical composers that includes Dvořák, Bartók, Copland, Britten, Ives, Barber, and Schoenberg. In 2016, a Princeton musicologist named Caroline Shaw, having won the same Pulitzer Prize in music as Copland, Barber, George Crumb, Elliott Carter, Virgil Thomson, Charles Ives, John Adams, and Steve Reich, was tapped by Kanye West to appear on his 2016 album, *The Life of Pablo*. In 2015, Lin Manuel-Miranda, the composer and star of the smash-hit Hip Hop musical "Hamilton," won one a MacArthur "Genius" Award, thereby joining a winner's circle that already included masters like Milton Babbitt, Ornette Coleman, and John Zorn.

This contemporary moment in musical history, then, affords an almost invaluable opportunity to widely survey rap music along its technical lines, in order to try and define the essence that makes it so widely popular. This book is just such a wide-ranging, empirical survey.

This technical reflection on rap will be centered around rap's interaction with, and approaches to, the aspects of music that are embedded in every type of music, no matter the genre. All music ever made can be parsed along the lines of how it interacts with the ideas of melody, rhythm, motivic development, structure, performance practice, texture, orches-

Introduction

tration, and instrumentalism. The following chapters are accordingly divided into separate orientations that each deal with one of those major aspects, or two, if the pair is sufficiently intertwined by the norms of rap. The interplay and interworking of all of these musical aspects are then discussed as a whole through the work of individual rappers in this book's final chapter, which is an extended, objective discussion of who the most musical rappers might be.

As just one example, the rhythm chapter will make use of traditional music notation's visual representation of melody in order to allow us to better digest the rhythmic results of certain rappers' performances. What we'll find, specifically, is a varied rhythmic land of duplets, yes, but also triplets, sextuplets, complex time signatures, double-time feels, metric modulation, and more.

As delicate societal debates over issues like abortion, mass incarceration, policing brutality, and censorship of free speech in rap lyrics only intensifies in our contemporary time, it is now more crucial than ever that we re-orient ourselves towards the facts. It's my hope that the present title might point arguments over rap's suitability back towards its true center: the fact that rap, above all, *is* art, and so is accordingly fully deserving of the respect and the seriousness that have typically accorded to the other mediums that have likewise earned that exulted distinction, in full and without question, even if—*especially if*—opposing sides shall still all come to different conclusions at the end of such debate.

1

Rhythm

Like many of the other musics that have emerged from the African-American community in the United States—whether blues, rock, or jazz—rap's own engagement with rhythm is of the foremost importance in its musical textures. As a preliminary comment, rap's views on rhythms, so to speak, might be summarized as always, for the most part, constituting the main deciding factor in any of the genre's musical textures. This structural emphasis on rhythm might be considered akin to Western classical music's own integral approach to polyphonic harmony. To an extent that is simply not found in many other genres of music, rappers are much more prone to explore rhythmic areas in music that have rarely been foregrounded in musical textures previously, as seen in these vocalists' extreme expressive rhythmic delays. In addition, a rapper who predominantly uses only one type of flow throughout their entire oeuvre will often be dismissed by rap fans as being one-dimensional, or simply unskilled. Over the course of the meteoric rise of their favorite genre towards widespread domination of the world's recording charts, rap fans have simply gotten used to being rewarded with a diversity of rhythmic expression from those vocalists who are considered of to be of only secondary importance in the genre.

A comprehensive investigation of transcriptions of the rhythmic melodies of a few rappers, such as Eminem, will bear out many of these assertions.

The Purposes of Transcription

A wide-ranging, general survey of this type is a straightforward way to take a quick measure of rap's various approaches to the kinds of rhythms that the genre contains within itself. The strongest reason that speaks for the use of this coming transcription system is the fact that it can account for any and all of rappers' various rhythmic techniques that will be documented herein—polyrhythms, rhythmic trailing, extreme subdivisions of the beat, polyphony, and so on. That goal can be achieved if, as in the following, rap scholars eschew the use of notated rap designed along the lines of what I call compositional purposes, and focus on the use of transcribed rap that has been designed along the lines of archival or cataloguing purposes. Although both purposes behind transcription make use of the same materials, what those materials are in themselves thought to be communicating to us will soon be seen to be quite different.

Music notation for compositional purposes is a system of notation whose norms and assumptions are crafted for the purposes of the performance of the music in a time and place that is different from the moment it was composed, by performers who are not the same instrumentalists that performed it. Music notation for archival, or cataloguing, purposes is a system of notation whose norms and assumptions are crafted for the purposes of capturing a musical performance that has already been executed as accurately as possible. The difficulties in establishing a standardized form of notation for capturing rap has largely been a result of the confusion of these two purposes of transcription. This arose because, although both purposes of transcriptions make use of the same raw materials (staves, systems, note heads, subdivision groupings, and all of the other symbolic trappings of notation), the assumptions behind such documentation are radically different; oftentimes, diametrically opposed. Somewhat counterintuitively, these dualistic approaches to the purposes of transcription can both be understood by comparing what each leaves unsaid. Compositional notation leaves mostly un-described such sonic parameters as specific metronome markings, percussive pitch, empirically-defined volume levels, and so on. These are the gaps that archival notation can fill in: since the performance has already been executed, an a posteriori transcriber can, in theory, define all of those unspoken gaps with the greatest exactitude. Thus, rather than shying away from trying to document rap for political or non-existent metaphysical reasons, all that was needed was a use of the same tools for different purposes. This is, in fact, the reason for which so many young music students take so long to appreciate differentiated performances of the same masterworks, or why so many young jazz performers can balk at the dearth of information presented in the performance of standards: they have yet to appreciate the different purposes to which notation can be put. Standards leave much unsaid so that the performers can maximally fill in the gaps with their own individualistic creativity in their continuation of an historical dialogue; Western classical compositions leave as little unsaid as possible, because the latter's own ideal largely continues to be that of the suffering Romantic auteur, and so the resultant differences from one performance of the same piece to the next are much smaller than those found in genres like jazz. As a small example, a compositionally-notated piece with a single-line stave meant for a percussion instrument is telling us that the specific manifestation of a notated-impetus is left to the discretion of the performer; an archivally-notated piece with a single-line stave meant for a percussion instrument is, conversely, telling us that that part of this previous musical performance is too unstandardized to be captured by Western music notation.

When notation is utilized for purposes of accuracy (as in archiving), and not for performance (as in composing), then the use of many extant but unusual norms in the system at hand here, such as noctuplet groupings, will be seen not only as not being unnecessary, but as even being demanded by stated scholarly goals. In this coming example of archival notation, those unspoken gaps can largely be entirely filled in by the transcriber with the corresponding amount of resources to do so, and anything left untouched is not unimportant, but simply being saved for a point in time when analytical tools have caught up to it.

The only reason that rap has not yet been documented in-depth in the form of sheet music notation isn't because it isn't possible, due to rhythmic complexity, or any kind of such inherent problem. The reason is that rap scholars have tried to apply compositional understanding to what is, in itself, an archival problem. This can all be understood in the light of a comparison of this rap notation with the more traditional conventions of Western music notation.

Consider, for example, the following music transcription of bars 165–173 from Eminem's 2014 song "Rap God." As the notation to come will show, Eminem's rhythms in this climactic section of music consist almost exclusively of the following speedy rhythm, repeated a full eight times. This image will be followed afterwards by a short explanation of this transformation of the Western music notation system into an adapted form that is able to encapsulate rap music's unique technical aspects, such as its lack of scalar melodies:

An example of Eminem's presto rhythms at bar 165 on "Rap God."

The notation above does *not* tell us, for example, that Eminem was "thinking" in terms of noctuplets when he wrote this verse. Instead, archival transcription is all presentation, and never interpretation: it does not reveal compositional methods to us, as the tracing of a tone row in duodecaphonic music might, but only tells us what the music *is*. The interpretation is left up to the scholar once they have internalized the facts that such notation presents to us.

Transcribing Rap

To sum up the discussion so far: this particular adaptation has been developed with the goal of creating a notational system for rap that captures its rhythms with accuracy that is so absolute that it allows a true comparison of this genre's melodies with the infinite amount of other types of music that have, for centuries, been represented with such familiar staves and note heads. This goal is achieved by retaining certain established norms of Western music notation with regards to rhythm, while largely declining to preserve the more traditional system's own absolute treatment of pitch. For example, if the reader considers the above notation, they will notice that there is actually just one long, horizontal line on which the note heads of individual musical attacks and impetuses appear. Because the norms of rap itself demand such a reduction for the scholarly purposes as heretofore stated, a more in-depth investigation of such norms is now demanded.

This single-line stave has been simplified from the more traditional form of sheet music that has transcriptions on 5-line staves, as with the bass or treble clef, in order to encompass the unique system of non-scalar, intonational pitch that most rap melodies abide by. Throughout the time of the development and codification of Western music notation, most of the musical compositions that included vocal performances—such as the melody of a Mozart aria, or a Schubert song—followed the well-defined notes of a musical scale. These classical music melodies rarely deviated from strict adherence to singing notes that could be found only in the 13-note chromatic scale. Once the standard frequency of the A below middle C had been established at 440 Hz, the amount of identifiable pitches available to vocalist performers in performance at concerts was restricted in practice even further.

The individual pitches that rappers rap, on the other hand, do not abide by any such traditionally-identifiable musical scale. Instead, the pitches of each note that a rapper pronounces are much less well-defined in mathematical or physical terms. As a result, the specific frequencies that a rapper raps in his or her melody have a musical effect that is much more similar to the timbral consequences of a percussion instrument, such as a snare drum. A snare drum sound is not heard as constituting any integral element of a tonal musical scale, such as C major or E minor. However, it nevertheless retains musical importance because of the more-generalized sonic and aural effect that it has on the ear—in very general terms, an emphasizing, underlining one. The rapped syllables of this genre's lyricists, even though they aren't created by a drum set, thus still manage to impart a similarly-timbral, impression on a listener's ear. This fact might account for the aggressive or rebellious tinge that colors many of this genre's main poetic themes, whether those themes themselves are inherently given to aggression and rebellion (such as political struggle), or not (such as romantic break-ups).

The pitches of rappers' melodies don't draw a quantitative melodic or harmonic significance from their position within a mathematically-defined musical scale's inherent tonality, such as the tonic note A in A major that begins in a certain octave with a frequency of 440 Hz. Indeed, rappers may rap such notes, but they are not afterwards interpreted in a scalar, tonal manner by listener's (i.e., as possibly being imbued with the function of a dominant that has a natural tendency to lead towards a tonic). Indeed, while rapper's might sing in such scalar patterns, these vocalizations within the genre are rather rare, and, in any event, might be said to constitute singing instead of rapping, resulting in a contradiction in terms.

Instead, the notes of rappers, when measured in frequency, draw their musical significance from relative comparisons among themselves. Just one example of this non-absolute understanding of rappers' own intonational pitch system would consist of a comparative test that results in evaluations of relative melodic height. Simply put, a straightforward comparison of two consecutive notes in a certain rap melody would be performed, after the two note's own distinct frequencies are described as being either ascending in pitch, or descending in pitch. This baseline rising or falling would then be matched and compared with the traditional, corresponding theories of the functional results of such intervallic leaps, as understood in the most fundamental way possible.

A specific example of such a comparative test will be helpful here. If, for example, a particular rapper's melody were to begin by slowly but steadily lowering its pitch over the course of its opening four bars, this should be heard as a decrease in dramatic tension that briefly suggests to the learned listener the possibility of a closing melodic cadence, which would itself be interpreted in light of the specific manner in which the rapper concluded this descent. This, perhaps, is the most empirical evaluation that is able to be clearly stated, to date, in which rap's non-scalar intonation is understood in terms of traditional aspects of contour, pitch, and structure. A specific example of such a study will be exposited in a following chapter.

In order to not confuse perceptions of the rap genre's prevailing system of intonation, then, the traditional stave in the transcriptional system used to represent Eminem's rhythms on "Rap God" above has been simplified to include only one horizontal staff line, instead of the conventional five. This does not indicate that a rapper is rapping the same pitch over and over, but, instead, that Western musical notation, as developed over the past several centuries, is so restrictive with regards to intonation that it cannot accommodate the frequencies found in rappers' own melodies. In this manner, this particular adaptation of Western music notation for the purposes of rap simply constitutes no more than yet another chapter in the evolution of this system towards the accurate representation of percussive elements like snare drums or bass drums. Notations for those instruments reduce the norms of Western music notation with regards to pitch in a likewise manner, while also still retaining its essential approach towards the representation of rhythm.

As mentioned previously, Western music notation's system for capturing rhythm is the most important element that is preserved in this new, rap-oriented adaptation. This is fully in evidence in the above transcription of Eminem's presto rhythms on "Rap God," as this system still relies on Western notation's own system of divisive rhythm.

A divergence occurs, however, in this system's normative utilization of noctuplet groupings for the rhythms of rap. These noctuplet groupings—a re-division of eight 8th notes in a 4/4 time signature into nine 8th notes—are not meant to be taken as an indication that the composers of these raps were "thinking" in terms of noctuplets when writing their music.

Compositional Versus Archival Transcribing

There are many reasons to resist these kinds of mechanical conclusions that might be able to be very constructively drawn when considering the conventional system of Western music notation, looking as similar as it does to this rap one. First of all, such a characterization of the rap composition process would largely be meaningless. This is because, unlike the method of composer-to-performer transmission that governed musical dialogue in the West for the past 1,000 years or so, the performer of a rap and that rap's composer are almost always the same specific personage. Even in instances where this is not true—known in the rap genre as "ghost-writing"—the use of oral, not written, transmission is utilized for communicating how a verse or chorus should be performed. A composer asking a separate performer to execute even the very same rhythmic noctuplets in supplied sheet music represents far different purposes and goals than these transcriptions being considered currently. These differences in goals, however, should only be addressed after this system has been explained in full, and so will be elucidated shortly.

Rather than any supposed ability to capture a composer's musical thinking in performance, it is the sheer flexibility of noctuplet groupings that encourages the use of two such groupings in every bar of this notational adaptation. Instead of being understood as consisting of nine 8th notes, the use of noctuplet groupings here should be understood as a re-division of the bar into eight 8th notes, with an extra one leftover. That leftover 8th note is created in order to allow for the cataloguing, archiving, and studying of one of the defining aspects of the rap genre: its vocalists expressive rhythmic delays. Without noctuplets, the inclusion of such rhythmic trailing behind the beat is either too hard to capture accurately, or reduced to the inaccurate ambiguity of a performance indication. Not all rappers rap behind the beat to the same amount; Kendrick Lamar's rhythms at the end of "Look Out for Detox," at time stamp 2:25, are much further behind the beat than a performer like Drake's are in his rap melodies from his 2009 song "Best I Ever Had." This is not an isolated incident that would demand no more than a mere accommodation on a case-by-case basis; the melodies of rappers, to a large degree, are defined by their distinguishing amounts of rhythmic delay. For example, the extreme delay of Talib Kweli on his 2002 song "Rush," at 1:24, or Mos Def's long wait on the beat in the seventh bar of his verse at time stamp 2:00 on the 1998 song "RE: Definition," would never be confused with the much more forward-leaning melody of someone like 2Pac on his 1996 song "Changes." To get specific, Jay-Z's first note in the thirty-fifth bar of his 2004 song "Dirt Off Your Shoulder" is .056 milliseconds behind the beat, which, at his song's BPM of 82, is equal to roughly the size of only a short 64th note. As extreme as it might be for performance in a Western musical genre, this is a much shorter rhythmic delay than that found in the aforementioned melodies of Mos Def or Talib Kweli. To ignore or explain away this fact is to reduce rap's melodic nature beyond recognition. As further proof that, because such rhythmic complexity are not isolated incidents within the genre, all transcription systems of rap that purport to communicate knowledge about its musical nature should be able to encompass perfectly accurate representations of its most extreme rhythms, there are the radical subdivisions of Talib Kweli in the 19th bar of his rap at 2:38 on "Twice Inna Lifetime," where he actually does rap in true noctuplets; the subdivisional-delay of MF DOOM at bar 20 on his 2004 song "Vomitspit," where he executes a kind of transformed tempo-accelerando onto beat one of the next bar at 0:54; the quasi-quintuplets of André 3000 in his first bar on the second verse of OutKast's 1999 track "Aquemini," at 1:50; and so on. To ignore these infinitely-small, but thereby fundamentally important, elements of rap melodies, such as by representing it only orthographically, is to distort this genre's actual musical technique.

Another advantage of the usage of noctuplets is that they can much more easily reflect the constantly-changing subdivisional groupings of rappers than traditional duplet organizations of the beat, since noctuplets are flexible enough to hold constantly changing groupings, or beamings. These two noctuplet 16th groups, found in every bar, can be cut up into wholes, or parts of, a division of two quarter-notes into not just two, three, or four, but also into five, six, seven, and so on, without ever needing to change the grouping. Unlike the eight 8th notes of a 4/4 bar, a division of a bar into two 16th note noctuplet groupings overcomes this prohibitively time-consuming problem of determining proper beamings for the reflection of the meter's quarter-note beat, since the four beats have been conjoined into two noctuplet groupings. There is, indeed, a small learning curve to reading and working within such a system, as in the fact that beat 2 lands not on the third 8th of the bar, but after a quarter note and a 32nd note; however, it's advantages are more than enough to at least call for a testing of it within a peer-review domain.

Perhaps it is this inability to accurately represent such a proliferation of expressive micro-timing that has encouraged music theorists like Dr. Kyle Adams of Indiana University to largely focus on orthographic systems of representation for rap, such as the flow diagram, even when considering rap's purely musical aspects.

However, the notational representation of rhythmic trailing of accent behind the meter's "proper" pulse was only ever a matter of overcoming heightened difficulty, and never an impossibility that would absolutely required flow diagrams a priori. Those flow diagrams, however, are extremely informative, and have advanced the nascent science of rap musicology extremely far. In the end, it still remained that an appropriately fine system of transcription, as well as an in-depth and thorough transcriber's metronome, would always be enough to overcome any such analytical obstacle.

Neither is the reading of noctuplets prohibitively difficult as it might seem at first, either. They conveniently divide the bar evenly into two halves of weak–strong beat pairs, and likewise are built on the rap genre's most widely-proliferated foundational rhythm: the 16th note. Furthermore, they communicate visually the expressive micro-timings that generate the delivery of rap melodies as well, through their slightly rightward delay of expected melodic entrances and rhythms. The use of an overarching subdivisional grouping in a ubiquitous manner similarly communicates not only rap's preferred method of oral history and person-to-person pedagogical methods, but, also, the fact that these transcriptions are meant for cataloguing, archival purposes, and not the accurate recreation of a composition in a different geographic locale and chronological time.

Moving on, the length of each note in the transcription is not necessarily chosen in order to most accurately represent the musical length for which the rapper is pronouncing each individual melodic note. Rather, the length of each note in this system of transcription is instead chosen in order to make the music as easy to read as possible, by filling in rests, and tying rhythms together across beats with ties. As a result, the difficulty of determining a single note's rhythmic duration—always of a chief concern to a priori composers, but of relatively unimportant to the oral-performance style of a syllabic vocal idiom, or an archiving transcriber—has not been solved, but, instead, is left to the side for the moment, as it is no more than a distracting stumbling block that can best be studied in other contexts with different scholarly goals.

Grammatical Syntax as Melodic Structure

One of the most important ideas contained in both this book and its transcription system is that, completely apart from the poetic or semantic meaning of a rapper's words, the syntax of a rapper's actual lyrics does, indeed, affect the ways in which their melodies are structured technically. The hypothesis is that where sentences stop and start can be taken to simultaneously indicate where the phrasing of a rapper's melody Eminem's stops and starts as it structures itself.

More traditional instrumentalists, like pianists, have musical considerations of articulation, as well as a wider range of longer rhythms, available to them when they are structuring their own phrases. Rappers, however, do not have such a huge palette available for their use as they go about performing their own music. To perform in such interpretively articulative ways, or to frequently rest for rhythmic durations longer than a quarter note, would come across as musically inept or awkward. This is because such hypothetical rap melodies would simply sound too different from the manner in which humans speak when they engage in everyday conversation, a stylized form of which the rapping genre works to capture and heighten, as can be gleaned from the genre's socioeconomic origins and constant activist concerns. Thus, rappers instead use the syntactical pairing of predicates with subjects, as well as dependent clauses, to give their melodies shape through musical phrasing. This is an essential point of evidence for the current discussion: the grammatical syntax of rappers' lyrics dually functions as a musical foundation for their melodic architecture. As such, the long, curving slurs under the note heads, instead of indicating a legato articulation, indicates the onset and arrest of sentence-phrases. This theory and its internal, logical necessity for the proper understanding of rap is further developed in this author's own contributed chapter to Scott F. Parker's 2014 title *Eminem and Rap, Poetry, Race*.[1]

A few more housekeeping, typological notes: the use of the accent sign, (>), is also used to a great extent in this transcription system. It is used to indicate on which note the rapper has placed the prosodic accent of their syllables, if it is somewhere other than directly on the beat. Furthermore, there is the feature of the treble clef, included at the very start of every one of these single-line staves. This treble clef does not indicate the range of the rapper's melody, as a treble clef would do in a piece of violin music, or a bass clef would do in a piece of piano music for a pianist's lower left hand. This treble clef, instead, is meant to call more attention from the reader to the fact that rap does indeed have a purely musical nature, which argument was fleshed out more in-depth in this book's introductory chapter. Finally, the positions of the impetus note head in these transcriptions indicate the onset of a syllable's vowel sound, and the length of each note is foremost decreed not by musical duration, but by convenient legibility. Although the omission of such musical omission, it might be the best compromise between the dualistic elements of repetition and variation that Adams so succinctly dissects in a 2016 articles:

> For hip-hop, though, there is as yet no form of transcription that captures both the linear nature of the lyrics and the cyclical nature of the beat. The beat can be

1. Rhythm

notated conventionally, provided we disregard the problems inherent in the transcription of sampled music. But the analyst must choose between notating one iteration of the beat, with instructions to repeat ad infinitum, in which case it is difficult to represent the various additions to the beat that happen inconsistently throughout the song, or notating it as we would notate any other musical layer, which obscures its fundamentally repetitive nature.[2]

It is also posited here that a combination of notation and typographical representation may also indeed be enough to not just "circumvent" these problems, as Adams suggests on page 132 of the same article, but to also "surmount all of those methodological obstacles."[3] For this reason, orthographic characters, such as symbolic letters, are frequently herein utilized to stand in for, and to make clear, the "repetitive nature" of the "various additions to the beat that happen inconsistently throughout the song," particularly in this book's "Motivic Development" chapter and Big Daddy Kane section. In this way, the flexible, interdisciplinary manner of rap representation presented here leaves ample room for its diverse textual, poetic, musical, melodic, repetitive, and cyclical natures, by purposefully combining the best advantages of all the representative systems (notation, transcription, text, etc.) that currently exist for capturing such incredibly different artistic phenomena.

To review, these transcriptions are meant to catalogue the archived performance of rappers for analysis, and not to transmit those performances in an easily digestible way for performance by different artists at a different time, and in a different location, by a group of musicians that does not include the composer acting in the role of a conductor. For these reasons, specific considerations, like those of specific musical duration, are not solved, but circumvented. This frees the notation from certain epistemological constraints that, while restricting its ability for per se interpretation, frees it up to do more for the communication of raw, unshaped information. Transcriptions, generally, work most optimally by executing only one of these two tasks, if the music-maker has not themselves notated their own creation, as Western art music composers do. Because rappers do not notate their own melodies in a transferrable form like Western music notation, whose norms and standards are largely understood by all professional musicians in the civilization, analysts are left to fill in the gap through devices such as transcription systems. This means that such analysts should not endeavor to read into the mind of the rapper to tease out what they were thinking, because such a project would inevitably result in confusing and accurate conclusion. What remains is the attempt to analyze the transcribed forms of the only musical event that rappers have ever unquestionably supplied to the musical community at large: their melodies in full performance, as recorded on a CD or album. Thus, if a reader might feel compelled to ignore this transcription system out of hand because of an alleged or supposed complexity, they might do well to remember just how much information in the standardized form of Western music notation is typically left to the performer's discretion, despite most composer's earnest attempts to minimize such ambiguity: exact tempos, manners of articulation, specific dynamic levels, etc. That is the stubborn, giant gap between creation and interpretation that this adapted transcription system is working to traverse.

As the proliferation of multiple, competing systems for representing rap represent, this is very likely not the final word in capturing rap's elements. Specifically, a project for extending it, and unifying all of these system's competing values, might consist in a dualistic notation similar to those of the school of New Complexity. In this manner, this current transcription system being proffered might appear to be only a start to the answer.[4] By representing rhythms on one line of notation, and pitch on the other, as in compositions like *Crutch Of Memory* by Aaron Cassidy, as documented by scholars like Stuart Paul Duncan,[5] treat separate aspects of the performance experience like articulation and dynamics, then one of the final steps to a uniform system of representing rap might ultimately have been taken.

Eminem's Presto Rhythms

Using these rudimentary sheet music skills, we can already say a few things about Eminem's rhythms on "Rap God," reproduced again below:

An example of Eminem's presto rhythms at bar 165 on "Rap God."

The most obvious thing to mention about Eminem's rhythms is that they are performed at a cadenza-like rate. In a tempo marking, it might earn a marking of presto. The speed of this song as expressed in BPM, indicated in the top left to be at 148, is going to be nearly the fastest BPM that will be considered in this entire book. Additionally, the rhythmic value of the notes themselves is very small, residing at the level of a 16th note. In this manner, Eminem's preferred rhythmic subdivision, as small as it is, is a melodic extension of the song's own structural speed, at a fast BPM rate of 148.

In addition to being incredibly quick, to a soloistic degree, the rhythms of this section of "Rap God" are also remarkably uniform and consistent. That is, 16th notes are largely the only subdivision Eminem utilizes in these eight bars. While rapping around one-hundred separate musical attacks in the space of just six chronological seconds, Eminem allows the strictly technical aspects of his melody to back up his claim for rap divinity that can be heard in the poetic and semantic interpretations of this song's own chorus and title.

However, it is by no means true that the melodies of Eminem's entire oeuvre rely exclusively on the 16th note subdivision. The next song, "Encore" (also known as "Curtains Down"), comes from Eminem's 2004 album *Encore*.

Eminem's Non-Subdivisional Rhythms

Eminem's rhythms on "Encore (Curtains Down)" can be termed as being "non-subdivisional," not because they don't make use of subdivisions, but simply because the subdivisions he makes use of are constantly changing. Eminem's twenty-fourth and twenty-fifth bars from this song have been notated below (see next page). Particularly informative notes have also been tagged with a representative letter, in order to make for easy referral in the below. These two songs have been purposefully selected in order to sketch the wide artistic spectrum of melodies that Eminem is capable of composing.

Here, we see rhythms that are vastly different from those on "Rap God." For one thing, many different rhythmic values are used, instead of just a presto 16th note. Instead, we get many different rhythmic lengths in notes. We have a dotted 32nd note, such as on the note above the letter J; there's also a 16th note, such as on the note designated by the letter A. We hear a dotted 16th note, as on note C; an 8th note, as on note G; and an 8th note tied to a 32nd note, as on note Y. Besides considerations of the sets of rhythmic class between the two songs, "Encore" and "Rap God" are equally delineated from each other technically by the range of tempo that they demarcate. Residing in the lower range of tempo, the BPM of

Eminem's musical rhythms, represented in notation, at bar 24 of his song "Encore (Curtains Down)," at 1:02.

"Encore" is down at 87 BPM, which is much slower than the 148 BPM of "Rap God." Qualitatively, it can thus be seen that Eminem's melody on "Encore" is more expressive and coloristic than his vocal work on "Rap God."

This technical survey was conducted along comparatively straightforward lines in order to provide a quick summary of Eminem's melodies along a very general rhythmic spectrum. With this information on Eminem's temporal speeds and rhythmic subdivisions in hand, a deeper investigation into the phrasing structures of his melodies is now possible.

Eminem's Constrained Rhythms

"The Way I Am" is notable for its extremely constrained approach to rhythm variety. Without fail, Eminem's rhythms on this song on "The Way I Am" consist entirely of the following 3-note rhythm being repeated in exactly the same way, over and over and over:

1. Rhythm

An isolated archetype of Eminem's foundational musical motive from his song "The Way I Am."

On "The Way I Am," this exact rhythm is repeated 216 times.

In a song with about four minutes of rapping, that means that this rhythm occurs once every 1.12 seconds. As the previous survey of other "Rap God" and "Encore" made clear, while Eminem is apt to repeat small rhythmic ideas from time to time, they are never taken to this quasi-serialist level of compositional control. Even the few notes that aren't a part of this song's basic tripartite motive turn out to be no more than derivations of its basic outline. In this manner, one sees Eminem's rhythmic world expanded from soloistic speeds, to coloristic syncopation, to a serialist's level of expressive restriction in terms of subdivision.

An essential concept in the understanding of melody in rappers' verses, whether those of Eminem or any other rapper, is whether such verses are broadly strophic, or, in general, through-composed. Strophic, while normally used to refer to a song's more global structure, is preferred here to descriptors like "motivic" or "thematic" because of the latter terms' connotation of development. What is probably a slight majority of verses in rap are built upon these repetitions of small, characteristic rhythms over a longer course of time. "Strophic" denotes just such an amount of limited, non-developed repetition that is much greater than the amount of repetition that would be found in through-composed musical material, where each succeeding bar would be broadly different from those that have come before. Along with the following sections' own focuses on textural function, tempo, meter, and the like, through-composition and strophism can equally be used to classify and understand the melodies of rap.

Eminem's rhythms on "Rap God" can now be considered once more in this new light (see next page).

The below bars of "Rap God" do consist of a rhythm that is repeated multiple times, the 16th note. However, this stream of repeated 16th-note rhythms isn't tied together, or unified among itself, in any motivic, developmental way, such as through metric transference, or rhythmic augmentation and diminution. In this way, while Eminem's rhythms on "Rap God"

Eminem's melody from bar 148 of "Rap God" displays an unstable type of rhythmic repetition, because its rhythms are not very unique or easily recognized on first hearing, since they are of such a common variety.

are repeated, they aren't necessarily strophic, since their rhythmic character is of such a passingly ordinary and common character on the subdivisional level.

The very same bars from "Encore" that were produced before, in addition to possessing strong syncopation, were also structured in a through-composed manner:

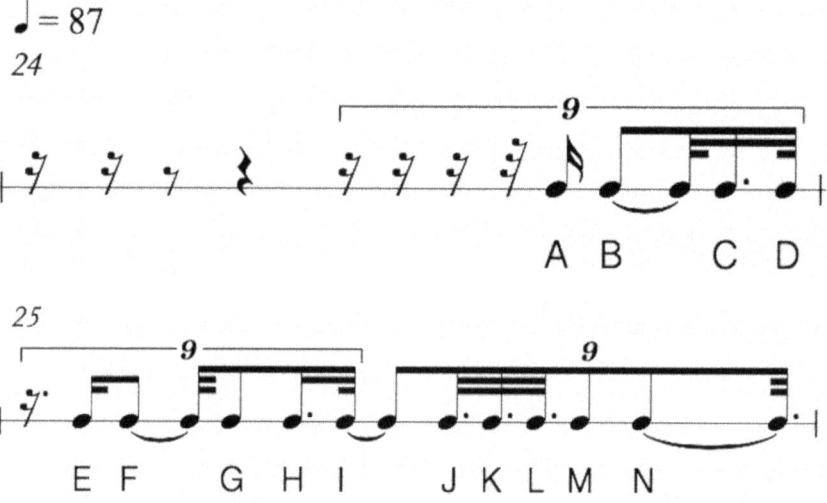

Eminem's rhythms from bar 24 of "Encore (Curtains Down)" begin a series of through-composed bars.

In these two bars, no exact rhythm is repeated from one measure to the next, and much of the same can be said for Eminem's entire melody on "Encore."

Eminem's Strophic Verse Rhythms

One verse's melody that is broadly strophic, however, is Eminem's final set of vocals on the 2002 song "Business." Here, Eminem repeats the same 1-bar, archetypal rhythm pattern eight different times across eight full bars. What follows is a sampling of the bars in question, starting at bar 64, around 2:47 into the song:

A transcription of Eminem's rhythms from his song "Business," whose final verse is strophic, due to its internally repetitive nature.

The vertical alignment of these bars right above each other underscores their strophic structure, particularly in the second half of each respective bar. Specifically, the final five notes of each melodic phrase are in exactly the same rhythmic position as each other, and each set of five notes lasts for exactly the same amount of time. The parallelisms between the two emphasize their close rhythmic relationship. Specifically, note I has the same duration and position as the note S; note J is the same as note T; note K is the same as note U; and so on, for the last two notes in each sentence. The large rhythm duration of both of these melodic phrases, when compared, are also equivalent: they both last for exactly one full bar. This similarity in multiple aspects of their rhythmic mean this verse is built on a strophically-repetitive foundation, as this archetypal gesture is repeated eight full times between bar 65 and bar 72.

However, a strophic compositional method can be made manifest in many different ways. Bars 89 and 90 from the Eminem single "Without Me," which at the 3:13 mark of the song, display a higher amount of repetitive density than "Business" did:

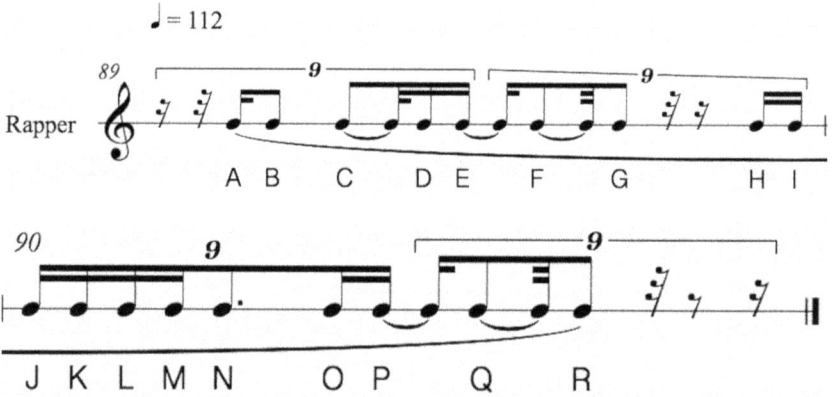

The rhythms of bars 89 and 90 from Eminem's song "Without Me," in addition to being structured out of a four-note gesture that is performed twice in each respective bar in the above, also transfers the metric position of that four-note gesture as well.

"Business" was made up of an eight-note, one-bar phrase that was repeated eight times over eight bars, while never transforming or departing from its prototypical structure in any fundamental way. "Without Me," however, is made up of a four-note, half-bar phrase that gets repeated six times in four bars, and does transform its technical aspects over time in a developmental manner. Specifically, the four-note gesture in question first appears on the letters D, E, F, and G. At the root of the situation, this gesture consists of a 16th note, followed by three 8th notes. It likewise occurs on O, P, Q, and R altogether, where it ends the bar in a corresponding manner to the first one. In bar 91, Eminem goes to rap this four-note, half-bar gesture a full two times. In its first iteration, the second note of the gesture lands directly on beat 1, and so receives a strong downbeat accent. In the second half of bar 91, however, Eminem shifts the position of this strophic material so that its second note is syncopated in its position on the fourth 16th note of this bar's third beat. This internal generation of recycled melodic material occurs in bar 92 as well, where this exact four-note gesture, having underpinned the previous three bars, is next repeated twice in the same exact way: once on the beat, and once completely off of it. As a result, Eminem's strophic repetition demonstrates an increase in developmental variation of the fundamental rhythmic structures in his melodies on both "Without Me" and "Business," whose own repeated rhythms never transformed in any kind of equivalent way.

The three-note motive of "The Way I Am" constitutes a level of rhythmic limitation, as well as an absence of developmental treatments, that the melodies of "Business," "Rap God," and "Without Me" do not quite approach. As a reminder, the following three-note motive is repeated a full 216 times on "The Way I Am," and any small deviations away from it in the melody are still no more passing derivations of it:

Eminem's basic thematic motive from "The Way I Am," isolated in the above, is an extremely heightened example of strophic constraints in a rap melody.

Beyond the strophic manner in which Eminem structured his melodies on "The Way I Am," "Business," and "Without Me," however, a large portion of this entire genre's whole output remains to be defined through its strictly through-composed elements.

Busta Rhymes' Through-Composing

While the raps of Eminem were a fertile investigative ground for strophism in rap, the melodies of Busta Rhymes can be just as fruitful for an equivalent look into rap's approach to through-composition. Busta's melody on his 2001 song "Break Ya Neck," in contrast to Eminem's structures on songs like "Without Me," almost never repeats its rhythms from one bar or beat to the next. The following rhythms come from this song's thirteenth bar:

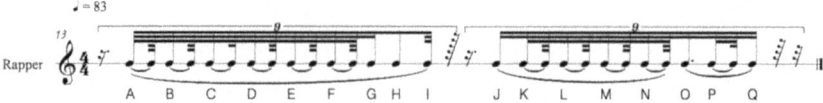

A rhythmic transcription of the opening bar of Busta Rhymes' melody on "Break Ya Neck," which demonstrates soloistic, extremely quick, and syncopated rhythms.

These rhythms are performed at an extremely fast pace, inviting comparisons to Eminem's own rap cadenza on "Rap God." Indeed, when counting this bar and the next on "Break Ya Neck," there is a total of forty-four notes that arrive within the musical space of just two bars. This quick pacing is something that Busta Rhymes keeps up over the entire course of this song. More notable, however, is the fact that Busta Rhymes also almost never repeats any small section of his melody's rhythms in the same strophic way that Eminem did on "Business" or "Without Me," even though he continues to utilize that noctuplet thirty second note, when it's tied to a noctuplet 128th note, as a foundational building block for his subdivisional level of rhythm. To be sure, this same bar's own basic rhythmic outline is not, for instance, repeated in the fourteenth bar, or any bar thereafter.

Even though Busta Rhymes' most well-known song was written in a through-composed manner, that does not mean that he is not capable of subjecting his verse's rhythms to strophic treatments.

Busta Rhymes' Strophic Verse Rhythms

In addition to utilizing through-composition, Busta can also interact with strophic approaches to intra-verse rhythms in a style that is more global in structure than Eminem's own more local sensibility. Consider, for example, the following rhythms from Busta Rhymes' 2006 song "Don't Get Carried Away," starting at bar 9:

1. Rhythm

N O P Q R   S T   U V W X Y

The musical transcription of the first two bars of Busta Rhymes' 2006 song "Don't Get Carried Away," which begins to demonstrate his global resizing of the proportions of strophic unity within a verse to the larger level of entire songs.

Busta's own strophism is based on his repetition of a four-note gesture at the end of each of his melodic phrases. In the above notation, this gesture can be found on the letters A–B–C–D, H–I–J–K, O–P–Q–R, and V–W–X–Y. On those letter groupings, it occurs in the following uniform order: a starting 16th note, followed by a 16th note, followed by a dotted 32nd note, and ending with 16th note. In emphasizing the strophic nature of his first verse on "Don't Get Carried Away," this very order of specific rhythmic durations occurs no less than twenty times.

In fact, the second verse of this Busta Rhymes song functions in a similarly strophic way. Not only is this second verse deeply strophic in its own right, but it even makes use of the very same four-note gesture that the first verse does. In the second verse, this gesture occurs over twenty times. In this way, Busta Rhymes has imbued this characteristic four-note gesture with a structural importance that extends throughout the entire song, and does not restrict its unifying effect to only the short moment of a single verse's own random selection of bars.

50 Cent's Intercantual References

Other rappers besides Busta Rhymes, such as 50 Cent, have even found ways to transfer the very same type of unique, recognizable, and easily-identified strophic gestures and their characteristic set of rhythms across separate songs, and not only separate verses (like Busta) or separate bars (like Eminem). In doing so, the use of a new word might help to avoid some of the pitfalls of ignorance or obfuscation that initially set the cultural context for a strong rejection of rap music in certain societal quarters. That interpretational confusion was originally due, in large part, to a misunderstanding of rap's dualistic poetic and musical nature, as documented in this book's introductory chapter. While focusing almost exclusively on lyrics and words in their dismissive critique of the periodically gratuitous imagery of many 1980s and 1990s rap songs, the earliest mainstream commentators on the genre introduced a large amount of misunderstanding and misinterpretation of rap's artistic essence and existence into communal discourse on the genre. By fully privileging rap's poetry over its music in the songs of artists like 50 Cent, the gatekeepers of societal propriety were preparing rap to eventually be dismissed as thoroughly non-musical and arrhythmic, as would be argued by pundits like Juan Williams.

In order to avoid the further propagation of such inaccuracies, the term that from here on will be used to refer to 50 Cent's transfer of purely musical aspects in rap between separate songs from separate time periods in his career will purposefully go to great lengths to avoid any misplacement of unbalanced emphasis on the lyrical, poetic, or textual elements of rap's nature. Because of this, the words "intercantuality" and "intercantual" are to be greatly preferred to the use of a similar (and, moreover, largely synonymous) concept, intertextuality, when discussing such historical conversations in rap. This is because these terms are founded on the Latin word "cantus" and its own purely musical connotations, which will help to avoid such pitfalls in analysis, due to its very etymological references.

Indeed, the term intertextuality has in fact been used to refer to purely musical phenomena, as in Michael Klein's *Intertexuality In Western Art Music*. However, since this book's argument relies on the basic premise that rap's textual elements can be divorced from its musical elements, it still seems necessary, as well as safest, that the distinction is made in order to remove any possible chance of confusion, conscious or otherwise. It should be noted, though, that what follows is not in anyway an argument for the adoption of the term "intercantuality" beyond the specific discussion at hand herein.

To comprehend how intercantual processes can occur in rap, it would do well to consider how an intertextual treatment of rap, carried out with the strictest possible definition of what a music's text is, would be handled differently from what is an intercantual treatment. On 50 Cent's 2003 song "If I Can't," he re-works and re-styles the opening line of Run-D.M.C.'s classic 1986 song "Peter Piper." In the latter song, D.M.C. and Run innocently exclaim their own harmlessly fun story as party rhymers in a classic tongue-twister about folklore's picker of peppers. When 50 Cent attached himself to this poetic lineage in 2003 by re-rapping it after he's imparted his own unique imprint to it, he makes the line much more semantically sinister by inserting descriptions into the text of how his own hobbies are more criminal than those of Run-D.M.C. In slightly changing the very recognizable opening of a song that he's referencing, 50 Cent is engaging in an intertextual process of conversation and dialogue with musical pioneers from the past.

However, such an orthographic interpretation is out of place when considering the strictly musical aspects of rap's nature. This is because rap's musical aspects are always informed and shaped by the structural elements of that very same text, such as prosodic accent. At the same time that 50 Cent is reworking Run-D.M.C.'s lines intertextually, he is engaging with them in an intercantual manner. That is, he is not just referencing Run-D.M.C.'s text, but also referencing their rhythms. It is the specific form of rhythmic organization, on both a metric and subdivisional level, that is preserved across these two songs. 50 Cent reproduces the rhythms of Run-D.M.C. in a musically verbatim way, as his own rap occurs in a way that is musically verbatim, being both note-for-note and pitch-for-pitch identical.

50 Cent's Self-Referentiality

On "If I Can't," 50 Cent can be considered to have structured his melody in a strophic way, if it is understood that his own song forms just one integral part of a pairing with the structure of Run-D.M.C.'s "Peter Piper." While those specific rhythms from "If I Can't" that are under consideration here aren't repeated on "If I Can't," they were repeated on a different group's own song. However, 50 Cent is also able to create strophic relations within his very own discography.

The next song at hand, "How We Do," comes from an album, *The Documentary*, that was released in 2005 by 50 Cent's previous bandmate Game. Meanwhile, the song that 50 Cent retroactively references on "How We Do" in an intercantual manner, entitled "Never Enough," appeared on an earlier, 2004 album release by Eminem, entitled *Encore*.

What defines the intercantual relationship between these two songs is the fact that 50 Cent has an extended direct quotation of the rhythms (but not the text) from "Never Enough" at the opening of the final verse on "How We Do." Accordingly, this reference to himself is unmistakably reminiscent of the earlier track in its use of the very same rhythms and melody. The following musical bar of 50 Cent's melody occurs at the 3:06 mark of "How We Do," towards the end of bar 77:

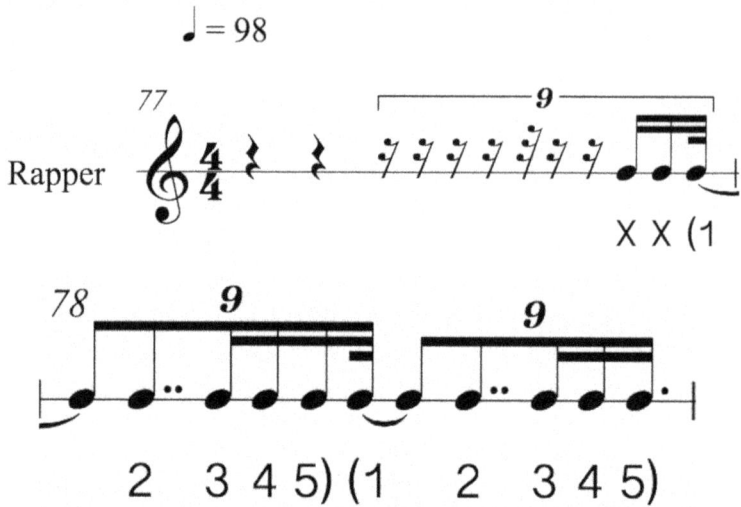

A demonstration of the intercantual, strophic nature of the five-note phrase on "How We Do" that 50 Cent had rapped, note-for-note and rhythm-for-rhythm, over a year earlier, on a completely different song and project.

This full bar here largely consists of one five-note rhythmic gesture that is repeated is two times. Its order of rhythmic durations is an 8th note tied to a 32nd not; double-dotted 8th note; 16th note; 16th note; and dotted 16th note. This rhythmic gesture is represented in the above by any full unfurling of the 1–2–3–4–5 ordering. In fact, these very same rhythms are also repeated another four full times over the course of the subsequent two bars that follow them as well.

As it turns out, 50 Cent has subjected this exact strophic rhythmic gesture to an intercantual treatment on "How We Do," recorded nearly a year after "Never Enough," since he has actually re-rapped the same musical melodic gesture from one song to the next. That strongly syncopated, five-note rhythm appeared back on "Never Enough" at 1:49, towards the end of bar 45:

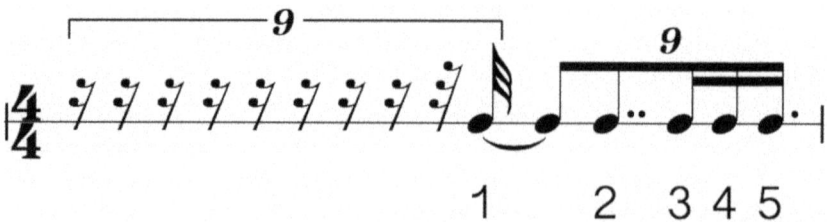

The same five-note phrase, heavy with 16th-note rhythms, which 50 Cent raps on Game's 2005 song "How We Do," was also utilized by 50 Cent back on the 2004 song he did under Eminem's headlining appearance, which was called "Never Enough."

Again, we see this same two-beat, five-note rhythm appear in the above transcription, wherever the notes 1, 2, 3, 4, and 5 have been once more grouped together in full.

It seems, then, that both of these two songs are connected to each other by more than the fact that they share the same producer, Dr. Dre. By preserving the purely musical aspects of his rap technique from a previous song, while purposefully ignoring the poetic elements of that same earlier track, 50 Cent engages in a particularly musical type of intertextuality in his raps.

Kendrick Lamar's Melodic Entrances

Whether the previous discussion was about differing approaches to intercantuality, strophism, through-composition, syncopation, or anything else, all of these rappers have, so far, simultaneously opened the beginning of their melodies in very standard ways. That is, in beginning all of their melodic expositions, those three rappers almost always and without fail began their melody right on the first beat of a bar that began at a larger hypermetric grouping of four bars altogether. For example, Busta begins on beat 1 of bar 25 of "Break Ya Neck," and Eminem begins his own first verse on beat 1 of his twenty-first bar on "Without Me." Meanwhile, the next rapper for study is a subtler artist who possesses a much greater tendency to skillfully present the introduction of his own orchestrational voice into the musical texture at large through means that are rather unconventional for this genre.

That artist is Kendrick Lamar, and he shows off this compositional tendency in full on his 2012 song "m.A.A.d city," which comes from the album entitled *good kid, m.A.A.d. city*. In the 105th bar of this song, which comes around 2:57, Kendrick starts his rap during a beat drop. However, he doesn't begin the exposition of his melody on beat 1 of bar 106, as would usually happen for the beginning of almost any other rap, from any other song. Instead, Kendrick inserts his voice into the texture directly on top of the fourth beat of bar 105. In this way, Kendrick foregrounds the musical aspects of his rap, by continually making them take innovative forms.

Indeed, the special way in which Kendrick begins his rap verses is not restricted to his work on "m.A.A.d city." Kendrick uses the same musical technique on the first song from the same album, entitled "Sherane a.k.a. Master Splinter's Daughter." Before the actual rap verse begins at 1:04, there comes a rhythmically free section that sets the dark, foreboding scene for this concept album. Immediately afterwards, the same musical dynamic that ordained Kendrick's rhythmic unbalancing of the 4/4 measure through a shifting of instrumental and vocal accent onto the previously-weak fourth beat appears once more. Rather than beginning his rap a beat early, on beat 4 of a preceding bar, Kendrick does the opposite on "Sherane a.k.a. Master Splinter's Daughter" when he waits a quarter note longer than usual to begin his melody. Kendrick's melodic exposition now begins on the second beat of the measure, not the first, which is the more standard beat that Eminem, Busta Rhymes, and the other rappers considered so far have been much more likely to begin their melodies on.

Kendrick, however, is not ignorant of the power of a measure's initial beat to rhythmically catapult the delivery of a rap melody by supercharging its driving accent. This is exactly how the beginning of his melody is structured on another track from *good kid, m.A.A.d city*, called "Swimming Pools (Drank)." Immediately before he enters right on top of the first downbeat of bar 9 on this album's ninth track, Kendrick raps a series of pick up notes that work to emphasize just how essential every measure's first beat is to this whole song's entire musical texture.

Even when Kendrick does begin his melodies in this standard, uniform way, he is apt to undermine or subvert the interpretation of that first beat. Another major radio single of his, "Poetic Justice," contains a second example of Kendrick Lamar beginning his melody with a strong accent right on the first beat of a musical section (but not, necessarily, what is the first beat of a 4/4 bar). This occurs in the very first bar, when the song begins at 0:00, whose own metric structure is briefly left in flux. This is because the role that Kendrick's beginning beat plays in terms of rhythmic accent is left in question for now, as Kendrick's melodic exposition has begun in an a cappella musical texture. With no backing musical accompaniment behind him at all, it is the rhythmic length and structural demarcators of his melodic phrases that will determine the metric structures of bars at first.

And, because his a cappella introductory section of melody lasts for an uneven number of quarter notes—nine of them, to be exact—it forces a new, non-symmetrical analysis of this melody's structure. As it turns out, the a cappella texture's subversion of accent results in a melodic introduction that is structured as an unbalanced period of a 4/4 antecedent phrase and a 5/4 consequent phrase. The consequent phrase of this opening melody might be better understand as having its own internal pairing of a 4/4 meter with a united and derived 1/4 meter, since this consequent is extended through nothing more than an extra iteration of a trochaic pair of weak–strong 8th notes, four instances of which comprise the entire antecedent.

This clever metric substitution is revealed as a delightful compositional ploy, and not the metric foundation of a song entirely composed in a complex time signature, when the full beat comes in on beat 1 of this song's true third bar. At that point it is revealed that, rather than beginning on the first beat of a measure, Kendrick's a cappella introduction was extended by a single, excessive quarter note. This shifting of metric position of the melody is much more digestible a re-interpretation than one that considers the musical accompaniment to starting on beat 2 of every subsequent measure, which would be almost unheard of in any popular music genre. When the only other competing solution for understanding the beginning of Kendrick Lamar's melodic exposition is so very unlikely, it is much more probable that the technical subversion of accent is in the hands of the rapper, and not the producer, on "Poetic Justice."

AZ's Ultra-Delayed Entrances

On "Poetic Justice," Kendrick Lamar waited an extra beat to begin his melody. But on the 1997 track, called "Firm Fiasco," the lyricist AZ actually waits an entire extra bar to introduce his own melody in the song's musical texture.

This song begins uniformly enough, as two-bar and four-bar ideas are repeated several times in an instrumental introductory section that lasts for a total of twelve bars. At this point, based on the prevailing norms of hypermetric, 4-bar groupings in the rap genre, AZ would be expected to begin his melody right on beat 1 of bar 13. However, AZ actually begins his melody on beat 1 of bar 14, which breaks strongly with the norms of rap's hypermetric groupings, since fourteen bars cannot be broken down into whole, undivided groupings of four bars. Thus, the beginning of AZ's melodic exposition is strongly at odds with, and disjunct to, the normal hypermetric groupings of the rap genre in terms of its musical structures. It can be left to commentators and musical personalities whose unexpected and delayed entrances work better, but in any event, such unexpected melodic entrances could not occur without a deep understanding of generic musical norms. In this way, AZ continues to explicate the musical theme of this survey: rappers, whether Eminem, Busta, AZ, 50 Cent, or anyone else, are constantly manipulating the musical norms of their own musical genre in new and unexpected ways.

Slimkid3's Tripartite Hypermeter

Just like AZ, the rapper Slimkid3 is another lyricist who responds to, interacts with, and re-interprets the normative 4-bar hypermetric groupings of his genre. He manipulates one of his genre's most fundamental musical standards on the song "Bom Bom Fiya," which comes from the self-titled solo album that he recorded with producer DJ Nu-Mark in 2014.

The English pidgin title of "Bom Bom Fiya" is a phonetic transcription of the vocal sample that is looped during the chorus. However, what is most interesting about this structural sample isn't its words, but the hypermetric duration for which it lasts. In contrast to the great majority of samples that have been used in rap, this particular loop does not repeat over an equal number of bars, like two, four, eight, or sixteen. Instead, this vocal sample repeats after three bars. Because of the tripartite rhythmic duration of this song's foundational sample, Slimkid3 is forced to respond to the nonstandard structure of the sample on "Bom Bom Fiya" in new ways.

Below is the structure of Slimkid3's first verse on "Bom Bom Fiya," as represented typographically. Each pair of brackets marks out the beginning and end of an individual melodic phrase. Inside each of those brackets is listed how long each individual melodic phrase lasts for, in terms of bars. The twelve total phrases of this entire first verse have all been divided up into sections of three bars, reflecting the length of the accompanying loop behind the rapper's melody. Meanwhile, each individual line of type represents the length of one bar in the music:

Three-Bar Grouping #1:
  [1/2 bar][1/2 bar]
  [1/2 bar][1/2 bar]
  [1 bar]

Three-Bar Grouping #2:
  [1/2 bar][1/2 bar]
  [1 bar]
  [1/2bar][1/2 bar]

Three-Bar Grouping #3:
  [1/2 bar][1/2 bar]
  [1 bar]
  [1 bar]

Three-Bar Grouping #4:
  [1 bar]
  [1 bar]
  [1 bar]

Here, Slimkid3 has unmistakably structured the onset and termination of every single one of his melodic phrases so that they always align with the structure of the three-bar loop behind him. In this manner, Slimkid3 mirrors his accompanimental background in his melodic foreground. Equally important in the above is just how each one of this group of three bars relates to the others. These three-bar groupings, when compared among themselves, show that the specific structure of any three-bar grouping is never exactly reproduced from one to the next. As just one example, the four straight half-bar phrases that open the first three-bar unit are never replicated in any of the other units. When this inventive melodic structure is combined with Slimkid3's unconventional tripartite approach to hypermeter, instead of quadripartite hypermetric groupings, this rapper's melody exhibits the same type of diversified compositional style that was already seen in Eminem, Busta Rhymes, Kendrick Lamar, AZ, and 50 Cent.

Black Thought's Temporal Range

So far, the subdivisions of rappers' melodies have been given much attention, while the tempo speeds at which those subdivisions are performed has received much less. In order to properly analyzing the work of the next rapper, Black Thought, this shift in focus must occur. Black Thought's own discography displays a very wide range of tempos at which he performs.

As a very broad generalization, the tempo of rap songs across the whole genre occupies a range that most often falls somewhere between about 60 BPM and 120 BPM, while aggregating most frequently in the low 90s. There are, of course, outliers for this range— Macklemore's "Can't Hold Us" comes to mind, with its BPM at 140—but, as a beginning departure point, is enough to get the following discussion of individual rappers' own specific temporal ranges off to an auspicious start.

In order to express this temporal range of song speeds in a much more empirical way for the coming discussion, the tempo-detection capability of the DJ music software program Traktor was used to calculate the tempos of nearly the entire oeuvre of Black Thought. A rapper who has been recording professionally since 1992 is bound to have a very large amount of recordings, both those accessible and those not accessible, so to gather every song was basically infeasible. The results, though, still managed to showcase an incredibly rich approach to tempo on the part of Black Thought in his capacity as lead lyricist for this Philadelphia supergroup. The songs studied were all of the ones on which Black Thought appears from nine Roots' albums called *Do You Want More?!!!??!*, *Game Theory*, *How I Got Over*, *Illadelph Halflife*, *Organix*, *Phrenology*, *Rising Down*, *Things Fall Apart*, and *The Tipping Points*.

The statistics for Black Thought's range of rapping speeds, once tabulated, demonstrate that his melodies come in a wide range: from the comparatively adagio, all the way up to the faster allegretto. While spanning almost the entire genre's own range within just his own career, it can also be seen that his slowest song occurs at a rate of 60.8 BPM (on "Boom!," from 2004's *The Tipping Point* album), while his quickest song is performed at a speed of 117 BPM (on "Here I Come," from 2006's *Game Theory*). In this manner, Black Thought's own oeuvre acts as a representative for the temporal range of the entire rap genre at large.

In addition to shedding light on the simple range of tempos in the rap genre, Black Thought's discography also contributes further understanding to which of the tempos inside of that range appears in rap most frequently. In order to help accomplish this, some simple statistical analysis can be introduced.

To begin with, a compilation of the different speeds of Black Thought's melodies into a single frequency distribution table, seen below, is a good way to start a discussion of the rap genre's general approach to tempo. This frequency distribution table is a graph that describes visually the tempos that Black Thought has performed at most or least often over the past couple of decades. The horizontal axis displays the range of tempo, from 60 BPM to 120 BPM, while the vertical axis counts the number of times that any Black Thought song has been performed at that specific tempo. (Any double-time songs of Black Thought that appear in this chart are represented in straight time.)

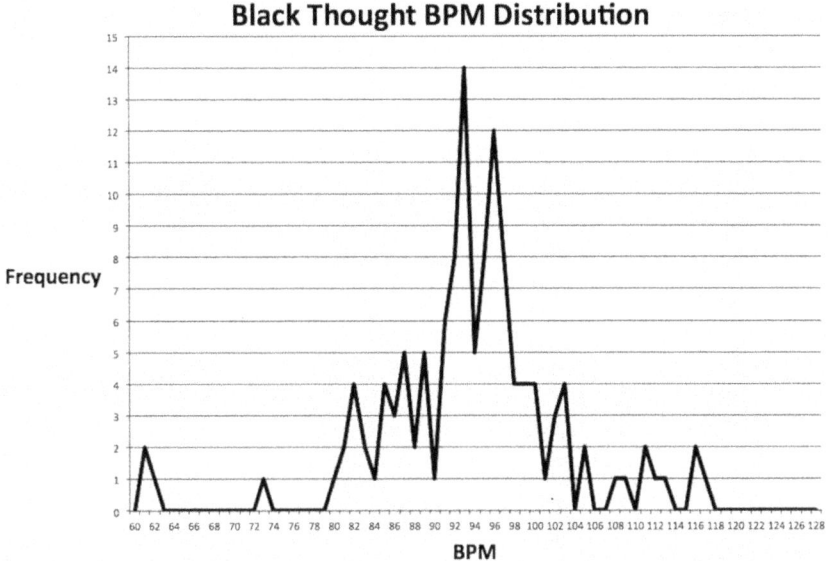

A frequency distribution of the different speeds of Black Thought's songs, compiled from the album releases in his career since 1992.

As a starting example for how to read it, one can begin by considering the chart's highest point in the middle, the one that is closest to the very top of the graph. While going down vertically from this point, one will find that it lands right on the horizontal BPM axis around 92. By proceeding to the left horizontally, one will also find that this high point in the middle falls right on the line that indicates a frequency of 14. What this part of the graph is communicating in total, then, is that Black Thought has rapped a total of fourteen songs with a BPM of 92 over the course of his career. This is the most common BPM that is ever heard over his entire oeuvre, and applies to songs as emotively diverse as "Stay Cool," "What They Do," and "Ain't Sayin Nothin' New," which all come from three different albums. By locating his most common temporal speed in the low 90s, Black Thought once again reflects a trend in the larger rap genre, especially those of more recent times, like the songs that Dr. Dre released after the arrival of his album *2001* in the year 1999. Indeed, all of this does seem to speak of some kind of large-scale shift in the focus of temporal speeds across the rap genre when viewed from its earliest days, as the most well-known songs of one of rap's famous pioneers show. "Planet Rock" and "Zulu Nation Throwdown," both released by Afrika Bambaataa in the very early years of the 1980s decade, are, on their own, on the faster side, occurring at BPMs around 128 and 108, respectively.

In contrast to that high point of fourteen songs at a BPM of 92 in the middle of Black Thought's frequency distribution table, there are also general temporal points in that broad 60–120 BPM range for which Black Thought has no corresponding song at all in the part of his oeuvre that's being considered here. If the reader considers the point of 66 BPM on the left hand side of the graph along the vertical axis, or 120 BPM on the right hand side of the graph, they will see that the graph's line doesn't rise at all above the horizontal axis, indicating that Black Thought does not have a song with that particular BPM inside the corpus of tracks under study now.

Just one of the takeaways from this technical graph of temporal speeds that are culled from the work of a single rapper is that, first of all, Black Thought's melodies display a comparatively wide range of BPMs. His slowest song is located at a lower, 60.8 BPM temporal speed. Meanwhile, his fastest song is almost 50 BPM faster in comparison, as it was performed at 117 BPM. This gives him an absolute BPM range of about 56.2 BPM. His average BPM overall, meanwhile, is 93.2. That number also fits in very well with the frequency distribution of his BPMs, since it is a number very close to the BPM speed that is found most frequently in Black Thought's musical speeds, which was 92, found at the mode.

Although conclusions about the rap genre as a whole might be accounted as being no more than tentative, at best, without some further analysis of a great number of other rap songs, many more conclusions can additionally be reached here if the same kind of statistical analysis is applied to a supermajority of the work of another rapper as well.

Waka Flocka's Temporal Range

Atlanta rapper Waka Flocka Flame has a much smaller discography than Black Thought, as he hasn't been recording for nearly as many years as that Philadelphia lyricist. In total, Waka Flocka has only about thirty-six official songs to be found over the course of both of his major record label studio albums that he had released by the time of this book's writing:

Flockaveli, from 2010, and *Triple F Life: Friends, Fans, and Family*, from 2012. The BPMs of all of these thirty-six songs were calculated and tallied in the same way that the corpus of Black Thought songs was analyzed. What results, however, is a much different statistical picture a rapper's favored tempo speeds, as well as tempo range.

In the graph below, the tempos of all thirty-six of those Waka Flocka songs, as tabulated by Traktor, have been mapped onto the same frequency distribution table as Black Thought. (Once more, any double-time songs of Waka Flocka have been counted in straight time, counting the snares and bass kicks of his songs that fall on the pulse as the constituting the true, underlying metric beat.) What results is a graph that demonstrates that Waka Flocka's own range of tempos is much more constricted than that of Black Thought:

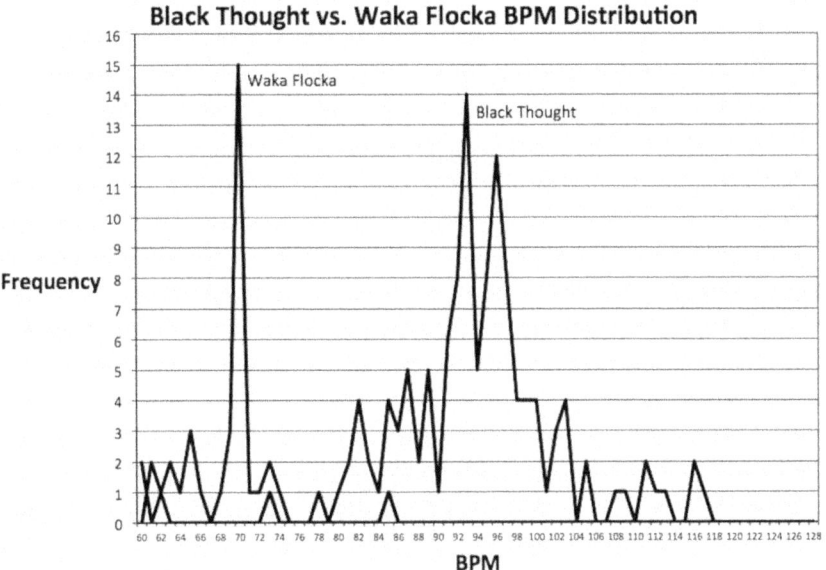

A comparison of how much more widely Black Thought's tempos are spread out across the entire range of songs speeds, as seen against Waka Flocka's own musical approach.

The difference in temporal range is accounted for by the concentration of Waka Flocka's speeds at the slower end of the spectrum. In fact, a full twenty-nine of his thirty-six songs fall between 60 and 70 BPM. Additionally, Waka Flocka's own slowest song, at 60 BPM, is slightly slower than Black Thought's own lower limit of 60.8. Another takeaway is that

Flocka's fastest song, at 85 BPM, doesn't come very close at all to Black Thought's own fastest song and its BPM speed of 117 BPM. As a result, while Black Thought's range of speeds is 56.2, Waka Flocka's own range is much smaller, at about 25 BPM.

As one of the final nuggets of information to be gleaned from this simple statistical analysis, it appears that the music of Waka Flocka is more limited than that of Black Thought in not only his own range of BPMs, but in the consistency of his own choice of musical speeds as well. That is, Waka Flocka's own most frequently-chosen tempo occurred on one of his individual songs a total of fifteen times, while Black Thought's own most frequent speed occurred only fourteen times.

To summarize, Black Thought raps over a wider range of tempo speeds than Waka Flocka, while he also tends to rap at a faster speed, on average, as well.

Variation in Rap Tempos

To further add to the revelations of this data range and data frequency, one more simple statistical tool, that of standard deviation, may also be introduced. Alongside range and frequency, standard deviation constitutes just one more helpful tool for describing the amount of variation there is in each separate rapper's own respective output.

A very common definition of standard deviation is that it constitutes a statistical measure of the variability of any set of numerical values about their average. As a general rule, if a set of numerical values has a high standard deviation, then the values are very spread out across the course of the entire data set. If, instead, those numerical values have a low standard deviation when it's calculated, the values are grouped more closely together with each inside of the data set.

With this information in hand, it can now be demonstrated that the standard deviation for the temporal speeds of a large corpus of Waka Flocka's compositional output, when calculated in BPM, is 4.77. Meanwhile, the standard deviation of Black Thought's own BPMs is much greater, residing at 9.16. Thanks to standard deviation, it can now be seen that Black Thought's own outliers are not as strongly anomalous as those of Waka Flocka are.

It should be noted at this point that, although certain words have been used in this discussion so far that can sometimes have negative connotations in particular contexts, they are certainly not meant to do so

1. Rhythm

here, in possibly judging Black Thought or Waka Flocka Flame to be the better (or worse) rapper through statistical method. Although words like "greater," "constrained" and "limited" have been used for describing the range, frequency, and standard deviation of these two rappers' temporal speeds when expressed in BPM, it does not in any way necessarily mean that one approach by one of the other rappers is better than that of the other.

Track Length and Song Structure

Another way we can empirically describe a rapper's musical technique is with the lengths of the songs on which they appear. Although counting or compiling the minutes and seconds that a rap song lasts for is a rather rote, artless exercise, it will simply be used here as a type of statistical shorthand for experimental song structures. That is, if a rap song is a very far outlier from the average in terms of its lengths, being either too long or too short—say, 16 minutes long, or only 30 seconds long—then it very likely has a quite complex song structure that enables such an anomalous chronological length.

As it turns out, that aforementioned average against which supposed outliers will be judged and identified can be calculated using the same software program that generated the exact BPM rates of the songs of Black Thought and Waka Flocka. Specifically, that length of the average rap song, when it was calculated from a corpus of 7,000 tracks by 195 different artists, is 3 minutes and 41 seconds.

Since the average length of those 7,000 rap songs is 3:41, it means that about 3,500 of them would have a length above 3:41, and about 3,500 of them would have a length below 3:41. And, if 195 artists were taken into account in this calculation, then each artist could be statistically expected to have made about 18 songs that are longer than 3:41. This is because when the 3,500 songs that are longer than 3:41 are divided by the 195 artists, 18 is the resulting answer. However, Black Thought's own musical group, The Roots, are responsible for no less than 162 songs of those 3,500 songs that last for a longer length of time than the average rap song. This means that, although he does not appear on every Roots song, Black Thought has created somewhere around nine times as many long songs as one would be lead to expect, based on probabilities. While being revealing of a particular genre's artistry in extremely broad, generalized strokes, this analysis is useful primarily because it tells the analyst where to look for what—but not, necessarily, what will be, or has been, found. This statistical analysis of an artistic phenomenon's empirical existence is convenient for finding identifiable outliers, such as The Roots song "@ 15" and its fifty-six total seconds of length, that demand a technical explanation, after they've first been located and identified.

Outliers in Rap's Normative Song Structures

Once this type of simple statistical analysis of Black Thought's music has been conducted, many outliers at either end of the song-length spectrum can be easily found and, afterwards, analyzed. They consist of, alternately, songs that are very short, or songs that are very long.

The shorter subset of outliers begins with songs like "@ 15" and its barebones musical structure, which consists entirely of nothing more than a monophonic texture with just one a cappella voice that raps merely one verse before concluding in under a minute. At the other end of the song-length spectrum from shorter songs like "@ 15" is "The Seed/Melting Pot/The Web," from 2005, and its own sixteen-minute length. When analyzed formally, this song turns out to be a three-part medley of different Roots songs, with instrumental solos in between Black Thought raps that are conducted by the group's band members in the manner of a classic jazz jam circle.

A final anomaly to be considered is "The Session (Longest Posse Cut in History)," which lasts for a full 12 minutes and 46 seconds. This song is of such an extended length, not because of intervening instrumental solos that arrive between rap melodies, but because there are no less than twelve fully accredited writers (including Black Thought himself) that appear on this song, according to its album's liner credits. Because more than ten lyricists trade verses back and forth in between the requisite hooks that fill out the song's standard verse–chorus structure, it makes sense that this song would have such a long chronological length as well.

Meter and Kanye West Melodies

Whether it was the musical analysis applied to the work of Eminem and other rappers like him in the beginning of the chapter, or the simple statistical analysis applied to Black Thought and Waka Flocka, almost all of the rappers have, so far, made songs that have a 4/4 meter. This section on Kanye West, though, as well as the ones to follow, will center around discussions of rap songs that aren't in a simple 4/4 meter.

In continuing this survey into the rhythmic techniques of rap vocalists, the next song from another rapper displays a very unique and identifiable rhythmic trait. The rapper is Kanye West, the song is "Black Skinhead," and the rhythmic trait is the triplet.

The repeated, gestural use of a triplet division of the beat can be heard in the rhythms of Kanye's melody from this 2013 song, starting at 0:36, which is bar 21. For the next couple of notations that follow, the defining rhythmic idiosyncrasies of rap, such as an expressive microtiming in trailing behind the beat, have been quantized in order to make their relationship to the compound meter behind them easier to understand:

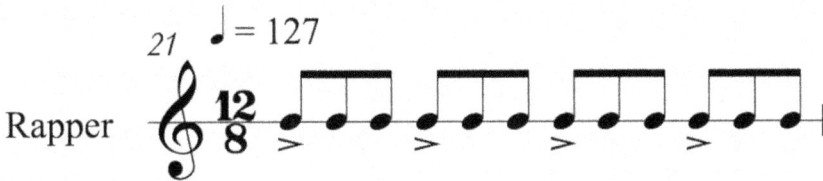

An example of triplet rhythms in the rap genre from Kanye West's song "Black Skinhead."

As Kanye West verbally explains his outsider position within his elite social circle because he's from a very different demographic than most other occupants, the musical traits of his rhythms immediately stand out as well. Most notably, "Black Skinhead" occurs in a 12/8 time signature, not the nearly ubiquitous 4/4 time signature that has been seen in almost every other song throughout this book up until now. This compound meter makes "Black Skinhead" something of an uncommon occurrence outlier within the rap genre. What is important here, though, is the fact that Kanye reflects this musical meter in his own melodic rhythms, and thus works to introduce a new rhythm into the melodies of rap that has not been seen yet in this discussion so far.

However, 12/8 is not the only meter, besides the traditional 4/4 of popular music, that Kanye's melodies can be found in. As just one example, Kanye's rap on "U Know" is in the rhythmic meter of 6/4. Although it might be able to be forced into the same notational scheme as the 12/8 meter of "Black Skinhead," the very slow tempo of this song is much more easily accommodated by the presence of a rhythmic subdivision larger than an 8th note in the bottom half of this song's time signature. Although both songs contain compound meters, they are put to much different uses in each respective context.

On "Black Skinhead," Kanye rapped only notes that fell directly on one of those three partials in each of 12/8 meter's four triplets. This is not how his melody on "U Know" was written, however. Instead, on "U Know," Kanye is much more likely to treat the basic pulse of the quarter note in ways that divide that triplet itself into compound sextuplets. This use of rhythms besides the triplets of 12/8 is allowed by the aforementioned slower tempo of "U Know." This begins when he starts his rap at bar 21, which comes around 0:34, after a free-rhythm opening:

Kanye's rhythms on "U Know" make use of a time signature, as well as a subdivisional structuring in his melody's rhythms, that is very different from the 12/8 triplets that are heard on his song "Black Skinhead."

As can be seen, Kanye sometimes fits four notes to a beat on "U Know," and not just three.

What West has done on "U Know" that he didn't on "Black Skinhead" is split some of the partials of his triplets in half, thereby creating sextuplets. This is indicated in the above notation by the beaming of the music into groups of three 8th notes, and the 16th notes that occur therein, even though the song has a quarter note pulse. In this manner, the beaming of the above notation and the song's actual meter are differentiated so strongly in order to drive home the various ways in which rappers can explore different parts of the same meter's pulse in separate ways.

In the transcription above, Kanye has split the third triplet partial of beat 1 in half on notes B and C, the second triplet partial of beat 2 in half on E and F, and the first triplet partial of beat 3 in half on H and I. On notes L, M, and N, he raps a note on each of the three partials of the triplet on beat 4. "U Know," then, can be contrasted with "Black Skinhead" in both its underlying meter (6/4 vs. 12/8), temporal speed (slow vs. fast), and predominant rhythmic subdivisions (sextuplets vs. triplets).

However, West does not, by any means, ignore the 4/4 meter in his

1. Rhythm

rapping melodies either. His first full, opening bars from the seminal 2004 track "Jesus Walks" are notated as follows:

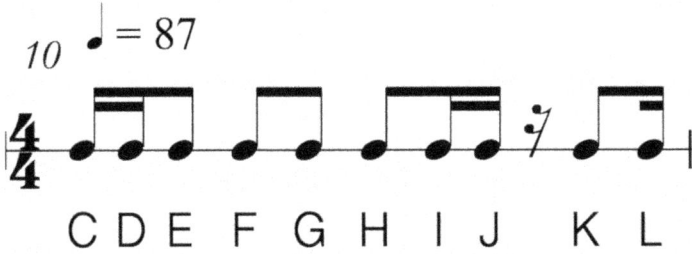

On his song "Jesus Walks," Kanye uses duplet rhythms, instead of the triplet rhythms that he performs on "Black Skinhead."

The time signature for the song is now 4/4, and the rhythms are much more regular than those that have been seen elsewhere. Here, all of the rhythms are based on simple divisions of the beat in half, not the tripartite division of the beat into triplets on songs like on "Black Skinhead" or "U Know."

Killer Mike's Triplet Melodies

Other rappers besides Kanye West also make use of what is called by fans from the rap community a "triplet flow." Another user of it is Killer Mike, as can be heard on the 2001 OutKast song "The Whole World." This song is more similar to Kanye's "Black Skinhead" than "U Know," because Killer Mike strongly preserves the triplet's identity as being made up of only three parts, rather than three parts that can be split it into two, thereby comprising sextuplets.

Killer Mike's opening lines, which start around 2:17, are below:

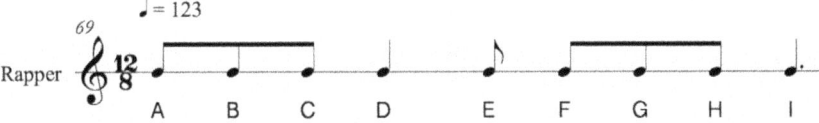

An example of Killer Mike's own approach to the use of triplets on the OutKast song "The Whole World," which is more strongly syncopated than the approach to triplets of a rapper like Kanye West.

Out of the four beats transcribed form this single bar, two of them contain a full triplet, on notes A–B–C and F–G–H. Killer Mike continues to frequently utilize this triplet subdivision in a structurally-important way over the rest of his subsequent bars. Interestingly enough, André 3000 and Big Boi both largely decline to follow this musical path on the same song. Instead, the OutKast duo themselves make use of duplet rhythms and the like, which are much more strongly disjointed from the 12/8 accompaniment's obvious suggestion of triplet melodic rhythms.

Kendrick Lamar's Triplet Melodies

However, a triplet compound meter in the rhythmic accompaniment is not necessarily a prerequisite for the occurrence of strong triplet rhythms in a rapper's melody. Kendrick Lamar demonstrates this fact on his 2012 song "Bitch, Don't Kill My Vibe," at 2:35:

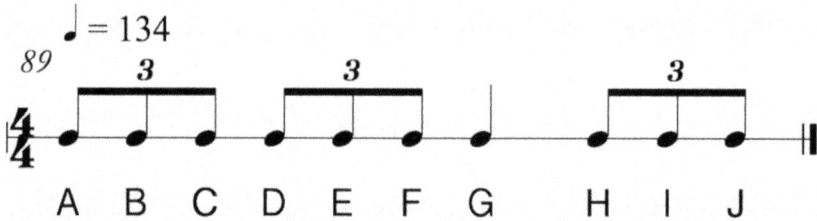

Rappers often fit triplet rhythms over songs whose meters aren't built on the tripartite division of the beat, such as Kendrick Lamar on his song "Bitch, Don't Kill My Vibe."

Kendrick's triplets here don't come over a time signature that is built around subdivisional groupings of three, like the 12/8 of "The Whole World" or "Black Skinhead," or the 6/4 of "U Know." Instead, Kendrick has inserted triplets into his melody over top of a standard 4/4 time signature, as defined by the musical accompaniment behind him.

Flobots' Complex Time Signatures

In addition to meters of 12/8, 6/4, 4/4, and 6/8, complex meters, such as 5/4, can equally be located within the rapping genre. As documented so far in history, there are at least three songs by relatively well-known artists who have rapped in 5/4, and gone on to release such tracks publicly and commercially. These songs are "Jetpack" by Flobots, "Dear Sirs" by El-P, and "Gone Fishing" by Captain Murphy. Although all of these songs share a meter, they all take radically different approaches to their melodies' reaction to that very same meter.

The rapper Jonny 5 from Flobots, on the song "Jetpack," actually structures his melodic phrases so that they completely align with the five-part groupings of quarter notes that is occurring in the meter behind him. That is, his sentences all last for the length of five beats, and continue to do so over a relatively long time period. Since the only important element here is the structure of the melody on a bar-to-bar level, and not the necessarily the expressive rhythmic trailing and microtiming of that structure itself, this next transcription has been simplified so that it lands right on the beat. The following rhythms occur at 0:45, at bar 37:

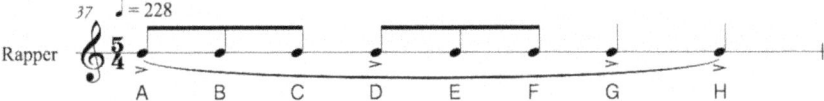

The Flobots song "Jetpack" makes use of a meter that has five quarter notes inside of every bar, instead of just the usual four, a fact to which the lyricist responds by grouping together his phrases so that they also last for five quarter notes.

Here, the rapper has started and ended his sentences, describing the difficulties of anyone sane trying to live in an insane world, exactly where the bars start and end. Specifically, the note A is the first word of a sentence, and that sentence's meaning, with both a noun and verb, is complete at note H. In this manner, the Flobots lyricist is completely abiding by the indicative structure of his 5/4 meter, which is completely unlike what other rappers have done in similar musical contexts.

The Flobot rapper has here grouped the ten 8th notes of a 5/4 signature into a repeating 3 + 3 + 2 + 2 grouping, as determined by what syllables the rapper accents, and as indicated by the beamings in the notation. In contrast, El-P and Captain Murphy instead choose to leave their groupings more open on their own respective songs, as mentioned before. Frequently, the rappers on these two new artists' songs change their phrasal groupings between one bar and the very next. Through this, the length of their phrases, as well as where their phrases stop and start, rarely (if ever) follow the length of the metric bar, or where that bar itself starts over again anew.

In summary, the lyricist of Flobots has responded directly, through his melody, to the 5/4 meter, while El-P and Captain Murphy choose, instead, to use it as a cleansing departure point for other, non-metrical musical happenings on "Dear Sirs" and "Gone Fishing." In fact, the melodies of those two rappers on their own 5/4 songs bear a stronger resemblance to the free rhythms of André 3000 and Pharoahe Monch, to be examined soon, rather than those of Flobots, even though their own respective recordings at hand here share a meter with the latter, not the former.

Hamilton's Complex Time Signatures

As another examination of time signature within the rap genre, the short song "Meet Me Inside," from the *Hamilton* Broadway musical, is written in 7/8. This complex time signature is combined with a tempo BPM that is at 180, as well. By combining a complex time signature with a pulse that is delivered temporally very quickly, the chaotic musical background perfectly fits the unbalanced dramatic action and psychological mindsets of the performing characters, who have just witnessed a duel. Two characters, exchanging lines of strong passion, toss the lead spot in the melody back and forth between themselves in the manner of a call-and-response texture. However, an analysis of that special kind of interpenetrating musical dialogue will be saved for this book's fifth chapter.

For now, it will suffice to restrict the discussion to how the combined melody of the two conversing characters interacts with the backing 7/8 meter. Most rap, as a rule, is made up of melodic phrases that all last for an even number of beats, whether two, four, eight, etc. Additionally, most rap also starts where the bar lines of the song's meter start, and end where the bar lines of the song's meter end. On "Meet Me Inside," an adherence to these conventions of rap by the characters might seem impossible, since the bar's meter now has an uneven amount of beats in it (seven). The question now is about how the songwriters have handled a musical time signature that would seem to make certain conventions in rap a priori impossible.

Indeed, the answer is supplied by this rap's composers through an adaptation of that convention into a new, non-symmetrical metric world. In order to preserve the inherent unity of their musical texture, the rappers on "Meet Me Inside" here preserve an alignment with the metric structures of their backing accompaniment by crafting their traded sentences so that they always add up to seven 8th notes. This describes accurately exact what occurs musically in the first four bars of this rather short, 1:24 song. As Alexander Hamilton, Aaron Burr, John Laurens, and the ensemble trade lines, a combination of their melodic phrases into consecutive pairs is always a preservation of this track's basic metric structure.

In bar 1, the first rap line from Hamilton, when combined with the ensuing rap line that's delivered by Burr, adds up to seven 8th notes, since both lines each last for seven 16th notes. The next two lines from Burr and Laurens in bar 2 also last for seven 16th notes each, and likewise start and end where the bar behind them starts and ends. These same considerations of complex meter and the melodic phrases that are overlaid upon it in "Meet Me Inside" are also borne out by the structures of bar 3 and bar 4 on this track as well.

In this way, the composers of "Hamilton" were able to carefully walk the line between convention and innovation. In his own rap melodies, Big Sean also shows an ability to light the way forward for the genre, based on where its been in the past.

Big Sean's Shuffle Melodies

To be added to our previous investigations of the triplet melodies of Kanye West, Killer Mike, and Kendrick Lamar is Big Sean, a rapper whose songwriting tendencies likewise lead to a frequent use of triplets. But although Big Sean's rhythms can be expressed in the form of a triplet notation, they are not necessarily always triplet rhythms, per se. This is because, rather than rapping constant triplets (like Kanye West on "Black Skinhead"), or rapping syncopated triplets like (Killer Mike on "The Whole World"), Big Sean sometimes repurposes that same tripartite division of the beat to achieve the swing or shuffle feel of the jazz's big band genre.

Although it may not derive historically from a triplet division of the beat, it is often the triplet form of notation that is used to represent the shuffle feel when it is transcribed in Western sheet music notation. This is because the shuffle feel resizes the two 8th notes of every pulse, so that the first one ends up lasting twice as long as the second, resulting in another tripartite division, but with only two of those three partials ever being fully expressed.

Detroit rapper Big Sean unfailingly uses the swing rhythm on the original version of producer-singer Mike Posner's song "Cooler Than Me," which appeared years before it became a hit on Posner's 2010 debut album *31 Minutes To Takeoff*. Before his verse was removed in the official remixed version, Big Sean had a cameo on this song that first appeared on Posner's unofficial mixtape *A Matter Of Time.*

Below are the bars that Big Sean starts rapping shortly into his verse, at bar 86, which comes around 2:38.

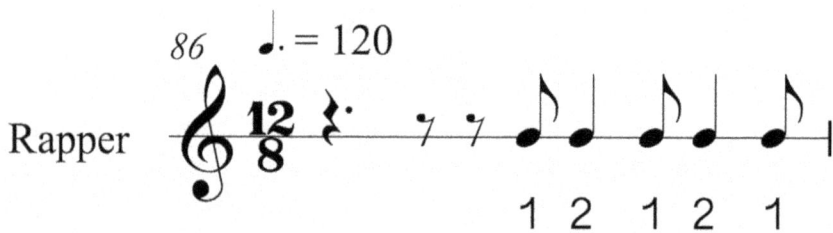

An example of Big Sean's shuffle-feel flow on the song "Cooler Than Me." Big Sean creates this feel by rapping notes only on the first and third notes of a triplet division, thereby completely skipping the middle note of the triplet.

For each two-note grouping of that swing rhythm that occurs in the notation above, the first note has been marked with the number "1" below it, and the second note the number "2" below it. In total, a full eleven of these swing groupings occur in just four bars. This two-note realization of a triplet division occurs much more frequently on the original mixtape version of "Cooler Than Me" than it did on either Kanye West's "Black Skinhead," or Killer Mike's version from "The Whole World." As a result, this particular use of the triplet notation denotes a two-note shuffle feel, rather than a true tripartite division of the beat. Even the notes that don't occur in a full, two-part swing rhythm, as indicated by the "X" marked below them, still always fall within one of those two subdivisional positions. Even as no more than a side note, it is intriguing to remark upon how a series of evolving transcriptions of Big Sean's melodic rhythms on "Cooler Than Me" can indicate a historical, societal, and cultural change in pure music.

An attempt to musically demonstrate that historical process of change and transformation is what determined the above notations' meter as being 12/8, and not 4/4, even though that duplet simple meter could also capture Big Sean's rhythms accurately. But to clarify the close relationship of these rhythms to jazz practice, those rhythms have been notated anew in the below transcription. The first two bars here capture Big Sean's rhythms as well, but with a different meter. The transcription now has a time signature that might eventually underscore where rap could ultimately be drawing its modern influences from:

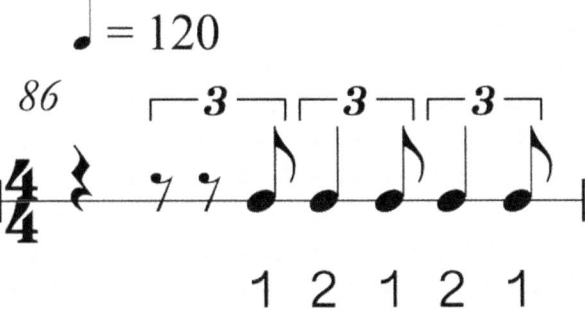

Notating Big Sean's flow using a 4/4 time signature and triplet groupings like in the above, instead of a 12/8 time signature like in the last notation, points out how similar Big Sean's flow here is to a very popular jazz rhythm from the middle of the 20th century.

Because of how prevalent these swing rhythms are in the genre of jazz, which many have posited is where rap springs from originally, jazz musicians often don't even need to be instructed to play the piece they're performing with this rhythmic swinging feel to it. Rather than notating this ubiquitous swing feel into the music over and over, jazz standards often come with a legend at the top of the notation that indicates this rhythmic feel. Thus, the swung triplet is visually simplified into the straight duplet, in order to make the notation easier to read. Having made the jump from 12/8 music to 4/4 with triplets, the representation of Big Sean's melody on "Cooler Than Me" can now make the jump to a 4/4 meter without triplets, but with an initial legend, or key, that indicates this rhythmic feel. In this form, Big Sean's rhythms would look like the following, with the necessary legend appended below the BPM symbols:

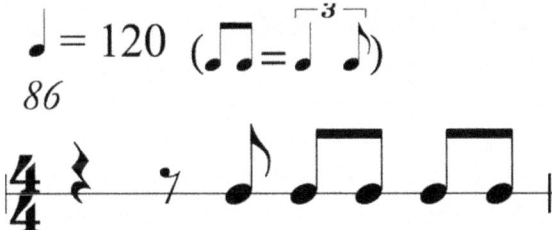

An example of how multiple forms of transcription for Big Sean's shuffle-feel rhythms from "Cooler Than Me" can be represented in modern jazz notation, thereby artistically underlining the connection between modern rap and its roots in jazz.

Thus, through this visual transformation from classical music notation to jazz notation, we see how Big Sean's rhythms are not just influenced by jazz, but also, in a way, comprise jazz itself. Conversely, songs from rappers like André 3000 and Pharoahe Monch display some of the musical influences on rap that come from places besides jazz. As different as these next few rap melodies are, they are all united by their peculiar approach to metric pulse.

Sprechstimme Melodies in Rap

As recent studies like Jeff Chang's 2005 title *Can't Stop Won't Stop* document, a heightening stylization of traditional Jamaican toasts often act as the informal introduction to songs from the dancehall genre. As Chang writes: "The blues had Mississippi, jazz had New Orleans. Hip-hop has Jamaica....' Them said nothing good ever come outta Trenchtown, [DJ Kool] Herc says, 'Well, hip-hop came out of Trenchtown!'"[6]

This historical connection has also been brought to the forefront of popular music consciousness through samplings of the work of Fuzzy Jones, as in the 2012 hit "Mercy," produced by the artist Lifted. Another source of rhythmically-free inspiration for the first generation of rap artists was the spoken word tradition of artists like Gil Scott-Heron. As Chang would go on to demonstrate, "...Public Enemy and Boogie Down Productions pointed back to the voices of Black radicalism, heard on the albums of the Watts Prophets, the Last Poets, H. Rap Brown, and Gil Scott-Heron."[7]

While such spoken word artists, both formerly and today, often perform with musical accompaniment, the rhythms of their words rarely if ever abide by the direction of the regularly-repeating, metrical pulse behind them in a traditional way. One can even hear this unique type of wonderfully uneasy co-existence between music and text in certain producers' sampling of the work of Scott-Heron. Kanye West's 2010 song, "Who Will Survive in America," incorporates extended samples of the Scott-Heron song "Comment No. 1."

Whether in its new Kanye West trappings, or back in its original context, Scott-Heron's rhythms are not performed *inside of* the meter. Instead, Scott-Heron sets up his own voice as a rhythmic counterpoint against the pulse, as he takes unexpected caesural rhythmic pauses that have no relationship to the meter's pulse or subdivisions, even while the music continues to activate itself. Scott-Heron's free rhythms even override the

1. Rhythm   57

foremost importance of the musical accompaniment's meter within the musical texture at times, in the form of an egalitarian give-and-take, quasi-improvisational performance partnership. The traditions of such artworks from the 1960s and 1970s are today carried on in the style of poets like Saul Williams, whose performance poem "When the Clock Strikes Me" bears many resemblances to both spoken word and rap.

In technical terms, the prosodic accents of rhythmically-free vocal idioms, like those of Gil Scott-Heron, do not line up with the pulse of the meter, and the structure of their melodic phrasing does not reference or respect the endpoints or beginning points of bar lines. As will be shortly observed, such artists' rhythms do have a musical nature, but one that seems to respond to a system of ad hoc, internal metric governance, rather than an explicitly aural one. It is a direct musical reference to these original roots of spoken word and Jamaican dancehall roots on Pharoahe Monch's song "Intro" and André 3000's opening verse from OutKast's "Return of the 'G'" that seems to be taking place.

A quick perusal of a sheet music transcription of André 3000's opening rap on "Return of the 'G'" will display this. The rhythms to come, even for archival or cataloguing purposes, border on the unintelligible. What follows is a transcription of the first melodic phrase from André 3000's rap on this 1998 OutKast song, at 0:30:

An example of an André 3000 bar from the OutKast song "Return of the 'G.'" His hyper-rhythmic melody doesn't follow along to the basic, repeating pulse of the music behind it in a traditional way.

The above music looks very different from most of the notated music that has been seen so far from the other rappers. First, there is a cadenza-like explosion of diverse notes. The bar in the above transcription actually has twenty-one notes within itself alone. Second, the note values are differentiated from each other in very, very small increments. For instance, the difference between the length of note J and the note of length K is only .021 seconds, or a mere 128th noctuplet note. Perhaps most importantly, the notes that have been verbally stressed by André 3000—notes G, M, P, and V—are spread out with apparent randomness all over the bar, rather than falling right on, or even close to, the pulse of the accompaniment's meter over which André 3000 is delivering his vocals.

As a result, it seems that on "Return of the 'G,'" André is not abiding by the guidance of the metrical pulse behind him. His prosodic accents do not fall on the beat, or even relatively near to it. He doesn't leave open rhythmic space in between his words in order to accommodate the musical space between beats; furthermore, his melodic phrases do not reference, in any way at all, the dictates of the bar lines behind him. Now, none of those rhythmic subversions of the meter's measural or pulse structure necessarily demand that André 3000's musical should be classified as displaying an untraditional approach to meter.

In fact, many rappers have melodies that display one or two of those exact characteristics. Notorious B.I.G.'s "Hypnotize," from 1996, is noted often for the way in which his melodic phrases constantly change their own positioning, using the structure of the bars behind them as little more than a tangential backdrop. However, rarely is such a wide bevy of metrically-subversive rhythmic details combined as in André 3000's opening verse here, and rarely does are they combined in a single verse so frequently. But when all of these technical subversions of metric structure are combined inside of a single melodic line over a duration of musical time, it seems to demand something other than an ensemble-oriented meter, audible to all, in order to explain how such apparent accentual chaos is able to retain an internally-coherent organization of rhythm.

Neither is this melody of André 3000—equal parts rapping, singing, and speaking—a quirky, idiosyncratic outlier within the genre. The first song from Pharoahe Monch's own 1999 solo debut album, *Internal Affairs*, is another example of how rappers have combined the methods of rapping with the methods of spoken word. Below is a transcription of the first few bars, coming around 0:23, that are performed by Monch:

The first full opening bar of Pharoahe Monch's melody on his rap song "Intro." Note the finely-delineated rhythmic durations that constantly change from one note to the next, and how the accented notes, such as G, J, L, etc., have almost no relation to where the four beats of the bar are.

In the above music, there are many similarities between André 3000's and Monch's rhythms. For example, the explosion of rhythmic activity continues unabated: Monch has a full seventeen notes in his second bar alone. Just like the work of his Southern predecessor, Monch's seventeen-note explosion is not easily fit into a single bar of music, especially at the quicker tempo of 93 BPM. There are also many melodic phrases that start and end here without any kind of proximal reference to the places where bar lines start and end in the music. The prosodically-accented notes on G, J, L, N, P, T, and V are radically spread out in a manner that bespeaks little or no reference to the fact that Pharoahe Monch, on this song, is performing with a metered musical accompaniment behind him. Finally, there are, once again, very small differences between the musical duration of these notes, such as between notes I and J.

Rather than communicating a need for completely new forms of analysis, these demonstrated connections between speech and singing on the one hand, and between spoken word and rapping on the other, communicate just how many steps on the continuum between music and non-music there are. On the one side of the arrhythmic, there is plain, everyday conversation, and at the opposite end, there is what one hears when they turn on their favorite artist in order to hear their recordings.

In between, however, there seems to be an infinite amount of small steps that move pure sound from one end to the other. First, there are the (mostly) unconstrained rhythms of everyday conversation; then, there is the pregnant pause for suspenseful effect; next, the comedic timing of a well-delivered punch line; afterwards, perhaps, the sprechstimme of Schoenberg, as will be observed in a following chapter; moving further towards music, spoken word performances are to follow; the non-metrical melodies of André 3000, Pharoahe Monch, and others like them might come next; then, rapping proper; and, finally, singing itself. The fact that André 3000 and Pharoahe Monch have simply picked an untraditional point along this spectrum where they would like to make a substantial portion of their music is in no way disqualifying for their categorization within the rap genre itself, once this music's evolution is understood historically.

Eve's Additive Rhythms

Influences from even other non–European music traditions can also be located in rap's technical aspects of rhythm, along with the jazz, blues, dancehall, and spoken word elements that have just been technically identified and located. Although the connection between Eastern musics, like Indian raga, and rap itself has yet to be documented or catalogued fully from a historical standpoint, the traditional elements that are commonly associated with such geographical identifications of music genres can certainly be documented, no matter how they might have actually come to be found in rap in the first place.

To be sure, many rappers make frequent use of the additive structure of rhythms within the context of the technique of metric transference. The rhythms of Eminem on "Without Me," at 3:18, even display such a tendency for an easterly focus on the small rhythm itself, and not how that rhythm fits into larger structural sections. On that song, Eminem proceeds to displace the very same four-note rhythm from first landing on the beat, to then being syncopated, as traced previously in the above. However, the extent of this special kind of rhythmic focus is often limited. Even in Eminem's example, it lasts for only about two bars, and is, in truth, no more than a transference of a rhythm's metric position within the system of divisive rhythm, rather than an approach that makes true use of additive rhythm itself.

But in actuality there are other rappers, such as the Philadelphia lyricist Eve, who utilize this system of additive rhythm to a much greater structural and formal extent. When Eve adds together small rhythms in order to build up large structures, she carries on this process for extended periods of musical times, and so makes it the very foundation on which large parts of her verse are built. In the music below, from bar 21 of her 2002 song "What," at 0:48, she uses one unbalanced rhythmic duration almost exclusively, the rhythm of a double-dotted 8th note, for two whole bars:

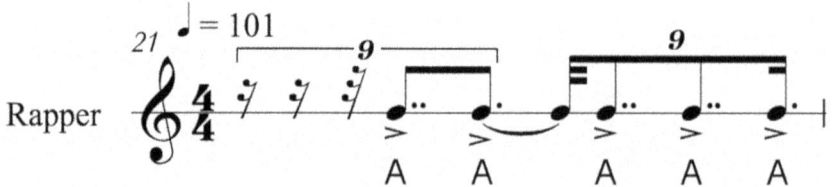

An example of Eve's additive rhythms on her song "What." Here, she adds together over and over a rhythmic duration, that of the double-dotted 8th note, to which the pulse of her musical accompaniment's meter is not closely related, since it is in 4/4.

The five notes in the above music, and all five of them—as denoted by the letter A underneath—have the length of a double-dotted 8th note.

Further establishing the importance of this rhythm, every note Eve pronounces is strongly accented. By largely declining to directly reference the regularly-repeating hierarchy of strong beats and weak beats with which Western musical cultures parses its temporally-organized sound, Eve has engaged deeply with the musical thinking behind additive rhythm.

Neither is Eve's engagement with the system of additive rhythm an isolated incident within the rap genre. Big Daddy Kane, almost thirteen years before Eve rapped on "What," had first laid the groundwork for such a transcultural reception of unfamiliar rhythms within the rap genre.

Big Daddy Kane's Additive Rhythms

Big Daddy Kane, on his 1989 song "Wrath of Kane," makes use of additive rhythms for a greater musical length than even Eve did. While Eve limited her own contributions to the length of about two bars, Big Daddy Kane extends his own two-note, additive-rhythm phrase over the course of four full bars, and, briefly, into a subsequent verse as well. And while Eve made her own additive phrase out of just a single note that lasts for a dotted 8th note, Big Daddy Kane makes his own additive phrase out of two notes: a first that lasts for a 16th note, and a second that lasts for an 8th note. Just like Eve, though, Kane makes no technical effort to fit the accent or position of his rhythms inside of the bar within the metrical hierarchy of the 4/4 time signature of the musical accompaniment behind him.

The additive phrase of Big Daddy Kane unfurls on "Wrath of Kane" at the start of the second verse, at 0:53. Here, Kane performs a section of his melody that has thirty-six notes, all of which can be divided into eighteen rhythmically-identical, two-note groups.

The first note in each one of these eighteen additive groups lasts for a 16th note, and the second note in each of these groups lasts for the length of an 8th note. Additionally, while the first note in each grouping is always unaccented from one of these eighteen groups to the next, the second is always unfailingly emphasized and accented in turn. This means that any single one of these eighteen groups will last for a total of three 16th notes. However, because there are obviously sixteen 16th notes in every bar of the 4/4 time signature over which Big Daddy Kane is crafting his melody, a number which can't be evenly divided by three, these eighteen additive-rhythm groupings very quickly become divorced and misaligned from the backing music's regularly-repeating meter.

To see this specifically in his rap itself, the first note of Big Daddy Kane's additive rhythm groupings will be designated in the below by the letter A, the second note will be designated by the letter B, and each single additive rhythm grouping made up of two notes will be denoted by brackets that surround those two letters. In this manner, then, the music can be notated as follows. This is a transcription of Big Daddy Kane's melody on "The Wrath of Kane," starting at 0:53:

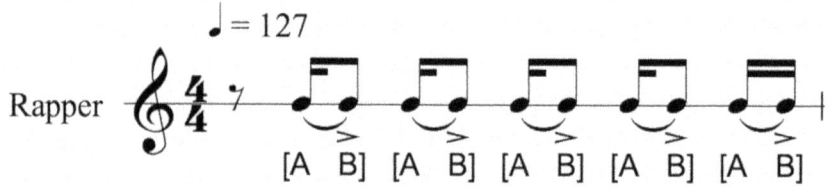

A notation of Big Daddy Kane's melody at 0:53 on his song "The Wrath of Kane," which is built on the combination of small units of rhythms—a 16th note and an 8th note—in a system of additive rhythm. The brackets surrounding each of the A–B groupings indicate where the structural additive rhythm that gets repeated can be found.

The astute observer will also have noticed that the beamings in the notated music above are, so to speak, "wrong." That's because the horizontal black lines over the top of the small, circular, black note heads here reflect the groupings of Kane's melody, and *not* the groupings of the meter. This is done in order to outline the presence of the additive rhythm, and not to indicate the structure of the backing meter, which imposes upon Kane's rhythms at this point with such little force.

In demonstrating his structural treatment of additive rhythm, Kane carries on this two-note, unbalanced rhythm on for a length of time that is so extended long—four bars—that its alignment with the backing meter actually comes back around into agreement, at time stamp 1:00. That is, this is the first point at which the second, accented note of Kane's additive grouping lands back on the accented first beat of the song's basic 4/4 meter. However, Kane continues the chaining of his additive phrase past this natural dividing line, which further communicates that his melody is being structured with additive rhythm, and not just an extreme amount of syncopation.

In the fourth bar of his second verse, Big Daddy Kane then performs two more of these special additive groupings, before bringing the melody back into alignment with the song's 4/4 meter by making his last melodic phrase last for the length of four 16th notes, rather than three. This ends the beginning of his second verse, as he afterwards goes on to make more use divisive rhythms, rather than additive rhythms, throughout the rest of his verse.

What's most notable, however, is that the same two-note additive grouping, lasting for a total of three 16th notes, that kicked off this first verse also ends it, at the 1:36 mark. Here, Big Daddy Kane performs four straight instances of this two-note additive rhythm. But over the course of the subsequent four bars, Kane shifts course suddenly when he goes on to regularize and normalize the grouping so that it now lasts for an even length of 16th notes, whether that number of 16th notes be two, four, or otherwise. The overall result, though, is a melody in the modern rapping vocal idiom that makes structural use of an additive, not divisive, understanding of rhythm.

Summary

As a final example, Big Daddy Kane's formal utilization of additive rhythm makes for an admirable endpoint to a survey of rhythms within the rap genre. This is because it demonstrates a fundamental element of the entire genre's most fundamental, inalterable guiding aesthetic: "Anything, from anywhere." This willingness to assimilate the most disparate artistic traditions into a single whole, even if it's not necessarily always coherent to its audience in a straightforward, teleological way, might be the main reason for which rap has catapulted to the list of the most popular music genres recently. Throughout this chapter, there has been catalogued a wide array of approaches to the deceivingly simple relationship of a beat to a bar, of a downbeat to an offbeat, of a subdivisional grouping to a song's meter, and so on.

A willingness to co-opt any style, from any music, and to then put that idiom towards an expressive end is what has been the driving force behind rap music for decades. Whether it was the Zulu Nation rapping over synthesized musical accompaniments under a borrowed international moniker back at the start of the genre, or the Wu-Tang Clan rapping in imitation of the broken English of bad kung fu flick translations under the flag of an ancient Buddhist martial arts temple more recently, rap draws no boundaries for itself. In the end, no matter the reason for its popularity, it is a safe bet to say that rap, as an art form, will continue to devour and repurpose traditional conventions for any expressive mission its artists deem sufficiently worth their while.

2

Melody

Melody in rap occupies a very unique place in the genre. While most of the focus on rappers-as-musicians is typically placed on their rhythmic abilities, most of the time their interaction with pitch, or even scales, is completely disregarded. When rappers like André 3000 are placing perhaps as many as twenty-one notes within a single measure, it is maybe understandable why such a case of critical tunnel vision might occur. Many people, for instance, don't even realize that rappers' contributions to a song even *can* be considered as having pitch-specific melodies.

In any event, rappers themselves are very aware of the new musical possibilities that a recitative-type of approach to their vocals, or even strict singing that follows the pitches of a mathematically-defined scale, can open up to them. In this chapter, a wide-ranging survey of the different types of melodies rappers have crafted over the years will be undertaken. In this context, the term "melody" may be understood as referring only to the aspects of rap vocals that engage primarily with elements of pitch, and not necessarily rhythm. It is from this perspective, then, that the rhythm of a rap is able to be constructively separated from its melody, which is itself a term that typically has a much more all-encompassing definition, one that simultaneously refers to both the rhythmic *and* pitch elements of the most important musical line in a particular piece of music at any given point in time.

This chapter will consider the melody of rap from a number of different perspectives, including how rap melody can determine rap structure, how rap melody can determine certain aspects of rap lyrics, and even how rap melody can sometimes impact rap rhythm itself. Because the specific pitch of a rapper's voice does not usually follow a scale, it is actually much harder to discuss the melody of rap than might be thought at first. As a result, melody within rap must periodically be considered in an indirect manner, and studied as a musical elements whose workings can be seen only through an observation of its effects on other aspects of the music, like structure.

What will soon be found, though, is that rap—far from being an unjustifiable musical innovation, bereft of both antecedent theory and practice, that came from nowhere in the late 1970s—can actually be understood as comprising a response to some of the most conventional musical traditions that are available to the modern audience, like opera. At the same time, rap also dually relies on some of the most radical innovations that the compositional treatment of the human voice has to offer, including those that come from the days of music's single greatest historical upheaval as it occurred around the time of composer Arnold Schoenberg's introduction of his sprechstimme technique in the early 1900s.

As it turns out, none other than Bob Dylan and his own musical melodies have extremely strong affinities and similarities to Schoenberg's own signature extended vocal techniques. Although he does not rap, the musical materials with which Bob Dylan makes his own music are so closely related to those of rappers that his vocals are a great place to begin to learn about the different types of singing.

The Speech-Singing Spectrum

Most of us are familiar with the type of straight, pure singing we hear from groups like The Beatles and other types of popular genre musicians. However, much of Dylan's own work makes use of the sprechstimme style of singing that is much more often documented in the work of classical composers like Schoenberg. Although it was until only recently that it was treated as a compositional consideration, and not as an analytical tool, the etymological roots of the German word sprechstimme in the compound word "spoken voice" are simply too informative and helpful to let it remain alone within the realm of performance. The performance term sprechstimme indicates a vocal technique that resides somewhere between the everyday cadences of normal speech and the heightened rhythms of stylized song, and so makes a wonderful starting place for beginning to understand how rappers shape the pitch and intonation of their melodies. To lay the foundation for the coming examination, it would do well to directly quote the composer who first differentiated sprechstimme from normal singing in the foreword to his magnum opus *Pierrot Lunaire*. Schoenberg there writes:

> The performer has the task of transforming [the vocal part] into a speech melody ["Sprechmelodie"].... He accomplishes this by ... being precisely aware of the difference between a sung tone and a spoken tone: the sung tone maintains the pitch unaltered; the spoken tone does indicate it, but immediately abandons it again by falling or rising.... The goal is certainly not at all a realistic, natural speech.... But it should not call singing to mind, either.[1]

Intriguingly enough, these ideas and directions could be directly applied in order to understand Bob Dylan's own idiosyncratic vocal performances on songs like "Like a Rolling Stone." Indeed, the effect of these writings as they manifest themselves in live performances of Pierrot Lunaire are not altogether that much different from Bob Dylan's own speech-singing. However, this could be more of an effect of subsequent generations' problematic interpretations, rather than an original composer's intent. As Pierre Boulez wrote in 1986, while recognizing the difficulty of this book's project in attempt to capture music-speech: "...The question arises whether it is actually possible to speak according to a notation devised for singing. This was the real problem at the root of all the controversies. Schoenberg's own remarks on the subject are not in fact clear."[2]

Whatever is the case, Schoenberg's musical intent seems to be reflected to an almost startling extent in a subsequent critic's commentary on one of Bob Dylan's most famous albums. The emphasis below is this author's own:

> "Cawing, derisive" was Philip Larkin's account of Dylan's voice on the 1965 album *Highway 61 Revisited*.... Larkin's adjectives ... suggest something of *the peculiar tonal quality* common to nearly all of Dylan's performances. Typically, the voice engages the line of the melody but its simultaneously jarring, atonal separation from the music, together with the relentless subordination of musical elements to the exigencies of verbal order, opens a space which registers a distance and an unease involving both singer and listener....[3]

Aidan Day's description of a "peculiar tonal quality" of Dylan's music might be just as accurately applied to the melodies that are performed in Schoenberg's own 1912 work.

These two concepts of "atonal separation" and "the exigencies of verbal order" are useful in defining two separate but interpenetrating spectra along which any vocal performers' melodies can be judged to fall. They will be particularly helpful here, since they help explain how most rap melodies should be understood by giving us a framework by which rap vocals can be compared to other types of melodic vocalizing.

The phrase "atonal separation" conceptualizes and defines a spectrum of continuous degrees along which a melody is said to be either strongly adhering to concepts of a tonal hierarchy, strongly averse to interpretation through a tonal hierarchy, or somewhere in between. Meanwhile, "verbal order" conceptualizes and defines a spectrum of degrees along which a melody is said to be strongly similar to speech, strongly dissimilar from speech, or somewhere in between those two poles. Traditional singers are set on one end, being a vocalization that has the smallest relationship possible to everyday speech in terms of both tonality and rhythm. (In simpler terms, traditional singers and traditional vocalizations can here be taken as referring to as performances of music that reside squarely within a musical scale, even unconventional ones.)

On the opposite end from them are rappers, whose work has the smallest possible relationship to singing in terms of the same demarcating factors. This also means, however, that rappers' melodies share much more in common with the melodies of Bob Dylan and sprechstimme vocalizations than the melodies of traditional vocalists.

Speech-Singing Visualized

This wide range of creative variety is compiled and visualized in the chart below for easy digestion. The horizontal x-axis represents, in increasing terms, just how similar each musician's rhythms are to singing, as judged by a relative standard. A position towards the chart's origin in the bottom left-hand corner indicates that that musicians' system of pitch isn't, comparatively speaking, very similar to strict singing at all. Meanwhile, a position that's further away from the origin horizontally indicates that that musician's intonational system of pitch is very close to strict singing, or, in fact, an exact example of it.

The vertical y-axis indicates just how close the musicians' rhythms are to strict speech. A position near the chart's origin communicates that that musician's rhythms aren't very similar to those of strict speech. At the opposite vertical end of the chart, towards the top, a musician's position will indicate that that artist's rhythms actually are quite similar to those of strict speech. Thus, in the top left of the chart, the following graph communicates that Kendrick Lamar's melody has little resemblance to the intonational pitch systems of traditional singing. Meanwhile, as his position in the graph communicates a close proximity to the origin in horizontal terms, this chart reveals the fact that Kendrick Lamar's rhythms are very close to those of normal, everyday conversation. This is true, even if they don't replicate those rhythms exactly. A representative for this rapping style from Kendrick Lamar could be his 2012 song "Backseat Freestyle." For now, the graph classifies and differentiates between five different artists, as well as one style particular tradition of singing, recitative, that helps to set the others in relief[4]:

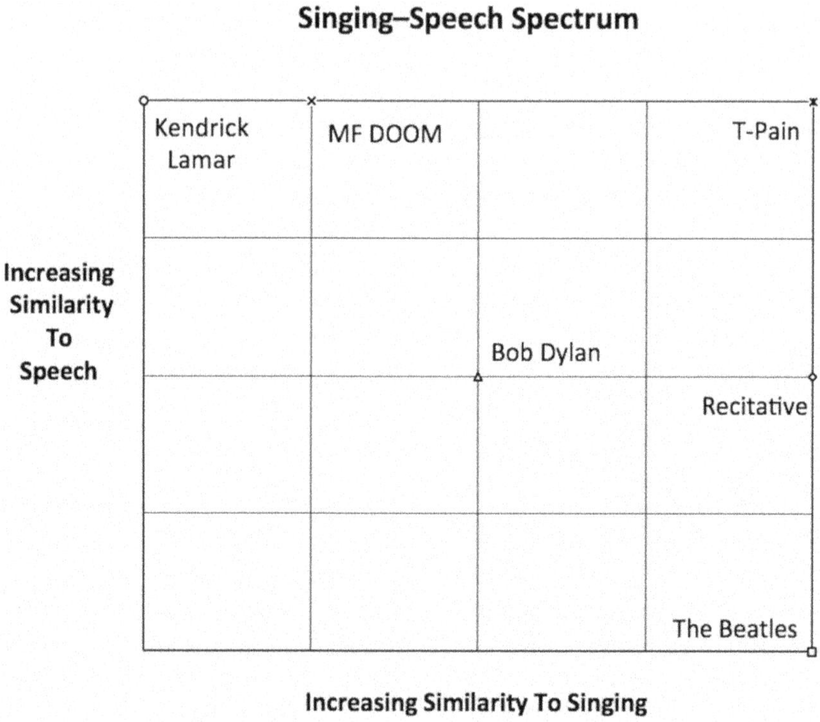

Singing–Speech Spectrum

Kendrick Lamar	MF DOOM		T-Pain
		Bob Dylan	
			Recitative
			The Beatles

Increasing Similarity To Speech (vertical axis)

Increasing Similarity To Singing (horizontal axis)

A comparison of the various vocal styles of different popular musical acts, as judged along a dual spectrum of speech (on the vertical axis) or singing (on the horizontal axis).

The second extreme of this chart, in the very bottom right of the chart, should also be examined, in order to better elucidate the cases of the rappers who fall between Kendrick Lamar and a traditionally-vocalizing group like The Beatles. (The revelations that considerations of T-Pain's melodies and recitative's melodies have to offer will be examined in a section to come.)

The melodies of the Beatles have rhythms that aren't very much related to the rhythms of speech. They are simply too heightened, too stylized, and too formalized by the dictates of a strict metrical pulse to be considered as such. However, their melodies also move up and down almost unfailingly through the scales of traditional musical keys, so their placement far away from the origin in horizontal terms reflects that their vocalizations are very close to traditional singing idioms of music. A song that's representative of this similarity to speech and similarity to singing is The Beatles' song "Octopus's Garden," or "Let It Be."

If The Beatles represent an approach to vocals that is almost the complete opposite of rappers, Bob Dylan represents an intermediary between the two oppositional vocalizations. That's because the specifics of his melodies on songs such as "Like a Rolling Stone" similarly refer to a system of intonational pitch that falls somewhere between that of pure singing and that of pure speech, just as rappers and Schoenberg's sprechstimme do. Dylan does move back and forth from a tonic home note, but he does so in ways that can't be easily understood or captured by traditional concepts of tonality. However, mixed in with his own rapidly shifting pitches—enhanced through portamento and other such techniques—can be found traditional singing in some of his musical sections, such as choruses. This nod to traditional tonality means that his system of pitch is more conventional than that of MF DOOM, even if Dylan's own doesn't tow the line as strictly as the traditional singing of groups like The Beatles. In addition to that medium value for his score on adherence to tonality, Bob Dylan's melodies can also be considered as falling somewhere between speech and singing in rhythm as well. Sometimes he follows the beat exactly, and sometimes he doesn't, so his melodies' rhythms have a relative, general designation that's halfway between speech and singing.

MF DOOM's Sprechstimme

With more familiar examples now in hand, the radical innovations of rap in its approaches to both "atonal separation from the music" and "the exigencies of verbal order" can now be considered. MF DOOM is located at the top of the chart with a high y-axis value, because the rhythms of his melodies so closely approximate those of speech, as on his song "Vomitspit." On this song, he does, in fact, organize all of his musical phrases to almost unfailingly coincide with the natural structure of order that the music behind him is supplying him with. For example, he ends his sentences on this song right where the measure ends, and usually begins his sentences right where a new measure starts. Additionally, he most often aligns the prosodic accents of his words so that they fall exactly where the regular pulse of the meter is falling.

The result is that much of what Day said of Dylan and what Schoenberg said of sprechstimme can equally be applied to the work of MF DOOM. DOOM's own voice goes up and down in that "peculiar tonal quality" of Dylan, while possessing an "atonal separation from the music." And, being rap, it is no surprise that the rhythmic elements of DOOM's delivery are subordinated to the "exigencies of verbal order." Meanwhile, per Schoenberg, MF DOOM's melody "indicate[s] [the pitch], but immediately abandons it again by falling or rising." Specifically, MF DOOM hovers around the very same tonic note of the jazzy musical sample behind him, whose organ is playing in the key of F. For all of these reasons, MF DOOM's music is not necessarily "realistic, natural speech," but it does not "call singing to mind, either." Therefore, his value for pitch system has been ascribed as being between somewhere between speech and singing—he is not necessarily comparable to Kendrick Lamar in terms of his vocal idioms, but that doesn't mean that he is overwhelmingly similar to The Beatles, either.

The unique delivery of MF DOOM, then, seems to have carved out a musical space that is original in the elements of speech and singing that it combines. He has defined a kind of melody that, while being almost completely like speech, also has strong elements of the intonation of traditional singing.

Another rapper, exceptional in this regard, has a style that seems to upend our interpretational framework here. It seems that T-Pain has a style of vocalizing that is almost completely similar to singing, while, counter-intuitively, also being completely similar to speech.

T-Pain's Sprechstimme

While maintaining MF DOOM's rhythms of speech in his own melodies, T-Pain also injects them with a certain amount of traditional intonation that would be quite out of place in DOOM's own vocalizations. Although this intonational effect is partially underscored by T-Pain's use of the much-maligned studio effect popularly misunderstood as Auto-Tune, T-Pain's vocals also maintain their adherence to musical scales of pitch without any type of digital magic or crutch as well.

T-Pain's historical moment in the early 2000s deserves to be addressed in-depth in a thorough study of rap analysis because the movement that he spawned by using Auto-Tune as an end in itself is carried on today by everyone from Young Thug, to Lil Wayne and beyond. That

2. Melody   71

effect's superimposition of a seemingly superficial, standardized melody in a normative diatonic key was so momentous because it laid bare the problems that usually surround any discussion of what the nature of rap truly is. To put it bluntly: is rap singing, or is it speech? And can it actually be both?

Rap is often defined by its very opposition to singing. Even the title of T-Pain's own album from 2005 implies that an artist can only ever do one or the other: *Rappa Ternt Sanga*. Even its detractors have defined rap as having no melody at all, as Duke professor Dr. Anthony Kelley did in an article that appeared in the student newspaper of Duke University in 2011.

As Dr. Kelley writes in "A melody? Word,"

> A musical culture dominated by rappers is virtually bankrupt. It is reassuring that even a pop venue like 'American Idol' recognizes the singer for vocally managing actual pitch, rhythm and a relationship to harmony—not the rapper, who creates a vocal art devoid of pitch specificity, unless assisted by the ludicrous crutch known as Auto-Tune. Rap requires no precise tonal specificity from the consumer/listener.[5]

This matters because melody, as Dr. Kelley defines it, is the highest virtue of music: "Melody, particularly in Western music, is one of the noblest offerings a musician can ever give to humanity. It is the precious, lasting currency of any musical culture that has ever explored the world of linear melodic art...."[6]

Elsewhere in this book, this book's author has endeavored to respond to arguments like those of Dr. Kelley by trying to show objectively that rap does have melody, just in a way that is hard to represent and recognize, which has resulted in its existence being unnecessarily passed over. With T-Pain, however, one can actually overturn that binary dichotomy, by showing how some rap does indeed have melody, even if it were to be held to the strictest standards of traditional definitions. In order to do this, we now need to define singing in this traditional way.

Pure singing, according to Dr. Kelley's formulation of the concept, is when a human voice moves its pitches according to a musical scale whose frequencies can all be expressed in proportion to each other's with simple integer fractions of the form A/B. For example, the opening of Harburg's and Arlen's 1939 ballad "Over the Rainbow" is singing because the frequency of its second note has an (almost) perfect 2:1 proportion to its first note. This definition of singing would obviously seem to leave behind the musical work of the artists that were examined in this chapter's previous sections on Bob Dylan and MF DOOM. This, in turn, might now beg the following question to be answered: is it possible to maintain an adherence to the cadences of speech, while simultaneously vocalizing an extended series of frequencies that all have strict, proportional relationships to each other?

This is the musical question that T-Pain answers in "Holla Holla," because this track actually does have a melody that falls fully within a musical key. In fact, all of T-Pain's vocals on "Holla Holla" appear squarely within the key of B major. At the same time, though, T-Pain maintains his respect for the linguistic rules of human speech that dictate the norms of quotidian conversation. For example, T-Pain does not ever highly stylize some heightened rhythms so that they fully abide by the structure of the pulse or bar line in his music's meter. Instead, his unpredictable rhythmic subdivisions float around the beat, while concurrently respecting the natural syllabic stress of each one of his words. As a result, it seems that T-Pain has unified the defining elements of rap with the defining elements of singing on "Holla Holla."

In T-Pain's opening bars on this 2008 song, a deeply melodic and musical logic is at work. There are moments of rest (bar 50), and moments of tension (bar 55); there are gripping, large musical leaps (bar 54); there are outlines of the underlying chords (bar 52–53); there is repetition (bars 48–52) whose impact is made driven home more strongly by a corresponding amount of measured variation (bars 53 and 55). Throughout it all, though, T-Pain is walking the dividing line between singing and speech much more evenly than Kendrick Lamar, MF DOOM, Bob Dylan, or The Beatles typically do. Moreover, T-Pain's dualistic vocalizing on "Holla Holla" comprises a golden opportunity for retrospective evaluation of previous approaches to the scholarly analysis of rap studies, breaking down, as it does, many of the barriers between pure rapping and pure singing.

Previous Approaches to Rap Analysis

One such wide-ranging methodology is admirably proposed by Adam Krims in his pioneering 2000 title *Rap Music and the Poetics of Identity*. At the beginning of his own discussion, Krims starts out by trying to avoid "well-defined and separable points" in favor of "terms [that] describe directions along spectra." However, his spectra are, counter-intuitively, overly constrained and restricted, thereby encouraging a top-down, cookie-cutter understanding of rap artists' creativity that would obliterate most distinctions between rappers within the same subgroup. Rather than allowing truly textured understandings of the individuality of every rapper's melodic technique, as music notation allows, Krims fits all styles of rap into only a select few taxonomic categories. For example, he considers his first categorization of rapping styles to be the "sung" style.[7]

Such a title might imply that it could encompass and explain T-Pain's work on "Holla Holla," but, in fact, Krims defines the "sung" rhythmic style as such: "[The sung rhythmic style refers] to rhythms and rhymes equivalent (or parallel) to those of much sung pop or rock musics."[8]

Meanwhile, this particular rapping style's approach to intonation and pitch is mostly ignored: "...[C]haracteristics of the sung style are rhythmic repetition, on-beat accents (especially strong-beat ones), regular, on-beat pauses ... and strict couplet groupings."[9]

As examples of this particular rap phenomena, Krims proposes Too $hort and Grandmaster Flash and the Furious Five.[10] While these groups' vocalists do sing, and while they do indeed rap, they do not sing *and* rap at the same time, as T-Pain does. The confusion and misunderstanding of rap that such broad taxonomies naturally create cries out for a deeper analytical appreciation of the fact that the modern rapping idiom's melodies are just as diverse and resistant to reductive categorization as any of those that could ever be found in any other type of music. For these reasons, it is here posited that only the given flexibility of an adapted transcription system, based on Western music notation principles (or another such established of archiving), could accomplish both goals of the proper scholar at once: to communicate accurate information, yes, but to also bequeath a true love and appreciation of the object under study to the learner.

Not even the finest delineations of a technical taxonomy for rap could accommodate the wide breadth of creativity that any professional lyricist is apt to display, as an attempted positioning of T-Pain's "Holla Holla" within Krims' system can demonstrate. This is because, in addition to not being easily fit into the "sung" style, neither does "Holla Holla" slide into place in Krims' other two broad categories for rapping styles (the "percussion-effusive," and the "speech-effusive").[11] Any discussion of pitch or intonation continues to be left aside in favor of further referral to only the rhythmic half of rap melody's dual nature, as Krims defines such styles as possessing:

> ... rhythmic boundaries [that] involve staggering of the syntax and/or rhymes; relentless subdivision of the beat ... repeated off-beat (or weak-beat) accents; or polyrhythms with four-measure groupings of 4/4 time.[12]

Again, the importance of pitch is passed over, once more resulting in a mischaracterization of rap that negatively affects its perception in the eyes of critics like Dr. Anthony Kelley, Juan Williams, and justice departments in cities across America, as this chapter's opening chapter detailed in-depth.

The Pitfalls of Rap Taxonomies

To further see the undesirable results of Krims' taxonomy, one needs only to consider what kind of comparisons and similarities they might result in if they were applied to real rappers. Take, for example, two rappers whose melodies, as documented heretofore in this book, are extremely different from each other, but whom Krims has both placed in the same "speech-effusive" category, according to his own definitions. These two rappers are AZ and Twista.[13]

Both of these lyricists do indeed create "polyrhythms with four-measure groupings of 4/4 time," and use "relentless subdivisions of the beat." However, their specific musical characteristics beyond these generalities are so different from each other as to make even finely the most detailed categories of taxonomy ineffective for understanding and appreciating their work.

The rapper AZ, as in his solo work, his early 1990s collaborations with Nas, or the album he released while he was part of the supergroup The Firm, is usually quite extreme in his rhythms, once they've been documented in terms of their large amount of expressive rhythmic trailing, fragmented subdivisional groupings, or misalignment of prosodic accent with musical accent. All of these conclusions can be accurately applied to his opening verse on the 1996 song "Firm Fiasco," as well as his other songs from the same time period.

Despite being placed in the same category as AZ by Krims, Twista's own melodies are so different from AZ's as to constitute a largely unrelated style. In technical terms, Twista's melodies make frequent use of very small rhythmic subdivisions that nevertheless remain related to his songs' underling meters, as well as a strong, recurring alignment of grammatical syntax with the appearance of bar lines. This can be heard on Twista's guest verses with Cam'ron on "Adrenaline," from 2004, or Kanye West's "Slow Jamz," released the same year. These conclusions imperfectly describe a very general melodic style is still, overall, quite different from AZ's own technical penchants, what with the latter's predilection for a widespread proliferation of unexpected prosodic accents that anchor and underpin complex subdivisions. In this way, Krims' system seems to be overly general to an extent that it might not be as helpful as possible for understanding the rap that it is said to be elucidating.

Recitative Melodies and Rap

In addition to using the melodies of luminaries like Bob Dylan and Arnold Schoenberg as a helpful analytical context for examining the work of rappers like AZ and Twista, we can also use the operatic melodies of composers, such as Mozart, in order to gain a constructive interpretive background. Indeed, much of what was just asserted about T-Pain's rap on "Holla Holla" might sound very familiar to the classical music scholar, with its discussion of a melodic line that contains verbal rhythms and a system of intonation based within a musical key. As it turns out, these very descriptions of tonality and speech might be applied as much to rap as to the idiom of singing called recitative.

In defining recitative, there is once more a recourse to the utilization of the previous two broad spectra that aided in the understanding of vocal idioms: a vocalization's similarity (or dissimilarity) to speech, as well as its similarity (or dissimilarity) to strict singing. The analytical graph from our previous sections is reproduced here once more in order to lubricate the following discussion (see next page).

Located all the way on the right between The Beatles and T-Pain, recitative might be considered as being closer to actual singing than the melodies of Dylan, DOOM, T-Pain, or Kendrick. This is because operatic recitative generally retains a definable, identifiable intonation of traditional pitch that still strongly adheres to a tonal musical scale. However, recitative is also, at the same time, a little closer to the speech side of the spectrum than the Beatles or T-Pain. This is because recitative's typical rhythms more closely approximate everyday human speech and that mode of speaking's declamatory, free, or independent rhythms. Likewise, Dylan, DOOM, T-Pain, and Kendrick are closer to the true-speech side of the graph, because recitative's rhythms are still, generally, more heightened and stylized than the rhythms of those musicians, following much more closely the guidelines of a meter and its organization of a pulse. It seems, then, that rap as a vocal form of music-making is actually much more familiar to us than it might seem at first.

Singing–Speech Spectrum

Kendrick Lamar	MF DOOM		T-Pain
		Bob Dylan	
			Recitative
			The Beatles

Increasing Similarity To Speech (vertical axis)

Increasing Similarity To Singing (horizontal axis)

A comparison of the various vocal styles of different popular musical acts, as judged along a dual spectrum of speech (on the vertical axis) or singing (on the horizontal axis).

Summary

Throughout this short survey, topics as varied as atonality, recitative, and sprechstimme were all called into action in order to help elucidate the manner in which rap vocals engage with concepts of pitch and melody. Such a diverse array of sources had to be called on because so many of rap's most basic assumptions about what melody can be are very different from the more common kind of scale-based melodies that are heard more frequently in other genres of popular music. In general, though, one has actually encountered a surprising amount of rather traditional musical conventions, already digested by listeners and composers, with which rap shares an unexpected amount of affinity. Throughout this discussion, Schoenberg's sprechstimme technique was found as constituting somewhat of a preparatory exercise for the eventual foundations of the rapping idiom, albeit indirectly. Alternatively, rap also seen as possibly constituting a form of operatic recitative that has had both its typical melodic constraints (a well-defined scale that guides the melody's pitch) and usual rhythmic constraints (its adherence to the regularly repeating pulse of a normal meter) loosened to a not-insubstantial degree.

All of these takeaways demonstrate two further conclusions in turn. The first is that rap is not always something completely superficial or iconoclastic in its newness, but, instead, a pristinely new unification of pre-existing musical concepts. The second point this analytical cross-section demonstrates is that fans can find in rap a bounteous wealth of artistic material that has an incredible potential for transformation into not just songs and freestyles, but into even more extended and complicated forms than many rap musicians might have yet fully imagined.

3

Motivic Development

A motive in music (used here synonymously with the term "theme") is a small, recognizable musical idea that occurs and re-occurs in a specific piece of music to such an extent that it can be considered as undergirding and underpinning that entire composition. Rather than belaboring and boring a scholar's understanding of a well-worn concept, this schoolbook definition is trotted out and refurbished once more in order to clearly outline the principles involved in thematic development that might seem to make it so a priori unsuited to rap melodies. If the fact that rhythm exists in rappers' vocals is somewhat obvious, and the idea that melody could exist in rap is scary and unfamiliar, then the proposition that certain masterpieces of rap could be built in a way that's similar to the masterworks of the great symphonists may seem downright outlandish.

However, as rappers as diverse as everyone from DMX, to Time Bomb, to Hittman, Xzibit, Defari, and B-Lo can attest, this is just what happens on certain rap songs. The themes of rappers, generally, inhabit one of two kinds of relationships to their musical accompaniment. The theme is either generated from a rapper's own freely-chosen rhythms and melodic pitches ex nihilo, or based on a unique, characteristic rhythm from the musical accompaniment behind them. DMX himself will choose to borrow a musical idea from his backing rhythmic section; the other rappers in the next part of this coming survey, meanwhile, will demonstrate different approaches.

Cyclical Motivic Development in DMX's "Who We Be"

The musical material that DMX crafts his theme out of on his 2001 recording "Who We Be" comes from the insistent, march-like rhythm of

3. Motivic Development 79

the electric guitar in the musical accompaniment behind his melody. The guitar rhythm in question consists of two notes: the first note is a single, solitary 16th note rhythm that occurs unaccented and off of the beat, which then leads to a second note. This second note is a dotted 8th note that is accented squarely on the beat. This simple two-note grouping is repeated once every beat, four times in every measure, during the entire length of almost the whole song.

When notated without pitch, this is what the rhythm looks like:

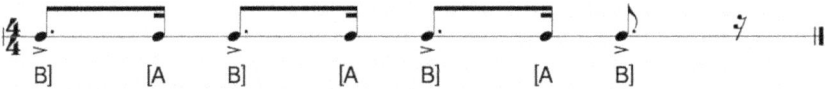

B]   [A   B]   [A   B]   [A   B]

The guitar rhythm from the backing musical accompaniment that DMX reworks to form his own musical theme on his 2001 song "Who We Be." The two-note theme is defined by its initial unaccented note, as denoted by the letter A beneath it, and then its second accented note, as denoted by the letter B underneath it.

This two-note rhythmic sequence might be described as consisting of a note that is soft, when judged in terms of its low dynamics and off-of-the-beat position, followed by a note that is hard, as determined by its on-the-beat positioning, and its own loud volume. Because this two-note rhythm is repeated over and over throughout the song, it forms a major backbone of the structure of the musical accompaniment. This rhythm is also very unique and immediately identifiable because of its strongly accented closing note. It might be for these two reasons, then, that DMX decided to place this straightforward guitar rhythm at the center of his melodic efforts to craft a journey of thematic development and evolution on "Who We Be."

DMX establishes the importance of his motive at the outset of his rap melody by repeating immediately. What follows is the opening of his rap at bar 9 (see next page).

One can immediately grasp DMX's initial musical intentions even from the very beginning of his melody on "Who We Be." This opening bar makes clear the central role that this flam-like rhythm in DMX's melody will take on. Over the course of "Who We Be," DMX will transform this nugget of a rhythmic idea in various developmental ways that are not teleologically or directly related to each other. For example, there will be no classical augmentation of rhythmic values, or discrete and absolute transposition of melodic pitches. Instead, one might say that this two-note

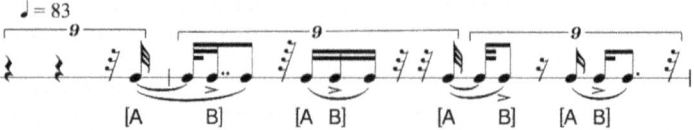

In DMX's very first bar of rap melody on "Who We Be," he repeats the motive that he's borrowed from the backing guitar a total of four times. Each instance of the motive appears only once during four different, separate sentences, as denoted by the A–B letter pairings that each represent one single instance of this two-note motive.

rhythm is treated more in the manner of foundational material from a set of variations that, while intriguing in itself, maintains only a loose evolutionary connection over the course of the piece.

The first change that DMX makes to this basic two-note idea is an increase in the number of notes in it, from two to three. However, if one considers only the most important structural rhythms in the above notation, then the theme's identity is still seen as being fully retained. The notes that are added to the previously two-note theme are of only a secondary importance, consisting of as they do of nothing more than unaccented syllables that happen off of the beat at the very end of a melodic phrase. Meanwhile, the core of that two-note off-beat, on-beat rhythm is still retained in the music above. In this way, then, DMX carefully walks the line between repetition on the one hand, and variation on the other. As he goes about evolving and developing this theme little by little over the course of "Who We Be," he is always extremely diligent about not changing it such a degree that the listener becomes unable to recognize his melody as being made up of that very motive in the first place.

It is these kinds of cyclical, non-linear progressions that DMX uses to extend his melody in his opening verse. For example, the artist here remains remarkably consistent in his rhythmic enlargement of the motive's quantity of notes (see next page).

In this second bar of DMX's first sixteen bars of rap, seen above, we once more observe the two-note guitar motive, now rapped a full four times.

So far, the most remarkable thing about DMX's verse is his almost neurotic repetition of the motive. Indeed, his obsessive use of the motive reflects well his obsessive poetic meditation on the details of how he himself perceives his own place in the rap industry, as well as just how hard he had to work in order to attain such pre-eminence. The bars that follow

3. *Motivic Development*   81

Rather than developing his motive in a linear, point A to point B manner, DMX is more apt to simply make changes to his motive in whatever order his artistic discretion directions him to do so. In the above, he has added an extra note to the archetypal two-note motive at different points, while still preserving its essential identity by retaining the unaccented first note and the emphasized second note that mostly define this theme.

will similarly do little to change this characterization because, by the end of bar 5, a listener will have heard the motive a full twenty total times. The paradigm shift in DMX's treatment of his theme is only to come later on, in bar 6.

This sixth bar is so important because it presents to the listener the creative tension that the rest of DMX's verse will proceed to melodically manipulate and play upon. The crucial changes here are two. First, instead of having the motive appear only once in a sentence, DMX now has it appear twice within a single melodic phrase; and, second, instead of placing his theme only at the end of a sentence, DMX now allows it to occupy internal structural positions within his melodic phrases as well.

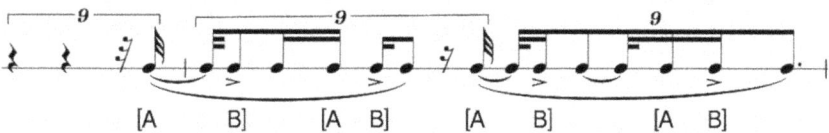

Beginning in his sixth bar, DMX begins to develop his motive by varying its appearance in terms of where in the sentence it comes—the beginning, or the end—and also in terms of how many instances of the motive are appearing in any given sentence—one, two, or more.

The structural changes that are made to his theme in this bar supply DMX with the essential variety and contrast that he needs in order to further develop it. Starting in bar 6, DMX begins to vary the grammatical position and numerical frequency of his motive as he starts to place multiple instances of it in the beginning, middle, and end of his melodic phrases. In sum, the central tensions in DMX's own thematic development revolve around where, and how, the motive will appear inside of his melodic phrases. In this way, DMX varies musical aspects of his rap motive that are different from the ones Time Bomb, King Tee, and Hittman will play with on the 1999 Dr. Dre track "Some L.A. Niggaz," as will be seen in the next section.

DMX's focus on thematic development continues to abound in bar 7. In these next two sentences, the motive is repeated four more times:

In bar 7, DMX inserts his motive three times inside of a single melodic phrase, both in the middle and at the end of the sentence. Both of these characteristics of the motive's context are new developments in DMX's treatment of the theme, because they differ from the motive's initial appearances on this song.

The same musical dynamic is still at work here, as that two-note motive now appears in increasingly varied contexts, whether such variety comes as a result of a change in motivic density, or a change in measural position.

After seven bars of contextual changes to his theme, DMX is next ready to make wholesale changes to the very core of his theme's definition. In his eighth bar, DMX temporarily upends the weak–strong accenting of his motive by reversing that order of relative accent:

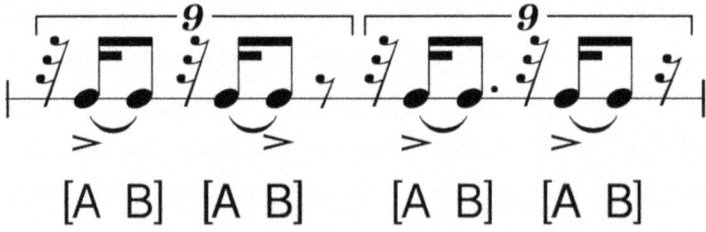

In his melody's eighth bar, DMX temporarily transforms the motive so that the first note—not the second note—is accented. However, because he has treated the theme so uniformly up until this point, a listener is still able to recognize the theme's appearance, even in this radically transformed musical shape.

DMX has just changed the rhythmic downbeat of the motive from being on the second syllable of his theme, to now being on the first syllable. While this overturns the previous definition of DMX's basic motive as

3. *Motivic Development*

being a two–note, weak¬–strong gesture, DMX began by repeating his theme so uniformly that the listener does not register this structural change as completely new material, but as just another thematic development.

Another type of rapper, such as Game, might next proceed by switching back and forth between these different versions of the motive. For DMX, however, this change was a complete feint, because his melody subsequently reverts right back to the original version of the theme in the very next bar (bar 9).

Bars 9–11 set the functional background for DMX's final variation and thematic development by uniformly and regularly repeating the standard, initial version of his motive quite frequently. This means that the final part of DMX's melody, from bars 12 to 16, have been set up as a potential thematic cadence point. Here, DMX can either resolve the melody's thematic tension by rapping the original version of his motive, or leave the cadential fall incomplete by rapping a new version of his motive:

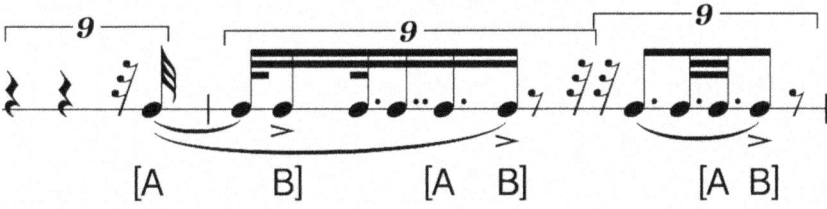

In DMX's twelfth bar of melody, he changes the length of his two-note motive's first note to last for different amounts of musical time that are both longer and shorter than the durations he has used up until this moment, thereby continuing his cyclical treatment of thematic development.

DMX's unique sense of rhythm here is what slightly obscures the multiple appearances of his two-note motive. Over the course of his entire discography, DMX is stylistically prone to falling drastically behind the beat, intentionally, when he inserts what seems like too many syllables in his musical line. However, he will always balance out this braggadocios display of unhurriedness by increasing the internal tempo of his rhythms, which resolves the problem by catching him back up the pulse. His song "Who We Be" is not the only example of this, because his deliberate rhythmic procrastination is also ticklingly apparent on his 1999 song "Party Up (Up in Here)" at 1:38, as well as on his 2003 song "Where the Hood At?" at 3:08. In the transcription above, this tendency manifests itself as extremely small variations in the length of the first note of our motive. Instead of lasting a 16th note, it lasts a dotted 16th note, or a dotted 32nd note. But if we look past these non-subdivisional rhythmic changes, the motive can still be found a full three times.

The important elements of DMX's motive are all to be found in full evidence at this point, with its two notes, a hierarchically-important downbeat position, and the weak–strong accents of a drum flam rudiment. Additionally, the same variations that first appeared in bars 6 and 7 continue to be put in play. Instead of appearing only once during each melodic phrase, motives now also appear twice inside of the same sentence, while, furthermore, showing up anywhere inside of the sentence, and not just at the end.

DMX, interestingly enough, ends this composition in a manner that leaves his thematic cadential point slightly unresolved:

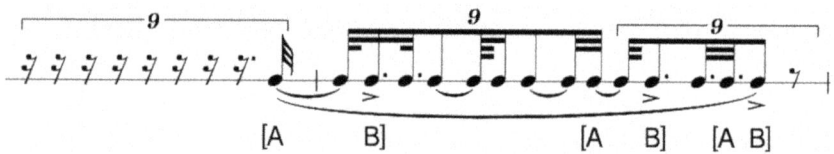

DMX's final bar, by delivering appearances of the motive in untraditional ways that haven't been seen consistently before, continues his non-linear treatment of developing his theme.

Looking past DMX's characteristic aspects of expressive rhythmic timing, the motive can be located another three times, in internal and external positions, inside of a single sentence that takes up an entire bar.

In sum, DMX has not structured the successive changes to his theme in an extremely goal-directed or teleological manner. At the same time that DMX likes to introduce changes to his motive, he largely declines to move back and forth between them directly, such as with clear departures and arrivals that might separate distinction sections of a long-form composition. Instead, DMX is prone to introduce variations on his motive, and to then never return to them again, if at all, while simultaneously refusing to squarely focus on the musical consequences that might result from those shifts, such as a key change. As just a single example, he treated his accent shift of his first note, from weak to strong, as if it were no more than a momentary diversion, thereafter reverting right back to the original version of his theme in the next bar, and never even registering it as a formal melodic division.

In this manner, a listener is unlikely to hear these changes as constituting discrete changes in the identity of DMX's motive at all. In contrast, they are more likely to hear DMX's thematic development as a type of extended variation on his initial two–note, weak–strong motive. This rather free handling of the aspects of his motive is what primarily separates DMX's own artistic vision from other rappers that engage and interact with theme in their melodies.

These assertions can be borne out through a quick summary of all the different forms, now isolated, that DMX's motive has taken in the music just transcribed. Sometimes DMX's motive from "Who We Be" is buried within a sentence with three notes; sometimes it is in a sentence with two notes, or even four notes; sometimes it lands almost directly on the beat; at other times it is off the beat, as almost always happens; sometimes it occurs frequently; sometimes it occurs only sparingly; sometimes it is in an internal phrase position; sometimes it is in an external phrase position. The crux of the musical matter, though, is that DMX does not predictably switch between all of these forms of appearance for his theme, but changes among them quickly and episodically.

But, as the next group of rappers will show, there might be close to an infinite amount of approaches to thematic development, whether in the modern rap song, or in the classical symphony of Western art music.

Linear Motivic Development in Dr. Dre's "Some L.A. Niggaz"

At the same time that it will elucidate certain truths about the advantages and limitations of thematic development in rap melodies, the next song at hand will also bring to the forefront of the reader's consciousness the inescapable intertextuality of music today. That's because the basic rhythmic patterning of the accompanimental backbeat on "Some L.A. Niggaz" will be heard as unmistakably jarring to anyone who's even passingly familiar with the popular music from 1950s until today.

Remarkably, there is actually no element of the drum set on this song that marks off the third beat of every measure, whether bass kick, snare, tom, or anything else. Furthermore, there is also not a single element of the backbeat that could even be said to imply the presence of the measure's third beat through syncopation, such as by falling on the 8th note partial either before or after it. This makes the beat of "Some L.A. Niggaz" singular with regards to its approach to the typical strong–weak, iambic patterning of modern popular music.

This song's producer, Dr. Dre, provides this song's backing musical accompaniment with zero rhythmic information in regards to that all-important, strong third beat. Instead, the backbeat contains only a snare sound that accents every measure's second beat, a snare sound that accents every measure's fourth beat, a couple of bass kicks on beat 1, and no more. This prevents the music from being strongly pinned to that third beat, which ends up greatly upsetting any kind of normalized interpretation of rap's usual 4/4 time signature.

The uniqueness of this beat's defining feature—that is, its omission of the measure's third beat from the accompanimental backbeat—comprises the same musical material with which this song's lyricists will craft and develop their own arc of thematic development. To be sure, every single one of the five different rappers who each has a full verse on this song musically interacts with, and technically responds to, that very singular rhythmic feature that's found in the accompaniment behind them.

The song's first rapper, Time Bomb, recognizes and brings to the forefront of the musical texture the accompaniment's missing third beat over the course of his entire melody. However, he initially opens the verse in his first bar by running out a melodic phrase that ignores that absent accompanimental third beat by continuing before, during, and after it:

In the very first line of Time Bomb's rap on the 1999 Dr. Dre song "Some L.A. Niggaz," Time Bomb doesn't in any way acknowledge or play off of the fact that the musical accompaniment behind him lacks a musical attack on the 4/4 meter's foundational third beat.

Even right afterwards, in bar 2, Time Bomb similarly fails to directly acknowledge or reference the absence of any third beat impetus in the accompaniment, as he once again strings out his melodic phrase continuously between beat 1 and beat 4. In his first two bars, Time Bomb has now twice laid out his musical phrases in ways that do not stop when the accompaniment behind him temporarily stops on the third beat. But in his third and fourth bars, this L.A. rapper allows his melody's technical structure to start to directly imitate the accompaniment's technical structure:

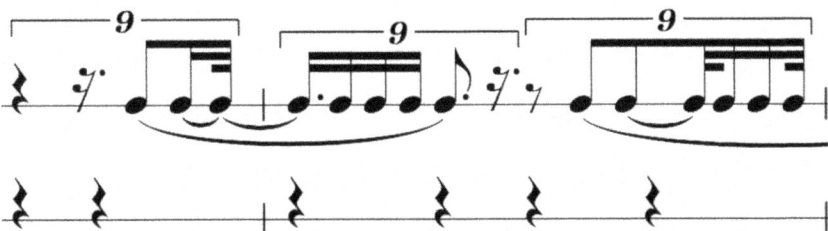

In contrast to his opening two bars, Time Bomb allows his melody to completely skip any acknowledgment of, or appearance on, the third beat of his third measure, in the very same manner that this song's backing musical accompaniment has likewise been skipping it.

In the above music, Time Bomb has placed a large rhythmic gap in his melody, right at his measure's third beat, that fully replicates the accompaniment's own rhythmic gap at the same metric position. Specifically, Time Bomb stops his first sentence right before the third beat, and only re-starts his melody that leads to beat 4 once he has musically referenced the marked absence of the third beat. Furthermore, his staccato articulation in this part of his melody serves to further reinforce the jarring effect of the conspicuously missing third beat.

Time Bomb continues this rhythmic imitation of his musical accompaniment's structure in his fourth bar as well. This next example begins halfway through his third bar, so that the notation can capture each melodic phrase as a complete whole:

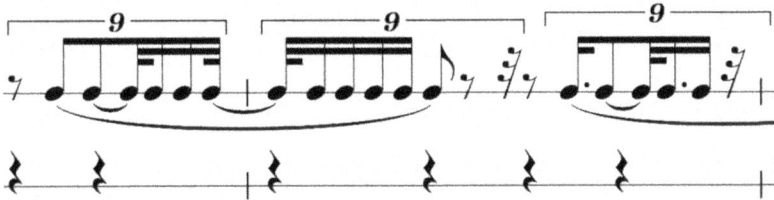

In his fourth bar, Time Bomb completely pauses his melodic phrases during his measure's third beat, making his melody coincide with this same gap in the musical accompaniment where, on almost any other popular music song (except this one) an impetus from the musical accompaniment—or at least the lead melodic voice—would almost always occur.

From this point in his melody on, Time Bomb is almost always cutting his rhythms short so that they end right before every measure's third beat, while then bringing his melody back into the large-scale musical texture on the beat that next follows. Sometimes he varies his phrase structure by fitting in two melodic phrases instead of just one before each bar's third beat, but he is always at pains to reflect, through the structure of his rhythms, the backbeat's omission of any strong impetus on the third beat of this song's meter.

In his next few bars, Time Bomb continues this song's basic musical theme by proceeding to never include any direct melodic reference to the measure's third beat.

However, Time Bomb does not just go on skipping that third beat forever, which might soon become tedious, even in its very uniqueness. Instead, Time Bomb begins varying his sentence structure from bar 15 until the end of his verse at bar 20.

In his last few bars, Time Bomb continues to reference and riff on this song's basic musical motive: an extremely weak third beat. Just as he opened his verse, Time Bomb now goes back to running his melodic phrases out over, across, and during that third beat (see next page).

In the penultimate bar of his verse, Time Bomb ends one of his last melodic phrases by rapping a series of pick up notes that lead right up to, but don't land on, the third beat of the measure. After he has picked his melody back up on beat 4, Time Bomb then transfers this subversive treatment of beat 3 to another strong beat within the 4/4, beat 1. He ends this melodic phrase with a series of pick up notes that lead right up to beat 1, without ever actually landing on it. Just like how he previously re-introduced his melody into the texture by rapping pick up notes that eventually ended up landing on beat 4, Time Bomb here re-introduces his melody after skipping beat 1 by rapping a series of pick up notes that end

3. Motivic Development

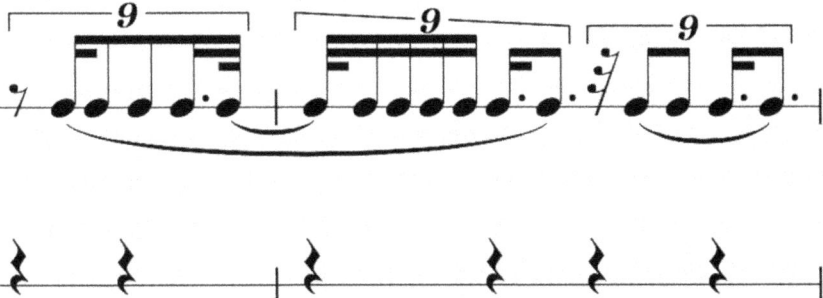

Towards the end of his verse, Time Bomb begins to once more include melodic references to the third beat behind him by placing notes right on top of and during it, in order to introduce some variation to this song's basic musical theme. This also sets himself up to eventually vary away from it in a developmental manner.

up eventually landing on beat 2. This means that Time Bomb has melodically transferred the accompaniment's dismissive treatment of beat 3 to the other strong beat in the bar, beat 1:

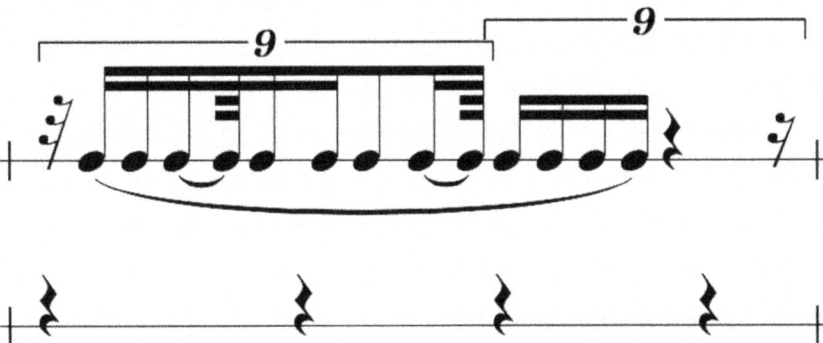

In his final bar, Time Bomb briefly but unmistakably transfers this music's characteristic omission of every measure's third beat to another, equally strong beat in the measure, the first beat.

However, this final sentence is also supremely important in the developmental process of this entire song because Time Bomb here brings his compositional dance around the third beat to a fitting close. He does this by finally placing a strongly accented syllable right on top of that truant third beat. Although he had rapped phrases across the third beat previously, he had simply extended his phrases across it with pauses, only rarely performing accented notes right on top of it. This closing gesture fittingly ends his verse by allowing him to put an accented rhythmic exclamation point on the musical drama's main character.

Each succeeding rapper after Time Bomb picks up on this same developmental and thematic imitation of the backbeat accompaniment in their own melodies, albeit in markedly different ways. The next performer to come once Time Bomb has finished his melody is King Tee, whose first measure actually interjects during the preceding lyricist's final measure:

Just like Time Bomb before him, King Tee picks up on the musical accompaniment's directions when he refuses to place any melodic material on, or even near, the third beat of every one of his measures, thereby continuing this song's thematic development.

In the above, King Tee has immediately picked up on that omitted third beat, ending his first sentence right before it, and only starting his next melodic phrase right after it. Just like Time Bomb, he has reflected the accompaniment's belittling treatment of the third beat's accent in his melody.

However, King Tee also introduces a musical trick on the first note of his second melodic phrase that Time Bomb did not focus on to the same extent. When the third beat is omitted in a backbeat, as it is on "Some L.A. Niggaz," that places a renewed emphasis on the fourth beat of a bar, because that is when the driving, accented backbeat re-enters into the musical texture.

King Tee makes extended use of this important disjunction. For example, he performs a strongly accented note right on that atypically important fourth beat in his first full bar. Since the fourth beat is a measure's final beat, King Tee strongly drives the music's motor rhythm forward, from one measure to the next, by placing the rhythmic focus of his strong accents here in such a manner. Moving on, the following section of King Tee's melody proceeds to treat the third beat with an extremely weak accent, as he continues to stop his sentences right before the third beat, only to restart his melody immediately afterwards.

But King Tee is also in no way monolithic in his treatment of the third beat. He does, from time to time, also include the third beat within his melody sometimes, by rapping right on it:

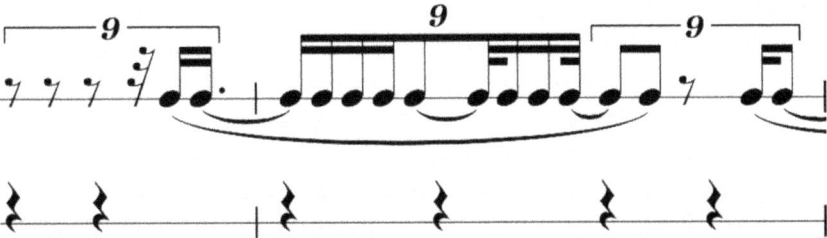

King Tee plays with the basic musical motive of "Some L.A. Niggaz" by not always strictly adhering to his musical accompaniment's ignoring of every measure's third beat. For example, in the above, he has structured his melody so that it includes a reference to the measure's third beat.

In this way, King Tee has reversed Time Bomb's own melodic opening, which at first completely ignored the fact that the third beat was missing in the accompaniment, and only afterwards started following its musical directions in imitating it. King Tee structured his melody in similar ways, but in the opposite chronological order: he begins by respecting the missing third beat, and only afterwards goes on to fill it in.

King Tee, in general, is freer in his treatment of his melody's phrasing than Time Bomb is. (Over the course of this, in fact, King Tee is probably the single rapper out of all five present who is most free and unpredictable with regards to his melodic behavior towards the all-important third beat.) This makes him a refreshing option to follow up after Time Bomb's own more tightly-wound arrangement. The listener can especially hear his stand-out approach before, during, and slightly after bar 23, when the length and positioning of King Tee's melodic phrases vary greatly (see next page).

In the below, the prevailing characteristic of King Tee's melody continues to be his skipping of that third beat. However, King Tee's respect for the missing third beat generally becomes looser and looser as the song goes on. He tends to end his phrases much closer to the third beat than Time Bomb ever ended his own sentences, as he sometimes leads right up to it with pick up notes, but always mostly declining to land right on it. Time Bomb might end his sentence as much as an 8th note before the third beat, while King Tee might end at a point that's no more than just a 16th note right before it.

In one of his middle bars, King Tee continues to treat the structure of his melodic phrases more loosely, by having them last many different lengths of beats, and by having them start and end in many different places within the bar.

We have now seen two clearly distinct, but closely related, approaches to the defining feature of this musical accompaniment's backbeat rhythmic structure. Time Bomb and King Tee both structured their melodies around alternations between ignoring or acknowledging the omitted third beat of the accompanying drum set behind them. Although they differ in just how regularly and consistently they did so, both rappers relied on the same basic musical material: heavy or weak melodic accents that either did (or did not) lead to the strong beats of a typical measure in the usual 4/4 meter of popular genre songs. The next rapper, Hittman, will himself also compose his melody using much of the same foreground–background dynamic, but in a more goal-oriented, predictable, and expansive manner.

As was mentioned briefly before, the extremely unique nature of the backbeat on "Some L.A. Niggaz" slightly transforms the usual interpretation of how a measure in 4/4 is structured. In the typical rap genre song, the four beats of a 4/4 time signature are structured so that the first and third beats of a measure are supplied with the strongest rhythmic accent. Meanwhile, the third and fourth beats are conversely heard as rather weak beats, with a smaller amount of emphasis on them. These facts are known to most rap scholars, and are only reprised here once again so that the ways in which these foundational interpretations of popular song meter are transformed on "Some L.A. Niggaz" can be better understood.

The lack of any reference to a strong third beat on "Some L.A. Niggaz" places an atypical amount of very strong emphasis on both beats 2 and 4. This reduction of the third beat to a quasi-weak-beat status, further emphasized by the underpinning bass guitar's ignorance of it, means that the second and fourth beats of every measure now take on a new level of unprecedented importance in rap.

3. Motivic Development

This musical anomaly is what Hittman takes full advantage of when he begins to transfer the musical accompaniment's ignoring of the third beat to every single one of the other three beats in the bar. Indeed, he will skip the third beat, but he will also structure the starting and stopping of his melodic phrases so that beats 1, 2, and 4 are treated in the same reductive way as well. At the same time, he'll loosen even further the normal metric dictates of popular song in 4/4 by not just ending his sentences right before any of those four beats, but by also beginning and finishing his sentences at any of those beats that he would like to as well.

While performing metrically-suggestive pick up notes, Hittman accomplishes all of this by structuring the rhythmic gaps between his own melodic phrases so that they can encompass any one of the four beats in a measure. Before that happens, though, Hittman begins his melody in the same way Time Bomb did, by refusing to respect the absence of the third beat in his phrase:

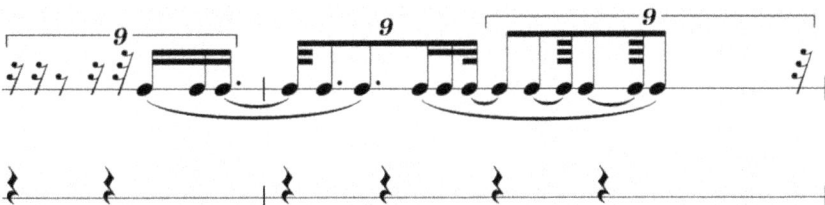

When former Dr. Dre protégé Hittman enters on this song, he will eventually interact with the same musical material of the alternating absence or presence of the third beat; for now, however, he begins by failing to reference the musical accompaniment's own omission of the third beat.

Immediately afterwards, however, Hittman reveals the mutating nature of his radically free global and local rhythms. At first, he cleverly uses the long pause in the accompaniment during the third beat to re-enforce his delivery of a joke he's telling by giving the listener the set up on the second beat, and then the punch line on the fourth beat. In a following bar (see next page), bar 44, Hittman then goes on to omit third beat from his melody for the first time, just as both Time Bomb and King Tee did.

In the above two bars, Hittman temporarily stops his melody twice, right before the third beat of both bars. He further emphasizes the third beat's absence by not just pausing before and during it, but by also using pick up notes that lead to a note on the third beat that never actually arrives.

Hittman not only leaves out the third beat of the measure from his melody at times, as the musical accompaniment behind him has constantly been doing, but also further heightens its jarring rhythmic effect by using onrushing pick up notes to head towards that missing third beat.

Now that he has built up, once and for all, the importance of this musical motive of missing beats, Hittman can now go on to transfer this rhythmic caesura to any one of the other three beats in the bar apart from beat 3. This is possible because Hittman has so strongly established the motive's existence as a sonic theme in the listener's ear by repeating it so intentionally and insistently.

What Hittman inevitably does afterwards, then, is omit the second beat from his melody, in the seventh bar of his verse:

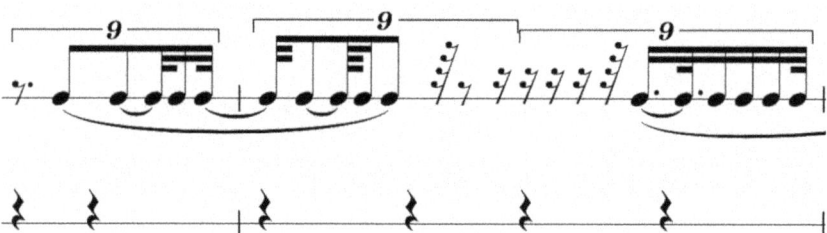

In his seventh bar, Hittman develops this song's basic musical theme—the absence of any impetus or musical attack on every measure's third beat—by transferring that structural absence to other beats within the measure, such as the first, second, or fourth.

In fact, Hittman likewise omits the second beat from his melody in not just bar 7, but bar 8 as well. By comparing the vertical position of the second line of musical rests with the notes on the first line above it, one can see that the notes involved in the melody on the top line land slightly right before the second beat, again acting as pick up notes that lead to something that is simply not there (a strong accent on beat 2 in his melody).

3. Motivic Development   95

Having treated the final notes of his melodic phrases as pick up gestures that emphasize the rhythmic absence of the third and second beats of the bar from his melodic phrases, Hittman afterwards ignores the meter's fourth beat with the same undercutting treatment:

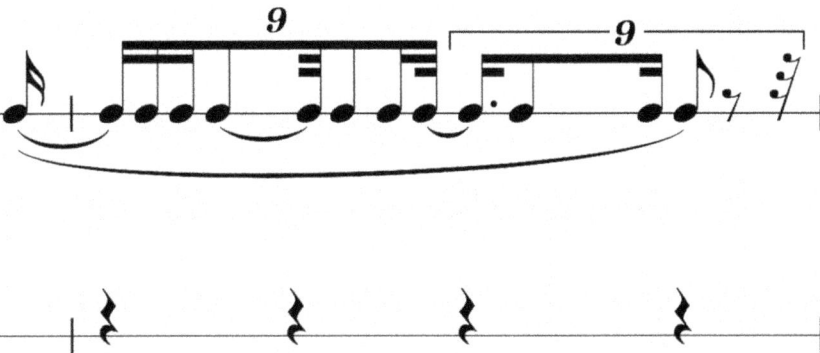

After initially omitting the third beat of the measure from his melody, and afterwards the second, Hittman then goes on to play with the interpretations of the measure's fourth beat through his melody's treatment of it. Specifically, Hittman does this by placing pick up notes right in front of it that are never rhythmically resolved by means of a strong beat 4 impetus.

In the above bar, the final note in the top right falls right before beat 4, even as it is accented. Once more, one sees that Hittman has transferred the musical accompaniment's reductive treatment of beat three to another one of the beats within the bar.

The fact that Hittman has omitted the third, second, and fourth beats from his melody in structurally important ways is allowed by, and supported with, the fact that many of his sentence-phrases last for lengths of musical time that are not altogether found very frequently in rap. Sometimes his melodic phrases last for two beats, and sometimes they last for three; at other times, they can last for four beats. With such a relatively free and independent approach to the structure of his melodic phrasing, it's almost as if Hittman can, conveniently, position his melody wherever in the bar he feels like having it at any given point in time. Additionally, he begins these uncommonly-structured sentences at uncommon starting points at well. For example, sometimes Hittman begins his rap on beat two, and sometimes he starts on beat three.

All of these melodically-free aspects come to a climactic head in his final few bars, where Hittman unveils a fitting end to his own developmental take on the evolutionary unfolding of this song's central rhythmic theme.

This penchant for starting his sentences wherever he wants them to, having them last for however long he wants them to, and then ending them wherever he would like—with little respect paid to where those bars are beginning and ending—reaches its apex of activity in his last several bars. Starting in bars 53–54, Hittman is constantly changing the subdivision of his notes at the same time that he is conjoining his verbal rhyme scheme in unpredictable ways:

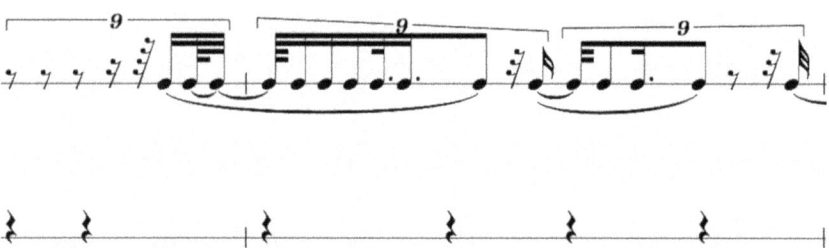

In his last few bars, Hittman's subdivision of his notes' rhythms becomes more and more complex, approaching free jazz, at the same time that the durational length and positioning of his melodic phrases becomes equally complicated.

It is interesting to note that this ultra-frenetic activity happens only right before Hittman gives us what the music's texture has been missing all along, which is a closing melodic phrase that finally places one of its strongly accented notes squarely on a measure's third beat, in bar 56:

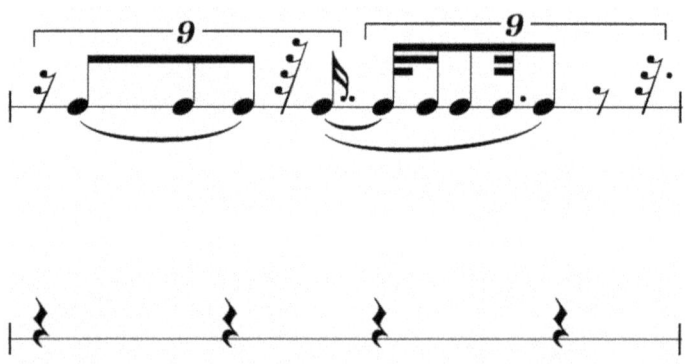

Hittman's last bar supplies a fitting punctuation to his theme's development by finally resolving his melody's central tension as he at last places a strong musical impetus right on the downbeat of the measure's third beat.

3. Motivic Development

This next chart is a musical summary of this technical discussion so far. It encapsulates all of the most important points in Hittman's thematic development by tracing the defining features of Hittman's melodic phrases. The necessary material with which he has supplied his audience to empower them to observe his theme develop consists of the details of the bar a certain sentence appears in; its length in beats; the specific numbered beat that it started on; and, finally, the specific numbered beat that it led up to, by terminating right before it. The column all the way on the left details which sentence is being examined in the corresponding row:

Sentence Placement	Its Length, in Beats	Its Starting Beat	The Beat It Ends At
Bar 43	2	2	3
Bars 43–44	4	4	3
Bars 46–47	3	4	2
Bars 47–48	3	4	2
Bar 50	4	1	4
Bar 54	2	3	4
Bar 56	2	3	4

This table gives a brief summary of how and where Hittman varied his melodic phrase's structure in order to develop the rhythmic theme of this song's missing beats.

As the table succinctly summarizes, the technical structures of Hittman's melodic phrases on "Some L.A. Niggaz" are extremely detailed and varied in terms of their rhythms. His melody contains phrases that last for two beats, three beats, and four beats; it contains melodic phrases that start on beat 1, beat 2, beat 3, or beat 4; and it also contains phrases that end on beats 2, 3, or 4, as well. Although such melodic variety might be not only frequent, but even expected, in other musical genres, this wealth of diversity in rap is certainly of a stand-out character. As a result, this table is a concise encapsulation not of Hittman's thematic development on "Some L.A. Niggaz," but the technical building blocks with which such a thematic development is built.

Hittman's metrical phrasing on this song is particularly apt, because the minimalist accompanimental backbeat places the rap's rhythms fully in the foreground. A more complex beat with lots of musical ideas, combined with a rapper with a more laidback rhythm like Snoop Dogg's on Dr. Dre's G-funk era work, would overburden the listener's ears with too many competing ideas.

Over the entire course of these three aforementioned rappers' work on "Some L.A. Niggaz," an astute audience will have observed a wide range of approaches to the singular musical gesture in this song's backbeat. Sometimes a sentence is laid right across beat 3; sometimes beat 3 is given lots of musical space. Sometimes that rhythmic respect (or disrespect) is transferred to beat 4, or transferred to beat 1; sometimes that ignorance is transferred to a beat other than beat 3. Sometimes the missing beat's effect on beat 4 is used to re-enforce a pun or double entendre, and sometimes the rapper fills in that beat 3 with an accented note right on top of it.

As a result of the fact that Hittman was so thoroughly focused on the same restricted array of variation operations while he went about executing his own musical program on "Some L.A. Niggaz," so to speak, his approach to thematic development on this song, as well as that of his collaborators, can most accurately be described as linear. To be sure, Hittman's thematic development was not carried out with the same kind of collage-like eye for strong juxtaposition as DMX's own thematic development was. DMX, in his own right, utilized every musical transformation, from note augmentation to accent inversion, in cyclical evolutions of his theme on the song "Who We Be." On that track, DMX constantly moved to musical places that were relatively distant from the original melodic theme that he had borrowed from his accompanying guitar. However, all the while that he did so, DMX also knew full well that he could balance out such embarkations by always eventually returning to the theme's archetypal form in between each and every one of those departures.

Hittman, in contrast, chose to maintain a strong, direct line between his rhythmic theme's beginning form and its ending form. Instead of treating the missing-beat theme as a core idea whose intrinsic nature could never be transformed or questioned, as DMX might have done, Hittman chose to thoughtfully pace out such transformations, without intervening reminders of where he came from. As a result, while the missing beat 2 in bar 49 and beat 4 in bar 51 might seem to be a disorienting step removed from the theme's archetypal form, since there is no intervening missing third beat in between them to make the connection clear, Hittman has so thoughtfully spaced out and handled the theme's continuous transformation with the same tools of phrase length and position that the listener is never left to founder on their own without a compositional helping hand to show the interpretational way.

The key element that has allowed all of this is the fact that rappers like DMX, Time Bomb, King Tee, and Hittman are all willing to think in terms of large, global lengths of musical time. By composing with a verse-to-verse mindset, rather than a line-to-line or bar-to-bar one, they have enabled themselves to create sonic structures whose rhythms and structures extend across vast tracts of time and musical space, because that is how they must be thought of in order to be fully understood in context. But since he was a featured guest on another main artist's own song, the rapper that will be studied next is going to reveal a more local, generative approach to thematic development than DMX or Dr. Dre's team on "Some L.A. Niggaz" do.

Organic Motivic Development in B-Lo's "U Know"

B-Lo's third verse on Kanye West's 2006 mixtape recording "U Know," starting at 3:10, works in a very unique way. As was gleaned from the first two themes presented in this chapter—a two-note, weak–strong theme from DMX's "Who We Be," and the missing-beat theme from "Some L.A. Niggaz"—rap musicians have a large amount of technical materials with which they can construct huge sonic structures of rhythm and pitch. This includes syncopation, strong and weak accent, the musical accompaniment behind them, melodic phrase length, phrase positioning, note frequency, and so on. The compositional materials with which rapper B-Lo works on Kanye West's own song is, to some extent, a widespread combination of all of these technical factors. For example, it includes a flexible approach to the phrase length and position of theme. Overall, though, B-Lo will put these same musical building blocks to a different purpose on "U Know."

B-Lo begins the melody of his guest verse on this Kanye West song by repeating his musical theme a few times in order to establish its preeminent importance within the musical texture, just as DMX, Hittman, Time Bomb, and King Tee all did. In fact, the first full bar of B-Lo's melody contains four total instances of the same three-note motive. Once more, B-Lo's expressive microtiming and trailing behind the beat has been simplified in the transcription below, in order to make his theme's appearances completely clear. As a reminder, the "greater-than" signs in the notation below, like so (>), denote the placement of a strong musical accent on the notes to which they're attached:

Even from his very first bar, the rapper B-Lo is making clear the importance of his motive on the Kanye West song "U Know" by repeating its three-note, downbeat heavy theme a total of four times.

In the above notation, all of the most fundamental features of this specific motive are showcased and presented for the first time in full. The five basic characteristics of this three-note theme are as follows:

1. The motive contains three notes, and, in the analysis to come, will be designated by the following letters in the musical notation: A will refer to the beginning note in the three-note motive, B will refer to the middle note in the motive, and C will refer to the motive's final note. It's important to note that, rather than referring to a specific rhythmic duration within the motive, these letters will refer *only* to any rhythmic duration's general placement within the chronological order of the motive itself, in an unspecific manner; i.e., not to a first, second, or third positioning, but to a beginning, middle, and ending positioning. This must be done in order to accommodate B-Lo's coming operations of thematic transformation.
2. The beginning note of B-Lo's initial three-note motive on "U Know" has the length of an 8th note, the middle note of the motive has the length of a triplet 8th note, and the final note of the motive has the length of a triplet 16th note.
3. The motive starts directly on the beat, whether that might be the downbeat of beat 1, beat 2, beat 3, or beat 4.

3. Motivic Development   101

    4. The motive consists of a single self-contained melodic phrase.
    5. The motive's first note is delivered with a strong musical accent.

B-Lo's motive here also deserves special mention because, on a song with a rather slow tempo of 69 BPM, it makes use of a shuffle, triplet 16th note feel. This makes the motive at hand a very intriguing outlier in the more uniform duplet rhythms that comprise most of the thematic structures that have been considered so far.

In fact, those exact same thematic characteristics just defined are repeated note-for-note and rhythm-for-rhythm in B-Lo's second bar as well:

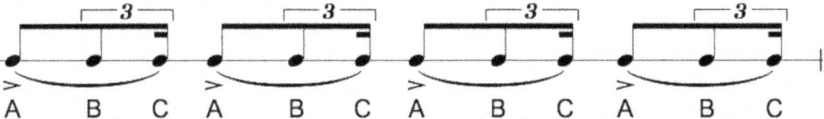

B-Lo uses his second bar of melody to strongly establish the rhythmic identity of his theme even further, prominently repeating it another four times.

Four more times, for a grand total of eight times in just two bars, B-Lo has performed a one-phrase, three-note motive that begins with a strong accent on the downbeat and consists of an 8th note, a triplet 8th note, and a triplet 16th note. Just like DMX on "Who We Be" and the California rappers from "Some L.A. Niggaz," B-Lo will now change, develop, and manipulate those five fundamental aspects of the motive in readily-recognizable ways, while still taking care to always allow identification of the theme's appearances.

Beginning in his third bar of melody, B-Lo expands his theme to encapsulate details of rhythm and accent that are noticeably different from, and yet still identifiably similar to, those with which his musical theme was first introduced. After first rapping his theme in the form of three notes that were repeated only once during the course of a single, one-beat long phrase, B-Lo now starts adding together longer, three-beat (or four-beat) phrases that are made up of multiple, chain-linked repetitions of this three-note motive that are joined to each other inside of a single sentence. At the start of the fifth bar, B-Lo takes this expansion of the theme even further when he begins to structure the theme so that it ends on a strong downbeat accent rather than beginning on a strong downbeat accent, as it used to do.

This change begins is jumpstarted by a very prominent musical rest on beat 1 at the start of bar 5. B-Lo takes advantage of this surprise tabula rasa of rhythm by starting his next run of melody on the weaker beat 2 of the measure, instead of his former beat 1 downbeat. By the time the music of bar 5 ends, B-Lo has re-balanced his motive so that it ends on downbeats, rather than beginning on them, by presenting his theme's same rhythmic durations in a new, re-assembled order. This is indicated by the shifted metric position of the letters A, B, and C in the below transcription:

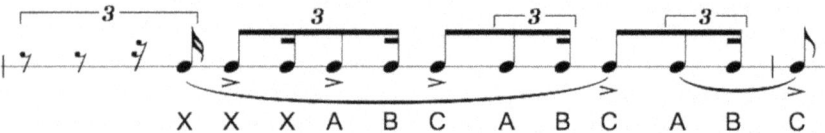

After establishing the archetypal form of his motive in the first section of his melody, B-Lo goes on to develop it by changing the order of its three notes so that its characteristic triplet 16th note now comes in the middle of the series, instead of at the end, as denoted by the shifted metric position of the letters A, B, and C.

After beginning the bar on a rest in the music shown above, B-Lo presents a new instance of his motive. However, he begins this new instance of the motive at the point in its rhythmic order that was previously at the theme's very end. Instead of hearing the usual first two motivic notes of a duplet 8th note and a triplet 8th note, which have now been replaced by a musical rest, a listener hears only that closing triplet 16th note. This is demonstrated by appearances of the letter X, which indicates that such notes do not make up any part of a self-contained instance of the full motive.

After that opening beat 1 rest, B-Lo places strong musical accents on the second X, as well as on the two notes on letter A and on the letter C that follow, both of which are rapped during the first full instance of the motive that is performed next. As a result, the theme should here be re-interpreted as having had its rhythmic balance developmentally changed in emphasis orientation from beginning on downbeat accents, to now ending on downbeat accents. As the motive now occurs, it does indeed still consist of an 8th note, a triplet 8th note, and a triplet 16th note. However, their order has now been changed and re-arranged. Instead of coming in its previous order, the order of the three notes in the motive have been re-arranged to now occur in an 8th note, triplet 16th note, triplet 8th note form. Although the rhythmic durations that the letters A, B, and C previously referred to specifically have been changed, their same A–B–C order in the transcription has been preserved, because, as a group, the same three rhythmic lengths are still being referred to.

B-Lo continues to develop his motive with these transformations in chronological order of rhythmic durations, thematic downbeat positioning, the weak–strong quality of accent, and melodic phrase length in his verse's sixth bar as well:

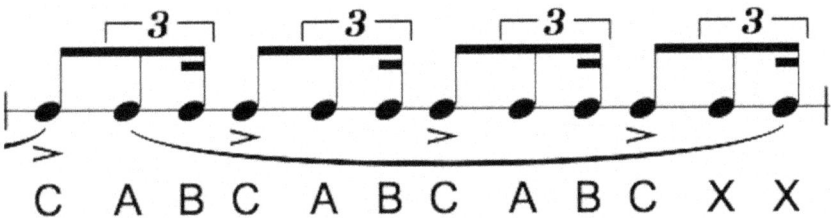

C A B C A B C A B C X X

In his melody's sixth bar, B-Lo continues to focus on the new importance of his transformed motive, as he proceeds to keep utilizing some of the changes that he's applied to it: the new order of the same rhythmic durations, as well as the new positioning of the accented downbeat during it.

In the section of bars, B-Lo starts to combine his previous musical idea of long, chain-linked melodic phrases with this re-worked motive's new rhythmic durational ordering, as well as its newly accented ultimate note. In the below notation, there is an almost two-bar long phrase that is made up of multiple repetitions of the initial motive's new manifestation:

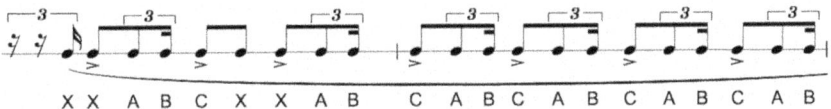

X X A B C X X A B C A B C A B C A B C A B

In his verse's seventh bar, B-Lo begins to combine multiple instances of the re-ordered version of his initial motive together inside of single melodic phrases in an example of phrase augmentation.

The As that occur in the above music serve to reset the onset of the motive continuously, and to place it back at a new beginning point of either the syncopated offbeat or the accented downbeat. This happens over the course of the six repetitions of the motive in the above transcription. In total, these bars bring the total number of motivic occurrences to a full twenty-eight times in just nine bars, and the number of total notes that are part of an individual motivic occurrence to eighty-four, out of a total ninety-four notes.

To review, B-Lo's thematic developments up until this point can be summarized as follows. In bars 1–4, B-Lo first began his melody by positioning the first note of each instance of his three-note motive on an accented downbeat inside of a single sentence. In bar 5, he then moved on to ending his three-note motive on an accented downbeat, instead of beginning it on one. At the same time, B-Lo began to string together multiple instances of his original motive together inside of the same melodic phrase, after he had first began by allowing only one motive to appear inside of each phrase. In bars 6 and 7 of his verse's melody that were just considered, B-Lo then combined these musical ideas of the ending, accented motivic note with his expansion of the melodic phrase.

Beginning in his penultimate, eleventh bar, B-Lo elegantly crafts his coming thematic climax by combining a final new element of thematic development—motivic elision—with his previous concepts of metric transference, measural positioning, emphatic accent, and phrasal expansion:

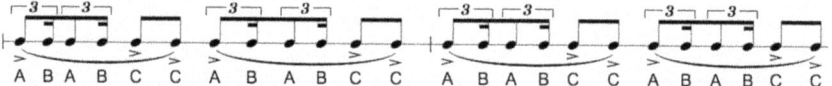

In his last bar, B-Lo organically expands the motive from three notes to six notes by rapping some of its characteristic rhythmic durations more than once, resulting in thematic elision.

In bars 11 and 12, shown above, B-Lo has organically grown and expanded the rhythmic length of his motive so that it now encompasses much larger tracts of musical time. B-Lo's motive can now take up two beats, instead of just one, because B-Lo has actually grown his motive in terms of the number of notes that occur within it.

When the letters A, B, and C were first introduced as helpful symbols to aid in the recognition of the different members of a motive, they were defined rather generally. Instead of referring to the first, second, and third notes of a tripartite motive, these letters were defined as referring to only the beginning, middle, and ending notes of what is, typically, a tripartite motive. The specific analytical situation for which this balancing act was performed can now be seen in full.

This minute but essential consideration is important now, as one strives to tease out the motive's occurrences and transformation in the order of the As, Bs, and Cs in the musical transcription above. Instead of always coming in an A–B–C order, the notes now come in a new A–B–A–B–C–C note order that's conjoined together within a single melodic phrase. Rather than indicating that B-Lo has introduced non-motivic rhythmic material into his melody, this new proliferation of As, Bs, and Cs instead indicates that B-Lo has elided multiple instances of his motivic rhythmic durations together so that larger melodic phrases, as well as an increase in thematic density, now result.

This conclusion, based on an increase in thematic elision and density (rather than a straight thematic transformation), relies on many points of evidence. First of all, while he is rapping these rhythms in a new order, B-Lo is still rapping the same monolithic rhythmic durations that he was using before: 8th notes, triplet 8th notes, and triplet 16th notes. Additionally, these rhythmic durations all still have the same amount of proportional frequency to each other, as for every single 8th note that is rapped, a single triplet 8th note and a single 16th note appears in the melody as well. Furthermore, as the slurs outlining his sentences in the above music indicate, all of these duplicated rhythmic durations still occur inside of a single melodic phrase together, which is exactly the phrasal manner in which the motive first manifested itself.

Furthermore, rather than placing an accented note either at the end or the start of his motivic rhythms—but never before doing both in a single melodic phrase—B-Lo actually does combine those dualistic, dichotomous structural positionings within the measures of music in question. In this way, the intertwining of multiple As, Bs, and Cs with each other inside of a single melodic phrase indicates that multiple instances of the theme are being performed simultaneously. By focusing on new combinations of traditional musical concepts in terms of rhythmic duration, melodic phrase structure, and masculine-feminine motivic prosody, B-Lo here increases the thematic density of his melody by eliding together multiple occurrences of his motive. As a result, B-Lo's final two bars of melody on "U Know" should be understood as a musical situation where a theme is grown organically, in terms of rhythmic duration, out of the technical parts that already constitute itself, rather than a situation where a theme is adding unrelated notes to itself, or some such unrelated transformation.

Because of this focus on the generative, the quintessential, and the substantial, B-Lo's mode of motivic development on "U Know" might be termed as comprising an organic approach. This stands in contrast to the cyclical approach of DMX on "Who We Be," or the linear approach of Dr. Dre's collaborators on "Some L.A. Niggaz." DMX constantly moved away, and back towards, his archetypal theme; Hittman, by transferring his missing-beat theme to other metric positions besides the third beat, actually ended in a different place than where he began. By applying the same cyclical philosophy of motivic development that DMX utilized to the sharply-defined techniques with which Hittman crafted his own transformative musical journey, B-Lo seems to have walked the middle path between two such approaches. That is, he does end up in a different thematic place, so to speak, just as Hittman did, but it comes off as a thematic place that has not itself changed, but as a thematic place that is now heard only with new musical ears that have themselves changed. In this way, B-Lo's compositional affinity might be most closely related to the work of the modern minimalist composers who try to make the most out of the least, such as Arvo Pärt or Philip Glass. In turn, Hittman might be identified with the teleological journeys of the great symphonists, like Beethoven, while DMX will have his day with the establishment party crashers who combine non–Western aesthetic philosophy with the Western building blocks of organized sound, like John Cage.

Summary

Throughout this rather short survey of rappers' approach to thematic development, there has appeared a rather wide range of assumptions and manifestations of musical thinking. On his song "Who We Be," DMX developed his own two-note, weak–strong theme in a non-linear, self-generative manner. He did so by contrasting elements of thematic density inside his melodic phrases with alterations to the normalized accentual structure of the theme as it was first presented. The theme of the rappers on "Some L.A. Niggaz," meanwhile, was not so much rhythmically-oriented as it was texturally-oriented. In their own melodies, these Californian rappers focused on developing the musical idea of their backing accompaniment's missing third beat in both new and familiar ways, such as by transferring their accentual "skipping" to other measural beats. Finally, the rapper B-Lo similarly made changes in the technical aspects of a motivic theme that he first presented in an archetypal fashion at the beginning of his verse on Kanye West's song "U Know." While preserving that three-note theme's subdivisional rhythmic durations, he presented them inside of new macro-rhythmic contexts that forced a re-interpretation on the listener's part. Then, through the augmentation of his melodic phrasing, he composed out a thematic elision inside of his rap that relied on an increase in thematic density.

Motives that are extremely similar to the three that were just examined have been central to the historical development of Western art music, as both a technical phenomenon, as well as an ingroup shibboleth that its composers, instrumentalists, and fans have used for centuries to not just identify the tradition, but to elevate it artistically. These rappers' utilization for technical purposes of the same fundamental musical principle that prevails in the music of almost every Western luminary—from Machaut, to Bach, to Beethoven, and all the way down on to Schoenberg, as well as to even more recent modern composers—would, as a result, seem to then cry out for a major disruption in any cultural distinction, of any kind, that's based on genre, pedagogy, consumption, or professionalism, to a similarly drastic and thorough degree. While there is a chance, very small (thankfully), that the minute descriptions and lofty verbiage at times employed in this chapter might be met with skepticism or cynicism in some quarters of the learned musical community, the full, accurate transcriptions of these three songs will always remain as their own strongest, silent reply. Perhaps, as a result, it is not the understanding of rap that needs to consequently be changed, but the scholarly or professional assumptions about cultural traditions and musical genres that are held with even the smallest amount of dogmatic belief by those of us who would make earnest attempts to more fully understand it in the first place.

4

Structure and Performance Practice

When taken as a whole, the global structures of verses, choruses, and entire songs, when examined across the entire rap genre, can often incorrectly come across as being rather simplistic, or, at the very least, exceedingly plain. Many times, a typical rap song does not extend or expand its structures beyond alternations of verses and choruses, as such songs often omit any kind of bridge section, as well as any texturizing introduction or coda section. Despite the fact that its structures might be rather straightforward, even at the very same time that the specific musical contents contained therein are quite often of a highly radical nature, many unconstructive critics have chosen to focus on some rappers' square structures to discredit the entire genre as being thoroughly non-musical. However, there are also many rappers who are incredibly aware and conscious of the musical power of their voices to bind together large spaces of sonic time in order to generate structures and forms that tie in with many trends in recent modern music.

To combine a discussion of a genre's structure with a discussion of a genre's prevailing performance practices within an analytical dissection might seem to be a mistake at first, since the two topics can be so different, and are often treated separately. However, the unique process by which rap is created and manufactured is what necessitates such a combination of topics within this chapter.

Rap's Division of Labor and Mode of Manufacture

Since the earliest days of rap analysis at the turn of the millennium, a dialogue that works to accurately describe the production process of rap

4. Structure and Performance Practice 109

music has been carried out by rap scholars. As it stands now, it is largely accepted that the musical accompaniment comes first, as the work of Dr. Kyle Adams shows.

As Adams concisely summarizes the debate in a footnote to his chapter in *The Cambridge Companion to Hip Hop*, edited by Dr. Justin Williams "The order in which hip-hop tracks are composed has been the subject of much scholarly discussion; in particular, the question of whether the lyrics are composed before, after, or independently of the beat. The most common model—as described in Manabe, 'The Role of the Producer,' and confirmed in my own discussions with rappers Freddie Gibbs, Josh Martinez, and Das Racist—is for some version of the basic beat to be composed first, at which point the rapper either writes suitable lyrics to it or uses pre-existing ones that seem to fit well, whereupon the producer may add additional layers to complement the lyrics."[1]

The needle has swung on this discussion before, though and is likewise to do so in the future.[2] For now, however, it seems completely reasonable to posit it as the normative standard that, at the very least, a barebones accompanimental framework for a musical beat is the starting point for a rap song, to which a vocalist then contributes their own work at a later point in time.

Not only does the beat usually come first in rap, but, additionally, the composer who creates the musical accompaniment, and the vocalist who later adds their own work to that pre-existing track, are, in the majority of cases, different people. One needs to hear only a short list of famous producer-composer duos in order to bear this assertion out: Eric B. and Rakim, Dr. Dre and Snoop Dogg, RZA and the other Wu-Tang Clan members (on almost all of their recordings), or Drake and Noah "40" Shebib. Although sometimes this is not the case, as in the case of producer-rapper duo Mobb Deep and its two members Havoc and Prodigy, the exceptions to this rule are on the rarer side.

Because of the rap genre's accompaniment–melody order of production, as well as the corresponding division of labor between the creation of the accompaniment by one artist and the creation of the melody by another, it is largely determined that, with such logistical restrictions in place, certain compositional results are a priori unlikely, if not bordering on the impossible.

For example, there is not likely to be a large amount of direct melody–accompaniment interaction, dialogue, or conversation. Such instances of direct give-and-take between a rapper's vocal and his back instrumental tracks are quite often restricted to no more than a cut-and-paste beat drop or two at the appropriate moment of dramatic tension, as on "Got Money." On this 2008 track, the moments at which rapper Lil Wayne directly responds to the musical accompaniment behind him, or vice versa, are restricted to two, at 1:09 and 1:53. At the former moment in time, Lil Wayne directly calls for the musical accompaniment to drop out, so that his own voice can take center-stage, and it obliges. At the latter point, the musical accompaniment introduces a snare which sounds like two hands making the sound of clap, thereby crafting a sonic pun, as it arrives at the exact moment that Lil Wayne uses that word. Even this small amount of direct interaction is relatively uncommon, as a slightly less-involved level of accompaniment–melody interaction can accurately describe the work of everyone from Black Thought on 1999's "Without a Doubt," Big Boi on 1998's "Skew It on the Bar-B" by OutKast featuring Raekwon, or Kanye West's 2004 track "Get Em High," despite the fact that, in the case of that last song, the producer and rapper actually are the same artist (West himself).

This results in musical structures that almost necessarily must be less involved and integrated than such complicated structures like sets of variations, or sonata form, all of where the relationship between a melody and its accompaniment is of the foremost importance. If the melody and the accompaniment were two be doing two completely things in such unified, textural forms, such as playing in different keys, the resulting take-aways of an interpreter would have to take stock of, recognize, and explain that disparity (as being a key change, a change in the emotive narrative, etc.).

Conversely, the balancing act in rap between accompaniment and melody almost demands that the relationship between the two main sources of musical information on a rap song will almost always place most of the listener's attention on the aspects of the melody initially, and not the aspects of the arrangement. That is, probabilistic scales will always be tilted in favor of a listener noticing first and foremost what the melody is doing. This is because the production is made first, and so must be kept on the simpler side, in order to allow the rapper enough sonic room to insert their own vocal line into the texture afterwards. If the production's rhythms, harmonies, or arrangement were too complex, then the addition of a rapping melodic line might, in fact, make the texture too complex for a proper hearing by an audience. Opposite approaches are not necessarily impossible, but only more unlikely, since a producer and rapper would have to have a very close working relationship, in both geographical and personal terms, to execute the opposite kind of balancing act, where the melody of the rap song supports that song's arrangement. Quite simply,

4. Structure and Performance Practice 111

this cannot be reasonably expected to happen in this genre very often, what with rap's professional norms of widespread collaboration, featured verses, and huge, interpenetrating collectives (like Odd Future, Wu-Tang Clan, or Black Hippie). In any event, a favoring of melody has largely been the manner in which this division of labor and chronological order of song-creation has been solved by producers and rappers.[3]

These musical findings are a direct musical correlation to the poetics findings of Dr. Adam Bradley of the University of Colorado–Boulder. In his 2009 title *Book of Rhymes: The Poetics of Hip Hop*, Dr. Bradley expertly describes the members of this balancing act as being the beat and the poetic line, rather than the beat and the melody:

> Rap's dual rhythmic relationship liberates the MC to pursue innovations of syncopation and stress that might otherwise sound chaotic, if it were not for the reassuring regularity of the beat. The beat and the MC's flow work together to satisfy the audience's musical and poetic expectations of rhythm: that it establish and maintain distinct patterns while creatively disrupting those patterns....[4]

By foreground an accentual dynamic that is simultaneously poetic and musical, Bradley has paved the way for ensuing discoveries about rap's rhythms. But back in the strictly musical domain, most of the structural forms that occur within the rap genre are ones that likewise respond to the pre-eminence of melody, such as the verse–chorus or freestyle forms, rather than ones that treat the texture as unified whole, like sonata form. This assertion will be made clear in the sections that follow. For now, it'd do well to note that, with zero exceptions, each and every one of the sixty-one songs that has been analyzed so far in this title has been in either a verse-chorus form, or a freestyle form.

The other results of this unique division of labor, as well as the new mode of manufacture, will be drawn out further in coming sections. For now, it'd do well to keep these two unique features of rap in mind over the course of the next few subheadings. This is because they might help explain why so often it might seem as if the best masterpieces from the genre are the result, not of a seamless integration of a melody and musical accompaniment that both work together toward the same emotive or technical goals, but, instead, are typically wonderfully chaotic, disruptive mediations of two sources of sound that are intentionally working at cross-purposes to each other, such as in the skits of Eminem that can sometimes span decades (examined further below). Additionally, it might cultivate that certain kind of artistic appreciation that might be necessary for a true love of this genre to flourish: an admiration for artists' unlimited creativity, yes, but also an admiration for their ingenious solutions to such "problems" under the desired, intended restrictions of such a division of labor. All of these considerations can be found at work, in abundance, in the songs of rapper Waka Flocka Flame.

Complex Meter in Waka Flocka Flame's A Cappella Intros

Waka Flocka Flame's own work will make an excellent departure point for an investigative dive into the producer–rapper relationship because of the contrast that it draws with the decision made by many other rappers in the face of the fertile opportunities that a division of labor between the creation of a musical accompaniment and the composition of a melody can affords artists. On "Karma," Waka Flocka Flame compositionally prepares his audience's interpretation of his own producer's forthcoming musical arrangement by means of a musical set-up that, without any other supporting information, plays upon his listeners' ingrained expectation that a piece of music will begin on the first beat of a measure.

Waka Flocka Flame begins this particular song with the simple, repetitive rapping of the vocable "pop," as he imitates the sound of an AK-47 machine gun. The listener naturally believes that Waka's first iteration of that "pop" syllable, coming at a BPM of 137, took place on the first downbeat of a bar, since this is a strong generic norm. This commonsense interpretation seems to hold up as the song progresses over the course of this short, four-second a cappella intro, where no other supporting musical information is supplied by any kind of separate musical voice. The introduction of that arrangement into the texture is held off on, for the moment, by Lex Luger, the producer of "Karma." While those "pops" are being rapped, they straightforwardly count off each of the 8th notes of Waka Flocka Flame's chosen quarter-note metric pulse.

If Waka Flocka Flame had stopped the number of repetitions of this onomatopoetic vocable "pop" at sixteen times, instead of at eighteen, then his melody would have had a very simple formal structure in its opening. It would have simply consisted of two bars of music in a 4/4 meter that contained sixteen 8th notes. However, this is not what happens, and so a much more detailed interpretation is called for.

Because Waka Flocka Flame raps his 8th-note "pop" vocable a full eighteen times, instead of a square sixteen times, he has strongly upsets the expectations for hypermeter in a typical rap melody. This structural disjunction is preserved when Waka Flocka Flame adds another four beats of actual poetic text to his melody, once he has finished rapping his opening vocables.

4. Structure and Performance Practice   113

When those lyrics are combined with the previous nine beats, the result is that Waka has begun this song with an opening monophonic section of music that lasts for thirteen quarter-notes, which is, of course, an asymmetrical length of rhythmic duration that cannot be easily broken down into even bars of 4/4.

If the first two 8th-note "pops" that are rapped on "Karma" were considered as together comprising the fourth beat of a pick up measure in 4/4, then these thirteen beats could be easily accounted for. However, this interpretation is not possible, since those two "pops" are unaccompanied by any other source of musical information that might supplement the understanding of this opening section by means of such details as harmonic rhythm, accompanimental figuration, etc.

If Waka Flocka Flame's rap is heard as beginning on beat 1, and, furthermore, that it has also lasted for thirteen full beats, then there is an analytical problem here. This problem is made clearer by the fact that, on the beat that immediately follows the end of Waka Flocka Flame's opening thirteen-beat melody, Lex Luger brings in the full musical accompaniment behind the rapper. Could this possibly mean that repetitions of Luger's musical accompaniment are starting on the second beat of every bar?

The rest of the song speaks strongly against just such a contrasting interpretation. This is because, as has been conditioned in the ear of a listener to the rap genre, the rest of the song is still strongly oriented towards a first beat that continues to occupy a supreme position of accentual importance. Specifically, most of the melodic phrases found throughout the genre of rap terminate on beat 4 and begin anew on beat 1, which is itself almost always aligned with the accompanimental backbeat's own bass kick on beat 1.

So, how is one to interpret Waka's rhythms, which themselves demonstrate little respect for the traditional time signature of the rap genre as its typically been structured in terms of hypermeter?

Here, because no supporting information is supplied by any backing musical accompaniment, a listener will hear Waka's unbalanced metrical phrasings as consisting of a conglomeration of various meters. Specifically, Waka has begun his song by rapping a series of three bars a cappella, each of whose meters are, respectively, 4/4, 5/4, and 4/4 again. The first bar has four quarter notes to it, because the rap genre has conditioned the expectation that its songs will be in 4/4, and will have its most important musical events occur on beat 1. The second bar, however, has five quarter notes to it. This is a result of the fact that, while the first eight 8th note "pops" have completely fulfilled the normative expectation of a 4/4 meter,

Waka actually goes on to rap those 8th note "pops" an asymmetrical number of times, five, right afterwards. To conclude his opening exposition, Waka strongly defines a new 4/4 bar's beat 1 by beginning his next line, a boisterous vocalization of his musical collective's name, on a strongly accented half note whose entire melodic phrase lasts for four beats. After this, the full musical accompaniment on "Karma" comes in, on beat 1 of the song's fourth bar. In this manner, all thirteen intervening values of the meter's pulse on this song can be neatly accounted for.

A major factor in all of this is that there is no supporting information from the beat when notating this music analytically. However, the full musical accompaniment does finally enter into the texture at 0:05. As a result, Waka's uniform performance of these same thirteen notes actually becomes re-interpreted when they are introduced back into the texture later on in the song.

This happens when Waka Flocka Flame brings his AK-47 imitation back at time stamp 0:14. Interestingly, Waka Flocka Flame does not change the rhythmic structure of his "pops" at this point in any way at all. He still raps a full eighteen of them, for a total length of nine quarter notes, when those notes are counted at the rapper's original BPM of 137 (the arrangement itself can be parsed in double-time). Once again, we have the same number of nine quarter notes that don't fit neatly into the divisions that a 4/4 bar naturally gives rise to. But, because the complementary musical accompaniment is now present to supply supporting information that can aid in metric interpretation, the backing voice in Waka Flocka Flame's semi-contrapuntal texture, consisting of these vocable "pops," can now be understood as ending on beat 4 of the seventh bar of this song's chorus.

To review, the second repetition of Waka Flocka Flame's AK-47 imitation isn't another 4/4, 5/4, 4/4 metric ordering of bars. Instead, these bars should be treated in a much plainer manner: that first pair of pops simply makes up one beat of pick up notes at the end of a 4/4 bar, which in turns leads to two more bars of 4/4. In fact, this is how Waka Flocka Flame arranges this unique musical idea whenever it occurs after its opening appearance, whether at 0:27, 1:23, 2:18, 2:32, 3:28, or 3:42. That is, Lex Luger never augmented any one of his chorus' bars by an extra beat, as Waka Flocka Flame did during this song's opening. Specifically, Lex Luger could never be said to have delayed the repetition of one of his musical accompaniment's loops by a beat in order to accommodate Waka Flocka Flame's metrically-extended phrase. Instead, Waka Flocka Flame continues to rap his AK-47 rhythms with the very same technical aspects after the full musical accompaniment has come in. It's just that he has made them fit into the more normal weak–strong structure of beats in a four-part meter, instead of a complex meter.

Waka Flocka Flame has also composed here a simple form of metric modulation. Due to the active, sharp, and loud nature of their dynamics and articulation, the snare, bass kick, drum, and keyboard synths are strong enough on "Karma" to structure all of this song's music into a 4/4 metric framework. Accordingly, they're also strong enough to almost singlehandedly define the temporal BPM of the track overall. If the reader has paid particular careful attention, they will recall that it was asserted that Waka Flocka Flame delivered his "pops" at a BPM of about 137. This is true, but only for the a cappella intro, and not for the song's entire texture in full. When it comes in, the drum set is playing at about half of Waka Flocka Flame's own original speed, down near the 68.5 BPM level.

So, in addition to utilizing a bar of complex meter, Waka Flocka Flame has metrically modulated away from the song's prevailing tempo in an accelerando direction. The metric modulation is a relatively straightforward one, from 137 BPM to 68.5 BPM, since a quarter-note at the former speed is the same as an 8th note at the latter speed.

By utilizing complex meters and metric modulation, Waka Flocka Flame is able to expertly support, through music, his rap's menacing poetic themes of violence and struggle. That's because the disjunction between the spoiled expectations for his opening a cappella melody, and the hypermeter of the arrangement that follows, are likewise structured in such a fragmented, chaotic way. This close marriage between poetry and music raises a strong resonance with the next rapper's own artistry, that of Wyclef Jean, whose work demonstrates a similar amount of appreciation for the effects that a careful balancing of rap's parameters can have on a listener's ear.

Wyclef Jean's Hook–Freestyle Integration

For "80 Bars," the fourth song from his third solo album, *The Masquerade*, Wyclef Jean actually did compose both the melody and the musical accompaniment. However, it this song's unique integration of oppositional concepts of structure, and not its defiance of generic production norms, that are the most notable aspects of this 2002 track. Indeed, Wyclef's adroit handling of the implications of structure and form is executed so masterfully on "80 Bars" that, in the end, he manages to largely redefine and upend previous conventional understandings of how verses and choruses can function within the genre.

On "80 Bars," he rearranges the opposing sections of chorus and verse inside of a freestyle context that relies on a blurring of lines between repetition and variation. (A freestyle, in rap, is a textual form that can consists of one long run-on verse, without any hooks or choruses to it. The term freestyle is sometimes used as a verb to refer to a rap that is composed improvisationally and on the spot, but that will not be the typical sense of the term as it's used herein.) In this way, the track ends up being a song with only one verse and only one chorus, a statement that would seem to be a contradiction in terms. However, Wyclef expands the traditional definition of verse and chorus by carefully handling not just these sections' chronological order, but their degree of repetition and variation as well.

Wyclef's compositional techniques on "80 Bars" are accomplished through a musical sleight of hand. By beginning his song in the form of a long stream-of-consciousness freestyle, and then unexpectedly introducing a new chorus section at the end of 80 bars, Wyclef merges the traditional forms of the rap genre. In order to capture this musical thought process, a simple representative system of brackets, apostrophes, and letters can be used. This typographical notation will tease out the true differences between the nature of a verse and the nature of a chorus, and just how it is that Wyclef Jean manages to manipulate their shifting relationship to each other.

The structure of Wyclef's rap on "80 Bars" is elucidated in the following breakdown, wherein the section of music, its function, and the sonic elements appearing there are enumerated:

1. Bars 1–4: Introduction Section; Instrumental Arrangement and Spoken Ad-Libs.
2. Bars 5–84: Verse; Wyclef's Rap.
3. Bars 85–92: Chorus; Wyclef's Rap.
4. Bars 93–100: Outro; Soloing Guitar.

What is striking about these musical structures is that their obvious function can be readily identified, even though none of the sections are ever repeated. That is, the definition of a chorus and the definition of a verse both fundamentally rely on whether the musical content of each is repeated or not. A chorus is defined as a chorus because it is repeated; a verse is defined as a verse because its musical content is not repeated. Meanwhile, a freestyle in rap is defined as a form that consists of only a long verse, with no bookending chorus section.

The question, then, is this: how has Wyclef managed to unify a functioning chorus with a functioning verse inside of a popular song structure, without ever repeating either section?

The reasons are twofold. First, the musical chorus appears on this song only after an unusually extended exposition of verse material, eighty bars long, that is thoroughly through-composed. The second reason relies on the fact of the prior existence of a specific song form, unique to the rap genre apart from all others, that is basically an extended verse (the freestyle).

Once the structure-defining melody of the song has been performed for about four bars, the section appears to listener as being no more than a simple verse, since none of the melodic material—in terms of its words, rhythms, or melody—are ever repeated. After about forty bars of this through-composed melody have been presented in this exposition, the song next assumes the form of a freestyle, which precludes the possibility of any chorus. Even if it were to be cut in half, the length of this eighty-bar verse is still far longer than most other rap verses on record in the genre.[5] While there may be rap songs of a comparable length, they are almost always proper freestyles, like Mos Def's "Beef." This is because such songs do not contain appended choruses that would force those freestyles to be re-classified as verses, albeit rather long ones.

When the pseudo-verse on "80 Bars" reaches its concluding eightieth bar, however, the song does not simply end. Instead, it is only at this tardy point in the track that Wyclef introduces an eight-bar chorus section that consists of a two-bar musical idea whose exact words, rhythms, and melody are repeated a full four times. Afterwards, however, Wyclef does not return to another verse, whether one consisting of eighty bars, or some other related length. Instead, the song ends with the sounds of a soloing guitar that brings the track to its conclusion.

By thoroughly re-working the traditional technical aspects of a well-known musical convention from his own musical genre and cultural tradition, Wyclef's music merges the technical aspects of a traditionally strophic musical section with a traditionally through-composed musical section in a manner that is not a pure verse–chorus form, or a pure freestyle form, but something of both. He does this by turning what sounds like a freestyle into no more than an extremely long verse, through the intentional delay of repeated chorus material. In a similar manner, the two members of the New York group Mobb Deep, Prodigy and Havoc, likewise innovate the relationship of common generic building blocks on their own song, "Shook Ones, Pt. II."

Disjunction in Mobb Deep's Accompaniment-Melody Relationship

The opening of the 1995 song "Shook Ones, Pt. II," from the Mobb Deep album *The Infamous*, is fairly standard, in terms of its technical aspects, for a rap song. It begins with an eight-bar instrumental introduction that consists of only the drumbeat playing, whose backbeat and accompanimental role will persist throughout the entire length of this song. Meanwhile, the piano bass line that underpins the contrapuntal aspects of the arrangement enters right on cue, at the beginning of ninth bar, a hypermetrically uniform position. However, similar to Wyclef, Prodigy next disrupts this generic uniformity by arranging the entrance of his own melodic voice into the texture in a hypermetrically-unbalanced manner.

Specifically, Prodigy orchestrates the structure of his melodic entry so that it first appears in full halfway through the second repetition of the piano loop, before that piano has completed its current loop. When compared against the norms of other melodic entrances in rap, this is thoroughly unexpected. This asymmetrical musical balancing supports the uneasiness that's found throughout the rest of the musical atmosphere: the too-slow piano bass line, the uncomfortably uneven reverb of the dominant snare, and the producers' stark, barebones treatment of the frequency spectrum in the skeleton stereophonic mix.

Rather than ever resolving this structural disjunction in his own verse, this half of the Mobb Deep duo chooses to retain that large amount of tension in the orchestrational balance of this song's arrangement. Havoc declines to end his verse in an even numbered bar, even though doing so would result in the exit of his own vocal melody from the musical texture. Thus, his rap would be brought back into perfect alignment and harmony with the new beginning of the next piano loop. The last three bars of Prodigy's verse, from measure 41 to measure 43, make this clear.

At this point, Prodigy actually ends his rap verse in the middle of the eighteenth repetition of the looping piano bass line that's played by the lower register's left hand, which is right where he began it as well. As a result, the most crucial aspects of the structure of this song's melody are prevented from being consonant or conjunct with the crucial aspects of the structure of this song's backing musical accompaniment. Prodigy has retained a traditional number of bars for his verse, as it encompasses a length of thirty-two measures, but he has unbalanced them in relation to the musical loop behind them at the same time.

4. Structure and Performance Practice 119

The other half of Mobb Deep, Havoc, likewise imitates Prodigy's own entrance and exit in the next half of the song. Just like Prodigy started his verse in the middle of a repetition of the piano loop, so does Havoc, after this song's chorus has occupied a space of twelve bars. At bar 56, in the middle of the twenty-fourth repetition of the piano loop, Prodigy inserts his own melodic voice into the musical texture. But instead of a full thirty-two bars, which is the length for which Prodigy rapped, Havoc now raps only twenty-four bars. However, just like the hypermetric, symmetrical balance of a section of music that's made up of thirty-two bars, a verse that lasts for twenty-four bars on "Shook Ones, Pt. II" would also preserve the strong structural misalignment between accompaniment and melody. At bar 80, in the middle of the thirty-sixth repetition of the piano bass line loop, the second hook of "Shook Ones, Pt. II" begins. Just like this song's first hook, it ends in the middle of the piano sample's loop as well, as it lasts for a full twelve bars.

The choice of Prodigy and Havoc to leave their verses unbalanced, with regards to the musical loop behind them, draws a sharp contrast to the work of other rappers. For example, an examination of a supermajority of the previous transcriptions in this book, such as Busta Rhymes' "Break Ya Neck," will show that almost all rappers begin their verses in alignment with a new loop of their backing instrumentation. In a similar manner, the next rapper under consideration further innovates his own music by upending generic expectations about choruses in his own oeuvre.

Eminem's False Hooks

In 2002, the rapper Eminem took the aggressive step of listing, for all to hear publicly, the rap lyricists that he considers to be the best ever on his track "Til' I Collapse." While Eminem doesn't list Prodigy, Havoc, or Wyclef as legends on this song, he picks up on the same technical themes that that trio played with in their own work. Indeed, Eminem performs a similar type of structural substitution as Mobb Deep on his own featured rap from the 1999 Dr. Dre song "Forgot About Dre."

On the hook for "Forgot About Dre," which occurs at 1:11 and 2:23, Eminem raps about how present-day rappers seem to have forgotten how important Dr. Dre was to their success and current music. This particular hook lasts four bars, and consists of two instances of the same two-bar lines. It first arrives on the song after Dr. Dre has rapped a verse that lasted for sixteen bars. After the end of the hook's first appearance, Eminem begins his own verse at the very same time that the musical ideas behind him also begin their new loops. So, instead of relying on a disjunct relationship between the backing voices and the leading voice, like Mobb Deep did, Eminem's artistry must find something else to manipulate. To be sure, Eminem's own structural sleight of hand will rely on the explicit transfer of the usual amount of polyphonic function between an accompanying voice and a melodic voice within the same musical texture.

This shift in musical focus substantiates itself after the first eight bars of Eminem's verse. At this point, Dr. Dre inserts a completely new musical instrument into the song at 1:54, which is a distorted guitar. Since this distorted guitar enters into this song's arrangement at the same hypermetrically-symmetrical structural point where a chorus almost always occurs on a typical rap genre song, it functions as a textural substitute for the leading melodic voice from what can be called a false chorus.

This guitar idea further cements its role as an imitation of a non-existent lead voice from a false chorus because both this distorted guitar riff and this song's chorus last the same exact amount of musical time on this track, four bars. It's also important to note that during this false hook, Eminem doesn't return back to the same rap that he originally delivered in the first chorus, which might, instead, make this a real chorus or interlude. Instead, Eminem continues the through-composed nature of his rap verse by fantasizing about all of his many violent capers when the false hook first begins. After this fake hook ends, Eminem continues his sixteen-bar verse as normal.

By cleverly structuring his rap in a through-composed manner at a point in the music in which a chorus-like idea is presented, Eminem slyly creates a new kind of rap structure. As the next section will elucidate, this is no new musical goal for Eminem to be achieving.

Hypermetric, Arrhythmic Interludes

In fact, there are very few domains in rap where Eminem's influence hasn't been felt. To count, he could have been included in this book's rhythm, melody, motivic development, structure and performance practice, texture and orchestration, and instrumentalism, and masters chapters. On the other hand, Eminem has also at times squarely placed his intense attention on just the technical structures of his music.

An essential technical descriptor of structure in rap is length, as the

4. Structure and Performance Practice 121

previous sections on Black Thought demonstrated. As it happens, even a routinely cursory perusal of the time lengths of Eminem's songs reveals that they can range anywhere from the very short (around just 11 seconds, for the skit "Paul," on 2000's *The Marshall Mathers LP*) to the very long (at a full 7 minutes and 14 seconds, for the song "Bad Guy," the introductory track on 2013's *The Marshall Mathers LP 2*). However, it's obviously not just when these songs stop and start that's important, but also what happens between their beginnings and their ends, that will reveal other descriptors that are essential for understanding a song's musical structure.

Ever since the very early part of his career, Eminem has frequently utilized unconventional popular song structures that largely work to eschew the quasi-ubiquitous verse–chorus alternations that can underpin so much of popular music. His oeuvre does indeed contain within it such standardized songs, like "The Real Slim Shady," that do not include a bridge, coda, instrumental solo, or any other diversifying musical section. But this is by no means the rule for Eminem, as there are a multitude of strong exceptions. On tracks like "Guilty Conscience," from *The Slim Shady LP*, Eminem shows more than a willingness to make free-form, open-ended structures the norm of his compositional technique.

"Guilty Conscience" might be more often noted for its extended multisyllabic wordplay, or just how intuitively Eminem verbally interprets and updates Dr. Dre's current position in the modern music industry. But it should also be recognized for the fact that its musical structure actually does contain chorus-like material, even under its false guise of an extended freestyle. However, such a designation would inaccurately relate it to countless other freestyles, such as The Roots' "The Lesson."

In reality, "Guilty Conscience" is actually a musical picture that has much more depth to it. This is because, if it's said that there are no choruses, than, arguably, there are also no verses on this song either. This interpretation is forced by the three full, non-musical interludes that intervene between the rapping dialogue of Eminem and Dr. Dre. During these skit interludes on the song, which themselves have no audible meter or pulse, an arrhythmic narrating voice sets up and introduces the good-versus-evil situations that confront this song's three third-person protagonists, whether it's an unfaithful girlfriend, late bills, or so on.

These interludes break up the flow and structure of the music by not organizing the sonic events within them by means of a recurring meter, as mentioned before. This means that, from the time slots of 0:00 to 0:15 and 1:10 to 1:31, as well as from 2:03 to 2:25, the sounds that are utilized are not organized into repeating patterns governed by a consistent pulse. While other rappers have frequently made use of non-rapping interludes, they oftentimes comprise no more than a skit that resides within the confine of its own track.

Such an example is the "Rob Quarters" skit of Ludacris' 2003 *Chicken-n-Beer* album. If the skits are, indeed, out of time with the music to come, then their appearance is usually only short and limited, such as the opening thirty-second skit of Wu-Tang Clan's 1993 song "Can It Be All So Simple." If the appearance of a non-rapping interlude on a rap track is neither short nor limited, then these interludes typically make up no more than a sidelined, non-thematic intro or outro to the track, such as the ending skit of Busta Rhymes' "Match the Name with the Voice."

For Eminem, none of these caveats of length, position, or importance are present to undercut the interpretation of his three intra-song skits. The essentially arrhythmic music of "Guilty Conscience" is heard by the listener as constituting an essential part of this song, which happens because of just how deeply Eminem and Dr. Dre weld these non-musical interludes to the song's hypermetric structure. However, that term, arrhythmic, must be partially qualified in this sense. While the interludes of "Guilty Conscience" are arrhythmic in the metric sense—on the quarter-note to quarter-note level—they are *not* arrhythmic in a hypermetric sense, on the bar-to-bar level.

This is because the start and end of these supposedly-arrhythmic interludes actually do unmistakably line up with exactly where the bars of the song's 91 BPM tempo, 4/4 meter occur when that meter continues to be counted off after the song's backing musical accompaniment has dropped out for the first time. The omniscient narrator who introduces this track's second moral dilemma, presented after this song's pulse has already come in for the first time, inserts his voice into the texture on the exact downbeat of the measure that starts twenty bars after the rap and musical accompaniment have established this song's prevailing pulse, back at 0:17. What's more, this interlude ends after exactly eight bars of 4/4, 91 BPM music have passed, at which point the musical accompaniment's pulse comes back into the song and is no longer implied, but directly felt.

A similar meta-rhythmic dynamic is at work for this song's third and final interlude. Introducing the plight of a young man who comes home from his job to find his wife cheating on him, this final interlude likewise lasts exactly eight bars, when counted at the song's underlying BPM of 91. These eight bars of interlude start at the same exact musical position where beat 1 of the forty-ninth bar of properly-timed music is be found.

Of course, eight bars also constitute the length of a traditional chorus in rap. Even more striking, these supposedly non-musical interludes even occur at the very points on "Guilty Conscience" where a traditional chorus would usually occur according to the norms of hypermeter in a normal, run-of-the-mill rap song. The traditional place for a chorus would be in between rap verses that last for some multiple of two or four bars, and the three verses on "Guilty Conscience" last, respectively, twenty, twelve, and then twenty bars again. Additionally, if this song's position in time is slightly shifted by a few milliseconds, so that its first timed section at 0:17 is placed on the downbeat of a hypothetical bar 9, these interlude-choruses are found to occur at the very same uneven bar numbers where real choruses would happen in the typical rap song. Specifically, these aforementioned interludes would occur at bars 29 and bars 49.

This begs the question: are these arrhythmic skits actually choruses?

The Structure of Eminem's "Guilty Conscience"

In a way, the compositional technique of the arrhythmic interlude seems to communicate the idea that Eminem thinks of choruses in an expansive, extensive way. This is because Eminem has here seemed to have expanded the strictly musical function of choruses to encompass arrhythmic phenomena. To Eminem, it doesn't seem to matter what the specific sonic content of a chorus actually is. The only technical aspect of the section that seems to matter is that the chorus continue to serve a connective, interlocking function between succeeding verses, as it introduces each new scenario, no matter what it might be. A chorus will always serve this helpful function as long as it is repeated in some manner; it makes little difference what sounds are being repeated, and the specific way in which those sounds are being repeated matters only slightly more.

In trying to put a name to Eminem's generic innovations on "Guilty Conscience," the relationship between different musical voices, in terms of their importance and number, should also always be kept in mind. At the same time that he's expanding the traditional treatment of the verse–chorus form, Eminem is simultaneously crafting an extended call-and-response musical dialogue with Dr. Dre, one where their two different voices are trading the dominant, commanding place in the musical texture back-and-forth continuously. In fact, these two rappers trade the melody back and forth a full twenty-two times on this song.

When the repeated arrhythmic skits and intensive call-and-response texture are taken together, the result is that the structure of "Guilty Conscience" lends itself to multiple interpretations. It could be said to have a free-form, experimental, A–B–C tripartite structure, since there are no conventionally traditional choruses that repeat in between each of the different verses, and all of the rap verses are different from each other in terms of their lyrical and melodic content. At the same time, this song might be considered in light of a strophic, A–A–A form. This is due to the fact that, while the rapped verses are never exact copies of one another, they are actually the musical sections on this song that are the closest to being real copies of each other. That is, the interludes are different from each other to an extent that is much greater than the differences between the rap, because of their respective rhythms and lyrics. From this view, the seeming randomness of the interludes places the verses in stark relief, and relates them all to each other. "Guilty Conscience" might also be considered as a new type of interrupted freestyle, where those sonic, arrhythmic interludes are really just breaks between which Eminem is delivering three different freestyles. This perspective would balance the chaos of the interludes with the straightforward interpretation of what a verse and chorus should be.

However, all of these interpretations fall short of the mark because they largely ignore the fact that, while those sonic, talking interludes are metrically arrhythmic, they do very much follow the structure of rap's traditional hypermeter and its organization of musical sections into groupings of bars whose total number is almost always a multiple of four. With this in view, it might be best to think of this song as a kind of rap rondo, in an A–B–A–C–A–D form, where the As, while acting as stand-ins for the place of the interludes, denote the fact that they are always performing the same connective function, even as they invariably contain specifically different (but not functionally different) content. At the same time, each of the three succeeding verses are denoted by the letters B, C, and D, since the content of each individual verses is always different from that of the others.

If the two oppositional terms are already being used freely, then this song might just next be reduced into only another instance of the verse–chorus form. A typographical representation of "Guilty Conscience" might then look something like A–B–A–B–A–B. However, this would overturn much of the foundational understandings of representations of structure. This is because, at the very least, that group of A letters communicates that every letter A is the same as every other letter A, and every letter B is the same as every other letter B. Nothing could be further from the truth for "Guilty Conscience," where no exact musical or lyrical material is ever repeated from one section to the next.

Perhaps the sections could be further differentiated by using the denotation of relationships through considerations of greater or lesser primes, in the form of A'–B'–A"–B"–A'"–B". However, this representation reaches such a level of complexity that it would call into question the entire enterprise. At the end of the day, the term rondo might be the best that a music analyst is left with, since it so carefully balances such considerations of repetition, variation, chorus, verse, freestyle, and notation.

Eminem's Intra-song Skits

Seen from one point of view, "Guilty Conscience" might also comprise the conjoining of two prominent traditions that run throughout the history of rap music: the skit and the freestyle. While the freestyle's interaction with "Guilty Conscience" has already been dissected, the idea of the skit, and how rappers utilize it musically, might bear a deeper treatment through a specifically-musical perspective.

A skit in rap can be many things. Fundamentally, however, it has the same basic purpose as that of a comedy skit: to make people laugh, and to tell a story. In rap, this has a long tradition that stretches back far in history, to even the very earliest rapping pioneers. For whatever reason, rappers were largely the first popular, modern musicians to fully embrace their dual roles as comedian and commentator in humorous ways in the era of digital recording. This comedic approach has led to some of the most memorable, quotable musical action in the entire rap genre, as in the delightfully transgressive "Torture" skit of the Wu-Tang Clan.

Eminem himself has played no small part in the development of a skit towards heights where the skit is much more than a comedic cast-off for cheap jokes. "Guilty Conscience" is just one part of this compositional puzzle, as Eminem herein manages to fully integrate the skit within his music to a large extent. The three arrhythmic, chorus–interludes on "Guilty Conscience" at 0:00, 1:10, and 2:03 can simultaneously be thought of as skits that have been thoroughly elided and merged into the traditional structure of a rap song. This is because those speaking interludes all display many of the usual characteristics of a rap skit. First, the narrating voice of those interludes is not in time with any repeating pulse. If satirizing rap skits are in time with the rhythmic pulse of a quarter-note beat, rather than the hypermetric bar, then they constitute musical parodies, and not skits. An example of such would be the extended outro of Kurupt's song "Who Ride wit Us," at 3:56. In addition, because skits do not have that essential music characteristic of rhythmic pulse to them, rappers generally do not perform an authentic rap over them. Instead, they simply talk, or, on the other hand, get new dramatic characters to speak for them, just as Eminem does. Finally, skits are, of course, humorous, and such a label can be applied to the stilted, stuck-up vocal delivery of the narrator on "Guilty Conscience."

All of these non-musical characteristics of a rap skit might seem to require that they be treated with non-musical methods, such as that of cinema, or even poetry. However, because these skits have been placed in the overriding master context of a musical album, Eminem's skits should be analyzed and understood from this musical perspective as well. Eminem's integration of the skit into the traditional verse–chorus popular song form on "Guilty Conscience" consists of an elision between the connective function of the conventional chorus and the rap skit's furnishing of comedic relief to act as a dramatic break between songs, whose place is here filled in by humorous verses of rapping.

Eminem's Intra-album Skits

But Eminem's use of the music-skit extends far beyond "Guilty Conscience," and even far beyond the one album that it appears on, *The Slim Shady LP*. From a count of the official studio albums he had released before the year 2013, Eminem has no less than twenty-six songs that can be considered skits in themselves. Neither does this number include the long list of skits that are included inside of other tracks. As the number of tracks across the course of his seven full albums between 1996 (*Infinite*) and 2013 (*The Marshall Mathers LP 2*) all add up to a total of one-hundred and sixty-two career songs, the fact that skits comprise more than more than an eighth of Eminem's total number of songs is quite remarkable.

On each one of these seven albums, these supposedly non-musical skits, fitted in between more traditional songs, often behave in ways that are very similar to how the real choruses on the songs themselves function. Take, for example, the three different skits, all entitled "Paul," that Eminem has released over the course of those eleven years. Each one of these skits features Eminem's manager, Paul Rosenberg, threatening to sue or disown Eminem for his latest lyrical transgressions against famous celebrities, American middle-class virtues, or some other societal sacred cow. These

4. Structure and Performance Practice

three skits appear, respectively, on *Marshall Mathers LP*, *Slim Shady LP*, and *Relapse: Refill*. In fact, the voice of Rosenberg also appears on the 2002 album *The Eminem Show*, on a track that is entitled, instead, "Paul Rosenberg." Acting in unison, this set of skits altogether function as a recurring, trans-album musical refrain that reminds the listener of one of Eminem's central poetic themes: the ingrained, incredible hypocrisy of middle-class, mainstream American culture.

On each one, Eminem's actual, real-life music manager, Paul Rosenberg, calls Eminem and leaves Eminem a phone recording on his answering machine that advises Eminem to tone down the ultra-violent and insensitive content of his lyrics. Just like a more traditional chorus on a rap song, it functions as a constant musical reminder to the listener that Eminem is always pushing the boundaries of what's acceptable in society, whether in music or poetic terms. Furthermore, this skit, just like a chorus, recalls that Eminem does so in the interest of artistic or personal expression, individual empowerment, and free speech. All of this applies to Eminem's verses on songs like "Bitch Please II" and "The Way I Am," or the chorus itself from "White America."

The "Paul" skits, seen from this perspective, then form a type of recurring motive of formal structure, rather than melody or rhythm, that reappears anew with each succeeding album release, which itself inarguably constitutes an incredibly important marker in any recording artist's career. At these crucial times, then, Eminem uses the "Paul" skits to re-orient the listener towards Eminem's own focus, simultaneously reminding both his fans and his detractors of where Eminem is, where he has been, and where he wants to be going. This is quite analogous to the functions of reminders that choruses play in the standard verse–form song structure.

If we consider the rap album to be nothing more than a grand re-formatting of the rap song when expanded to larger proportions, then we can see skits as being extra-musical choruses, and traditional rap songs as the verses between them that serve to elucidate and texturize the messages we find on those skit-choruses themselves. The four different recurrences of the skit "Paul" across an eleven-year stretch explain the musical quintessence of Eminem's career, as he's explained it not just in his rap, but in interviews as well it.

Apart from the skits, then, the other ten or so songs on any of his albums will subsequently serve to show just how he will specifically do those things, thereby playing the texturizing role of verses. It's to Eminem's credit that he elevated the arrhythmic rap skit into the musical sphere by being the first to utilize multiple recurrences of the same type of skit in different forms across his entire career, which does, in itself, form a sort of über-album.

Eminem's Extended Song Structures

In stark contrast to those very short skits, Eminem's song structures can also extend in the opposite direction, when he takes the popular song form and maximizes its proportions, rather than shortening its parameters. In fact, it only takes three of Eminem's longest songs—"Beautiful," "Wicked Ways," and "Kim"—to add up to a timeline that's a mere shade under a full twenty minutes if played consecutively. Those three aforementioned songs each last for 6:33, 6:31, and 6:18 minutes, respectively.

"Beautiful," coming at a rhythmic speed of 132 BPM, has a total length of two-hundred-and-seventeen bars. Out of that total number, a full eighty bars altogether comprise the length of Eminem's three verses in sum. This is a length of rap that is almost at least twice as much as the normal number of bars that a rapper performs on a typical song, where there are typically three verses that each last sixteen bars. When one furthermore considers the fact that Eminem also performs the same twenty-four-bar chorus three different times here, it means that Eminem raps for a total length of one-hundred-and-fifty-two bars on "Beautiful." He even adds sixteen bars of outro ad libs at the end of the song, which means that Eminem is rapping, in one form or another, for about 306 seconds, when there are only about 396 total seconds available to him in the first place.

However, Eminem also utilizes structural truncation in his compositions as well. For instance, his song "Never Enough" might be considered as the ultimate economical use of the rap art form. Over the course of this song, there is not a single bar that doesn't have rap in it, as it clocks in at a comparatively stunted time frame of 2:40. Here, we receive another consistent artistic message from Eminem in a strictly musical form: "only the rap matters."

Elzhi's Musical Tributes

A Detroit rapper by the name of Elzhi did something similar to Eminem on his song "Never Enough" when he expanded the idea of the rap mix-tape-remake to encompass the extended format of an entire album. On an album he released in 2011, Elzhi declined to simply add new

4. Structure and Performance Practice

melodies over a musical accompaniment that a different rapper had previously consecrated as being particularly important in the history of the genre, either through their words or rhymes. Mos Def's re-working of the backing music from Notorious B.I.G.'s song "Who Shot Ya" constitutes just such an example. On this song, Mos Def added his own words and rhythms to a musical accompaniment that Notorious had previously made classic a few years earlier.

Elzhi's compositional trick was to extend this idea of covers to include an entire LP, instead of just a song or two from another famous lyricist. That 2011 Elzhi album was entitled *Elmatic*. That title makes the influence of the 1994 Nas album *Illmatic* on Elzhi clear not just in its public presentation and branding, but in its musical technique as well.

As it turns out, Elzhi's producer didn't just rip re-assembled, looped instrumentals from that classic 1994 Nas album. Instead, his producer re-recorded each and every element of the musical accompaniments from all of the ten tracks that appeared on Nas' album seventeen years earlier. Using a wide orchestration that included basses, guitars, organs, pianos, strings, live snares, and live bass kicks, Will Sessions, the song's producer, was able to recreate all of the musical samples that were used on Nas' own 1994 project. On that track, producers as legendary as Q-Tip, Large Professor, DJ Premier, Pete Rock, and Nas himself sampled a wide range of music: Michael Jackson (from the pop genre), R.E.M. (alternative rock), The Soul Children (soul), Steve Miller Band (classic rock), Joe Chambers (jazz), Grand Wizzard Theodore (hip-hop itself), and still others.

As just one specific example, the skulking piano bass that first appears at 0:12 on Nas' "N.Y. State of Mind" was originally pulled from the Joe Chambers' record "Mind Rain," at its own 1:06 mark. On Elzhi's "Detroit State of Mind," a live studio session musician plays the same notes of that adagio left-hand in the low bass register. The same process unfolded for the ringing alarm sound at 0:01, from the same Nas song. That sample comes from Donald Byrd's "Flight Time," at the point that's thirty-one seconds into its own song. When Elzhi's backing musical section recreated it for "Detroit State of Mind," they used what sounds like a modulated, synthesized guitar.

However, Elzhi's own 2011 albums takes as its foundation not only re-workings of Nas' own musical accompaniments, but the melodies of Nas as well. Particularly striking is Elzhi's many instances of direct imitation of Nas' melodic phrasing structure. In fact, this next example of Elzhi's melodic imitation is just one of several wherein he imitates and expands upon the musically-unique aspects of Nas' own vocals, which, in turn, made them such influential musical precedents for generations of rappers to come.

Nas' 1994 *Illmatic* song "N.Y. State of Mind" is remarkable for its sudden truncation of the chorus at bar 47. While each of his previous two choruses on this song had always lasted for a full four bars, Nas unexpectedly interjects during the final instance of this song's chorus with a through-composed melodic line that starts the next verse. At the start of what was previously the chorus' fourth bar, Nas jumps in with his own melodic idea, thereby augmenting his subsequent verse structurally by adding a single bar onto its beginning.

Elzhi himself does not fail to likewise interpolate his own structural truncations and augmentations into his melody when he imitated Nas' own melody seventeen years later. All of what was just said about Nas' extension of his third verse, and shortening of his third chorus, can likewise be applied to Elzhi's own song "Represent." Just like Nas, Elzhi here truncates the final instance of the chorus by removing its fourth bar, with which he subsequently augments his final verse.

However, it is important to note that the re-workings from *Elmatic* are not any kind of crude, plagiarizing copies of the rap rhythms from the original *Illmatic* album. For instance, on "Detroit State of Mind," a play on Nas' own "N.Y. State of Mind" song, there is a key change during the verse of the tribute song, first heard at 1:08, that is not found in the original model.

Elzhi's unprecedented level of imitation of a forebear might raise the following question: is there a body of compositions in the rap genre that comprise a set of shibboleths and code words with which the genre's musicians can recognize each other, akin to the standards found so ubiquitously in jazz? To answer that question, it would do well to first survey how previous oral practices of music and repertoire have existed and been communicated from one group to the next throughout the recent history of popular music.

The array of ideas by means of which rap's own performance practice will be judged consists of the concepts commonly termed as remix, cover, and standard. The use of any other similar adjective or noun throughout this discussion, such as "re-working" or "re-styling," are only meant to be able to refer to this entire group as a single whole. These three terms will be differentiated from each other by answering the following three questions as specifically as possible:

1. Does this particular class of performance practice re-workings eventually assume a definitive version, or will it always be con-

stantly evolving throughout succeeding generations of musical history?
2. Does this performance practice directly quote that historical material in the form of electronic sampling, or only indirectly paraphrase it in the form of performance interpolation?
3. Does the song remake the previous song's melody, the previous song's musical accompaniment, or both?

These questions should now be directly applied to the first term, "remix."

Popular Music Remixes

The particular class of musical re-stylings called remixes most often occurs in the context of contemporary electronic genres like techno or electronica. It incorporates the idea of remaking precedents that is essential to the entire class of performance practices, whether the specific practice be a standard, remix, or cover. However, remixes are largely defined by their exact re-appropriation of a pre-recorded sample that is neither manipulated, nor changed in any way at all, in its new context. For instance, when Radiohead member Johnny Greenwood remixed his fellow Radiohead Thom Yorke's 2006 song "A Rat's Nest" in 2010, he still retained in his own composition not only Yorke's melody, but the exact audio recording of the specific take of Thom Yorke's sung melody that Yorke had used previously on his own musical track.

Most remixes are identifiable as re-workings of earlier songs not because the entire musical accompaniment is borrowed, but because a substantial portion of the vocal melody has been sampled exactly. Additionally, remixes, meanwhile, are apt to eventually assume a final form that exists unchangingly forever as a definitive, authoritative version that will eventually stand on its own, all the while co-existing uneasily in competition for an audience and for recognition with its predecessor.

Popular Music Covers

All of this differentiates the remix in important ways from the cover of the rock music genre. The Beatles, hailed today by many as the greatest band of all time, started out early on in their career with the same kind of extended borrowing that the members of Radiohead have periodically utilized, but in the form of covers, rather than remixes. Such a specific example is their song "Roll Over Beethoven." Chuck Berry's original 1956 hit song of the same name was eventually re-made into the first track on side two of The Beatles' 1963 album *With the Beatles*. However, "Roll Over Beethoven" was far from the only cover on the album. In fact, "Till There Was You," "Please Mister Postman," "You Really Got a Hold on Me," "Devil in Her Heart," and "Money (That's What I Want)" were also remakes of songs that had been published previously. The original versions of those Beatles covers were written by people as diverse as Smokey Robinson, the R&B singer, and Meredith Wilson, who originally wrote "Till There Was You" for a musical.

Seen from this perspective, covers can be differentiated strongly from remixes. While remixes sample previously-recorded audio takes of prior performances, covers largely do no such thing. Instead, they opt to partially remake a previous song's musical accompaniment and melody, oftentimes retaining the basic harmonic and melodic structure as inflected by chordal extensions or harmonic ornamentation. For example, Robinson's "You Really Got a Hold on Me," in the hands of The Beatles, had a warm groove based around a pensive acoustic guitar, while the slow ballad "You Really Got a Hold on Me" was transformed by more assertive, aggressive guitars. Additionally, covers are more likely to inhabit a definitive position of artistic authority than jazz standards, but less likely to do so than remixes. This is due to the fact that covers are often made of the same original song, while the focus of remixes consist of a much more widespread array of diverse models and precedents. For example, the Beatles' own version of "Roll Over Beethoven" is by no means the only cover of Chuck Berry's original hit, as The Electric Light Orchestra likewise re-worked the same basic compositional materials in 1973.

With an understanding of the ways in which electronic remixes and rock covers have approached the domains of authority, sampling, and found materials now in hand, jazz standards can be considered next, as an examination of rap's own approach to musical tributes is slowly worked towards.

Jazz Music Standards

With The Beatles is not the only album of musical borrowings to come from an up and coming artist who would later become a legend. Frank Sinatra's first two albums, *The Voice of Sinatra* and *Songs by Sinatra*, from 1946 and 1947, were comprised completely of recordings of jazz standards. On the first album, the song "Someone to Watch Over Me," originally by George & Ira Gershwin, was from 1926; Cole Porter's "Why Shouldn't I" came from 1935; and "I Don't Stand a Ghost of a Chance with You," by Ned Washington, Bing Crosby, and Victor Young, was from 1932.

Sinatra's own unique take on popular jazz standards exists in a way that is both different from, and similar to, the way in remixes and covers act as conduits or vehicles for the inter-communication of musicians who all share the same generic. Unlike electronic remixes in most instances, and rock music covers in some instances, jazz standards never assume a definitive, authoritative version. Additionally, unlike remixes or covers, standards do not electronically sample previously recorded material. Similar to covers and in opposition to remixes, however, jazz standards most often retain the basic melodic and harmonic framework of their predecessors. On the other hand—similar to remixes, and in opposition to covers—jazz standards often can depart from their forebears in extremely radical ways. For example, few people would ever confuse Coltrane's own 1962 version of "All or Nothing at All" for the original version of the jazz standard that had first been penned decades earlier by Arthur Altman and Jack Lawrence.

When jazz musicians get together to play, an aesthetic element of the prevailing performance practice is that, even if they've never played together before, they can still begin a practice session at once. This is the communal element that the borrowing and sharing of jazz standards allows. The ideal is largely one of a shared, mutually-enjoyed musical history that's unbroken, rather than a succession of iconoclasts, intentional or otherwise, who redefine musical paradigms in the manner of the Bach––Beethoven–Brahms family tree of music. It turns out that, although this type of musical discussion among jazz musicians most often occurs in a live-performance setting, a similar type of constant process of ingroup identification occurs throughout the entire discography of the rap genre as well, and this historical conversation unsurprisingly includes Elzhi's *Elmatic* album.

With this historical backdrop to the advent of the rap genre in hand, the ways in which the modern rapping idiom combines the prevailing performance practices of cover, remix, and standard can now be investigated.

Rap Remakes

A rap-specific performance practice that borrows the assumptions of the electronica remix, the rock music cover, and the jazz standard is strongly at work in the recording careers of many rappers, particular during the early stages of their public life. This performance practice in rap will herein be referred to as the remake. Although rappers do not need to always be carrying their musical history on their backs, as it were, in order to be able to rap with others, they do show off their education in a very parallel way when they remake hits and beats from other past legends of rap.

When Mos Def adds his own verses to the Notorious B.I.G. hit "Who Shot Ya," or when Kanye West recreates the legendary Souls of Mischief beat from "93 'Til Infinity" and calls it "03 Til Infinity," a rap fan will immediately recognize that those musicians are "real" rappers, with all attendant ideas of authenticity and talent, simply because they know who *other* good rappers are. That is, Kanye, Mos Def, or whoever else it might be in this case didn't choose to re-fashion just any rap beat; they chose to re-fashion a rap beat that has achieved classic status in the larger rap community for very good, musical reasons. This is extremely similar to what jazz musicians do when they "talk" to each other, even during the first time that they meet, using the vehicles of standards. It is simply rap's focus on studio-recorded releases that might prevent the musicologist from considering this kind of ongoing, historical musical dialogue between contemporaries and their forebears to be the same exact entity as a standard.

Instead, the modern rap re-working might be more accurately called a "remake," or "re-making," an ambiguous term purposefully used here in order to indicate the extent to which this performance practice unifies and reconciles previously competing concepts of historical modeling. These concepts are, specifically, whether or not electronic samplings of historical recordings—previously considered as authoritative, non-negotiable musical material in the hands of re-mixers—can be treated in the same flexible fashion that the composers of rock music covers and jazz standards treated the melodic or harmonic frameworks of their own historical precursors.

Take, for example, one of the mixtape recordings of Kanye West from the early 2000s. When West sampled the entire musical accompaniment of the Tribe Called Quest's previous 1993 song "Electric Relaxation," his new song, "'03 Electric Relaxation," turned out to be largely built on the technical aspects of a previous, historical composition. However, on top of that extended sampling of a prior recording, he added his own completely new rapping melody. In this way, rap remakes manage to strike a balance between both the iconoclastic and conservative ideals of standards, covers, and remixes. At the same time, Kanye's own "03 Til Infinity" assumed a quasi-authoritative stance in the minds of many listeners, since the Souls of Mischief version and the Kanye West version are rarely compared to each other adversarially. That is, Kanye West did not sample "03 Til Infinity" in order to display artistic disrespect for another group. In contrast, those are the exact reasons Jay-Z supplies on his 2001 "Takeover" as an explanation for his artistic re-working of a Nas line, from the 1994 song "The World Is Yours (Tip Mix)," on his own 1996 track "Dead Presidents."

Perhaps, in the coming decades, if enough people borrow the entire beat from A Tribe Called Quest's original song, then it could drift into what musicologists would eventually deem to be a new repertoire of rap standards. In this manner, then, the answer of the rap genre to the three defining questions posed at the start of this discussion is a balanced mix of the affirmative and the negative.

In sum, then, rap remakes borrow the idea of a shared musical history from the jazz standard, while marrying it to the more iconoclastic tendencies of the rock cover, as well as the sampling techniques of music genres that came of age in the digital world of sampling, like electronica. To the extent that standards, covers, and remixes are defined by the position that they occupy within the genre in terms of proliferation or supremacy, it would seem that rap remakes are, once more, something of an in-between case. That is, they do not play the central role in rap that standards do in jazz, but neither are they relegated to the B-sides of rock records.

It would do well at this point, then, to describe some of those historical sources for rap music's backing musical accompaniments. This will help the critic and fan gain a better sense of just what those historical sign points, anchors, and guide posts that have been referred to all along throughout this chapter actually are in specific terms, and, accordingly, how they function in rap remakes of them. One artist in particular will serve as an excellent exemplar for the wide array of historical sounds and tastes from which rappers often choose to pull their inspirations or influences, in both his solo and collaborative career: Wyclef Jean. In doing so, Wyclef's songs will make clear the unique historical existence that rap remakes take on.

Wyclef Jean's Rap Remakes

The eventual direction that Wyclef's music would take in his solo career, including songs like the previous "80 Bars" examined in the above, might not be much of a surprise to those who followed closely his career with the group The Fugees. On this group's 1997 album *The Score*, the musical tracks they re-worked include Bob Marley's classic hit "No Woman No Cry," as well as the 1970s hit "Killing Me Softly." This musical potpourri echoes what is found on the group's *Besides* mixtape, where Wyclef, along with Lauryn Hill and Pras, remakes the song that is often used to mark the chronological point at which mainstream rap split off from other popular music genres. At this evolutionary branching in the late 1970s, the rapping lyricists of The Sugarhill Gang chose to record an extended 14-minute version of a re-worked take of The Chic's 1979 hit "Good Times." Sugarhill's new song, familiar to most listeners as "Rapper's Delight," is now largely recalled as being rap's first mainstream hit.

However, the beat from "Rapper's Delight" isn't the version that the Fugees trio chose to flow over on *Besides*. Instead, they go back to the original source and rework the version first made by The Chic. Referencing the lineage of a song important to not just rap, but other genres as well, "Fugees on the Mic (Remix)" turns out to be a singular example of many rappers' knowledge of the imitative category of songs, and how they can function in educational, entertaining, and reputational ways.

After his work with The Fugees, Wyclef would continue to build on the themes of this historo-centric artistic form of expression. Over the course of his recording career, he would go on to re-style the chords and melodies of everyone from Bob Dylan, to the Bee Gees, Kenny Rogers, Pink Floyd, and The Four Seasons, and these artists' home genres of rock, blues, soul, funk, jazz, psychedelic, barber shop a cappella, and more.

An example of this comes from 1997, when Wyclef released his first solo album, *The Carnival*. The eighteenth track from this album is entitled "We Trying to Stay Alive," which combines imitative elements in the form of what has been so far termed the rap remake. Like many categories of imitative song, Wyclef's "We Trying to Stay Alive" takes a final, definitive form, that won't be treated in inventive ways by future musicians. Unlike the aesthetic ideals of a rock cover, however, Wyclef chooses to compose his own new, original melody for this song, instead of trying to bring his own unique voice to a melody from the past. However, in combining the norms of a remix with the norms of a cover in the form of a true rap remake, this "We Trying to Stay Alive" utilizes both previously-recorded audio material and completely new material. Many listeners will automatically recognize the groovy bass line and screaming vocals of the Bee Gees, but the bass kick and snare behind that surface orchestration are additions of Wyclef's own. For these reasons, Wyclef's imitative songs, and those of

4. Structure and Performance Practice   137

many other rappers, seem to fall somewhere outside of the regular protocols of covers, standards, remixes, ad standards.

Wyclef's other voyages outside of rap take a similarly chimeric approach to his sonic canvases. On his sophomore album *The Ecleftic: 2 Sides II a Book*, from the year 2000, Wyclef chooses to keep the same instruments playing the same lines and chords. At the same, though, he also decides to re-record those exact musical ideas so that he can manipulate them more finely, just like Elzhi and his backing band did on their *Elmatic* album. On Wyclef's "Kenny Rogers–Pharoahe Monch Dub Plate," a live appearance from Kenny Rogers has the country singer still vocalizing the same melody that he performed on his own legendary 1978 song "The Gambler." However, the artists have now oriented the musical scope towards subjects and themes that are more appropriate to rap here, as they reference turntables and microphones, rather than the countryman's card tables, as a metaphor for life's most serious issues. Kenny Rogers' expansive chords now float over a stronger drum set and backbeat accompaniment that in turn allows Wyclef Jean and Pharoahe Monch to rap comfortably. "Kenny Rogers—Pharoahe Monch Dub Plate" might even be considered a remake-within-a-remake, as Wyclef combines Kenny Rogers' song with elements of Pharoahe Monch's own 1999 track, "Simon Says." This Wyclef song again walks a line between covers and samples, having combined a new melody from the modern rapping idiom with an extensive live band accompaniment.

The song "Knockin' on Heaven's Door," from 2002's *The Masquerade*, completes this trinity of Wyclef's first three albums, as he continues to strongly define and re-define the functions and aspects of a rap remake. Over a studio translation of the picked guitar that is heard on Bob Dylan's 1973 song of the same name, Wyclef transforms this traditional musical tribute into an emotional eulogy, as he quotes a litany of rappers whose time on earth was ended prematurely. Again, the instrumental is both new and old, combining the previous guitar with an updated drum set accompaniment that allows Wyclef to substitutes a melody from the modern rapping vocal idiom for Bob Dylan's own vocalizing style.

These few songs, however, are just a small sampling of the technical examples by Wyclef of the rap remake. "Guantanamera," from *The Carnival*, goes all the way back to 1929, and all the way down to Cuba, for its own musical forebear. "Oh What a Night," from *Masquerade*, is turned from The Four Seasons story of an early 1960s one-night stand into a celebration of the day that Wyclef signed his first recording contract with The Fugees. Wyclef also throws in a reference to John Denver's "Leaving on a Jetplane" at the end of this track as well. "Wish You Were Here," from *The Ecleftic*, becomes a love letter to the legendary psychedelic band Pink Floyd, who recorded a song by the same title twenty-five years earlier. A common pet name changes from being something innocent and cute to an invitation for something much more adult on Wyclef's "Pussycat," which apes Tom Jones' 1965 hit "What's New Pussycat?"

All of these songs take a definitive form when each uses an original rap melody accompanied by a live backing section that is based on a previous historical popular music song, but one that's contemporaneously re-recorded with real instruments. The result is a historical tribute that combines the communicative functions of jazz standards with the commercially-definitive stature of electronic remixes and the romantic, anarchical creative aesthetics of the rock cover.

Thematic Quotations in Classical Music

Classical music is yet another musical tradition, along with jazz, electronic, and rock, that has valuable information to yield for the understanding of rap's unique forms of historical tribute. Far from hiding their influences in hopes of avoiding hypothetical charges of plagiarism or unoriginality, classical musicians of the past and present oftentimes foreground found materials in their compositions. This can frequently take the form of a piece of music that is a set of variations. Oftentimes, the musical element around which these variations revolve consists of a theme that another composer had previously generated and treated in their own work.

For example, Frédéric Chopin wrote a set of variations on a melody that comes from the first act of Mozart's legendary 1787 opera *Don Giovanni*. It was only the second piece Chopin ever wrote, when he was just seventeen years old in 1827, and is notable in that it was one of the few works Chopin ever wrote that included an orchestra. As another composing great, Robert Schumann, wrote in a review after he heard this set of variations, "However little need of such intentions Chopin's talent may have, I too bow my head to his genius, his steady striving and his imagination."[6] Indeed, Schumann himself was fully immersed in this lively tradition, having written a set of variations on a theme by Beethoven. In a set of works published after his lifetime, a piece was found that was based on the theme in A minor from the second movement of Beethoven's Symphony No. 7.

4. Structure and Performance Practice

Beethoven himself not ignorant or detesting of what, in the wrong context, might be called stealing. In fact, Beethoven himself wrote no less than four different pieces that were variations on themes from Mozart operas. Written between 1792 and 1801, these four variations, for a variety of orchestrations, borrowed material from *The Marriage of Figaro*, *Don Giovanni*, and *The Magic Flute*, which was quoted twice. It must be emphasized, however, that all of these thematic quotations are just a few of the many examples that can be pulled from the literature.

This long tradition of musical dialogue between composers, when seen against the background of popular music's own modern interpenetrating musical conversations, raises an obvious question. How does classical music's thematic quotations compare to the rap remake, the jazz standard, the rock cover, and the electronic remix, when it is judged through the same tripartite prism of the imitative song class' level of commercial authority (i.e., can it be sold?) its use of harmony versus its use of melody, and the presence or absence therein of audio sampling?

First, classical music's own type of musical borrowing usually focuses on a quotation of melody, rather than harmony or accompaniment, even though that is obviously perfectly possible in other contexts. Additionally, it clearly makes no use of electronic sampling, while simultaneously assuming an authoritative position in the repertoire as a composition that stands on its own, in that cannot be remade in the same quotational way without compromising its quintessential identity. This means that the tradition of thematic quotation in classical music is, just like the rap remake, a conglomeration of some of the protocols and processes from other imitative song classes, such as the jazz standard, the rock cover, or the electronic remix. When seen through these lenses, thematic quotation participates in the communal aspects of the standard, the rock genre's romantic ideal of individual compositional achievement, and the cultural authority of the remix—or, rather, those popular genres partake of classical music's thematic quotation in a like manner, due to obvious chronological difficulties.

The question now, then, is this: does the convention of classical music's thematic quotation shed any new light on the nature of rap remakes?

The answer, if affirmative, is most likely an indirect one, in that thematic quotation is a heretofore unseen combination of the same decisions that have to be made when executing any musical borrowing. The jazz standard consists of a conservative self-effacement through musical paraphrasing of both background and foreground musical materials that already were existing previously. The rock cover consists of iconoclastic authority through musical paraphrasing of, mainly, foregrounded musical materials that also have historical existences. The electronic remix consists of iconoclastic authority through direct quotation of foreground musical materials; that is, the melody from a previous song. The tradition of the rap remake, in its own right, is built on an iconoclastic authority through direct quotation of accompanimental background musical materials, but not melodic foreground musical materials, that did previously exist.

The thematic quotation, in its own right, accordingly consists of iconoclastic authority through the paraphrasing of historical, foreground material, but a simultaneous arrangement of that paraphrase within a very unfamiliar context that can be radically different in degree from the new contexts of rock covers. Specifically, a composer might begin by exactly quoting the melody of a previous composer through interpolation, not digital sampling, and end by re-working that paraphrased quote so that it eventually comes to be expressed in their own words, so to speak.

In this manner, classical music might act as the cinching link between all manners of historically-imitative song classes. Sets of thematic variations paradoxically express paradigmatic shifts, through paraphrase, by means of the pre-computerized era's own version of electronic sampling. Rap oftentimes expresses a similar iconoclastic authority in its re-working of historical material, but is apt to do so mainly through the actual digital displacement and rearrangement of electronically-recorded audio material from the past. In this way, all five classes of imitative song compositions can be seen as continuously participating in the same ongoing, subconscious historical discussion about what music is, and how it can be changed for the better.

Digital Production in Rap Performance Practice

The fact that rap's own aesthetic values surrounding historical tributes would only be possible in the digital age of electronic sampling in the studio calls for a further discussion of the specific ways in which today's potent technological capabilities effect rap's aesthetic ideals of live performance. In its current modern reception by contemporary critics, rap sometimes runs up against the specific tastes of arbiters of the establishment, whether they are music critics at established newspapers and magazines, professors at well-reputed colleges and universities, or the leaders of world-famous orchestras. Such arbiters, being naturally conservative

4. Structure and Performance Practice 141

in their artistic tastes due to their institutional positions, oftentimes prefer music that can be performed and recreated, rhythm-for-rhythm and note-for-note, just as its original composer would want, in a live concert setting. The defensible and worthy argument of these gatekeepers might run along some such lines: "If you can't reproduce your music without any unnatural technological support at all, then you can't really call it music."

Such a stance is largely antithetical to the coherent, consistent performance practice values of rap, ever since it first came into being in the 1970s. The responding argument from rap fans to those establishment gatekeepers might run along the following lines, as they rejoin: "A live performance is no doubt full of emotional immediacy and human communion, but what if we worked to marry those artistic virtues with ultra-fine musical control through technology, instead of taking it for granted that one must necessarily undermine and replace the other?" In this manner, rap works to reverse a presupposed disadvantage into being one of its great strengths: it creates music that could *never* be performed live.

The six separate string sections on Dr. Dre's song 2002 "Business" could never be teased apart by our ears in a live setting, where it wouldn't have the help of stereophonic mixing to separate them, or to make them sound so impossibly large. Although this discussion might come across as no more than an unprincipled iconoclast's raging at the landed class for the attainment of cultural concessions that would do no more than act as a salve for the egos of a certain genre's fans, it is much more than that. Such class values surrounding authenticity are often used to cut short any discussion of rap's worth, or even technical aspects, before it can even begin, and so must necessarily be addressed in as direct a manner as possible.

This live-versus-studio debate is one of the criticisms that rap, along with other studio-oriented genres like electronic dance music, have had to consistently respond to over the course of its history. As progressive house producer Joel Zimmerman, better known as deadmau5, put it in his 2012 Tumblr post, entitled "We All Hit Play": "I just roll up with a laptop and a MIDI controller and select tracks, and hit a spacebar."[7] After a summary dismissal of his critics, Mr. Zimmerman goes on to make the argument for the performance practice of not just prog house, but rap as well, when he ends his article by adding, "My skills, and other producer's skills, shine where it needs to shine: in the ... studio, and on the ... releases."[8]

That is the ultimate argument for why musicians and fans within the rap genre simply do not mind that their music can't be fully fleshed out in the live performance context, wherein all of the music that existed for the hundreds of centuries before the advent of computers was judged for its worthiness. If a listener must temporarily live in a physically-impossible stereophonic world in order to hear and enjoy rap and all of its identifying musical characteristics, many seem to think that such a trade makes for a fair deal. Such an equal trade-off adeptly mediates between a free suspension of disbelief on the one hand, and the inability to ever conveniently and fully experience rap music live, with human eyes and human ears, on the other.

Summary

Rap's approach to technical sonic structure is more conventional and traditional than perhaps any of the other aspects of music in question here, whether it's rhythm, melody, motive, or any of the other ones to come. This might be because of the typical division of labor in rap: the producer makes the beat, and then the rapper goes on to add their own melody to it afterwards. This special division of labor, as mentioned previously, is what ties up the technical aspects of rap's music—particularly the sources for its sonic accompaniments— so inextricably with its studio-centered and digitalized norms of performance practice.

Rap's pre-occupation when dealing with structure seems to be, ultimately, one that focuses on making sure that the spotlight on their rather radical melodies shines bright and clear, so that even their most atypical rhythms would not catch even the most musically-illiterate listener off-guard. Structures are kept to the bare materials most of the time—chorus, verses, bridges—so that, perhaps, the rap vocals can be even more delightfully radical and untraditional. Sometimes, however, the rap vocals can be radical even in their conservatism, which can be seen in the long tradition of rap remakes based on iconoclastic authority, new melodies over old arrangements, and digital sampling.

Indeed, a varied number of approaches has been observed: non-repeating choruses by Nas, rhythmicized skits by Eminem, and non-freestyled freestyles by Wyclef. However, in the entire rap genre oeuvre, these shining examples largely constitute a group of large outliers. Again, this is only to support the derring-do of the melodies, wherein, at the same time that verses are almost bound to alternate with repeated choruses, the vocals are apt to fly afar afield. This could be to places as unfamiliar as additive rhythms over complex time signatures, as was seen in the first chapter on rhythm. Because of this, although song structure and performance practice are probably not going to be the first things that will hook a newcomer to rap, their importance in the entire genre should never be relegated to a lower level of importance.

5

Texture and Orchestration

Texture and orchestration, although they might be covered in separate sections in other books on the basic technical aspects of music, are here together joined as one. This is because the manufacture of rap, described in the above section, occurs in such a singular fashion. This unique production mode, wherein a melody is added by a songwriter to an extant accompaniment that was previously composed by a separate artist, comes with the result that the musical texture of a rap song is usually of only two types, either monophonic or homophonic.

The term "texture," here, rather than relying on a definition that connotes an infinite amount of ways in which music can be felt, restricts itself to a more straightforward meaning. That meaning, specifically, constrains itself to considerations of the number of voices in a piece of music, as well as how independent they are or are not. Subsequently, the word "orchestration," when applied to rap herein, restricts itself to an arranging of specific manifestations of those voices, in the form of pianos, synthesizers, guitars, basses, organs, and, obviously, the rapping human voice. In this manner, the term orchestration can be taken herein as being synonymous with the terms instrumentation, accompaniment, and production. What would be most helpful to the coming discussion is to begin with an examination of a certain artist's song orchestrations, since doing so will make clear how orchestrations in rap differ from those of other genres and traditions.

Jean Grae's Borrowed Orchestrations

New York City rapper Jean Grae is an excellent example of a lyricist who shapes her melodies with the history of rap always in the forefront of her compositional mind. Additionally, she is always more heavily attuned to the advantages her outsider status in a hyper-masculine community can afford her, rather than any supposed disadvantages that might result from it. However, the intriguing aspect of her discography that's under examination here is her penchant to borrow, in full, the orchestrations of other rappers and to use them as her own accompaniments. This artistic dynamic becomes plainly manifest at many points throughout her career.

In particular, her re-styling of the poetic narrative from Jay-Z's 2002 *The Blueprint 2: The Gift & the Curse* song "Excuse Me Miss" turned out to be a particularly adroit repurposing of a beat. "Excuse Me Sir" appeared the very year after, on Jean's own 2003 album *The Bootleg of the Bootleg*. Unlike Kanye's mixtape remakes, "Excuse Me Sir" was formally released on an actual album. But in addition to also slightly changing Jay-Z's story, Jean's musical accompaniment also makes in-depth use of the trippy phasers and synths from the original beat, which was orchestrated by The Neptunes.

"You Don't Know," both in musical content and title, is a play off of another Jay-Z song, "U Don't Know." While "Excuse Me Sir" went back to *The Blueprint 2*, "You Don't Know" goes a little further back, to Jay-Z's original *The Blueprint* album, from 2001. While Jean Grae references and restyles much of Jay-Z's poetry on her own song, the musical orchestration behind her is, more importantly, still the same as that over which Jay-Z added his vocals.

After Jay-Z, Jean turned her attention in a more northwesterly direction, to the locale of Detroit. Along with Jay-Z, Eminem did not evade Jean Grae's rap études either, as the ninth track from *The Bootleg of the Bootleg* shows. "You Don't Want It" doesn't re-spin one of Eminem's more recognizable arrangements, like "My Name Is" or "Real Slim Shady." Instead, she turns her attention to *The Slim Shady LP* and its musical beat of "Role Model," which does not belong to the list of radio singles from the album. Uncoincidentally, Eminem's "Role Model" song is also the ninth track on its album as well, bespeaking Jean Grae's ever-constant sense of artistic purpose. While Eminem's "Role Model" had a full pop music structure with both hooks and verses, Jean's "Role Model" is a shorter freestyle. The same musical elements are still all there, though, with its bubbly sound FX and ornamental, non–Western instrumentation.

In fact, the artistic and communal function of *The Bootleg of the Bootleg* seems to be very similar to those of The Beatles' *With the Beatles* album, as discussed in a previous chapter. Both albums seem to proclaim a new musical act by associating them with legendary acts of the past, while proclaiming their expertise by taking pre-existing musical material and making it sound completely new. In addition to the three songs just considered by Jean Grae, other tracks on *The Bootleg of the Bootleg*—"High," "A Little Story," and "Breathe Easy,"—actually do sample the musical work of various rap legends, such as Nas and Big L, in their own orchestrations. Any corresponding similarities between Jean Grae's own orchestrations and those of her forebears, however, are usually just the set-up for the melodic methods by means of which she will celebrate her predecessors.

Jean Grae's Borrowed Lead Voices

Take, for example, the very first instance of direct tribute that was posited in this chapter from Jean Grae, called "You Don't Know." In this song's forty-sixth bar, she re-raps the basic rhythms from Jay-Z's own twenty-fourth bar, note-for-note and pitch-for-pitch. The specifics do vary slightly—for instance, there are seven notes in the bar in question from Jean, while Jay-Z's own bar has ten notes in it. However, these are a result of an augmentative elaboration of Jay-Z's rhythms, and not an upsetting or overturning of them. Both rappers preserve the same basic 7-note structure that places two 8th accented notes on each of the first, second, and third beats of their own respective bars, and then a final quarter note on the measure's final beat. In this way, both the arrangements and lead voices in Jean Grae's musical orchestrations are frequently based on those her own favorite artists.

These conclusions are also borne out through an examination of another Jean Grae track that has already been previously mentioned, "Excuse Me Miss." In fact, the imitation here occurs at the same exact point in musical structure on both song, in the eleventh and twelfth bars. In a small contrast to her tribute from "You Don't Know," Jean Grae's adherence to Jay-Z's own melody here is much more strict. While changing the words to apply to her own romantic situation in life, Jean Grae maintains each and every one of Jay-Z's accents and rhythms. Both, for example, have the very same number of eighteen notes inside of the melodic phrases in question. In fact, both Jean Grae's rap and Jay-Z's rap are themselves exact rhythmic imitations of an earlier rapper's work. Back on the 1995 song "Big Poppa," the rap legend Notorious B.I.G. delivered these very same rhythms in the exact same singing style.

It would seem that even while the musical nature of rap's existence is debated by some, rappers themselves are very clear in their thinking on the matter. Jean Grae does not restrict her musical tributes to Jay-Z's poetry, or his public persona, or his views on the rap industry; she also trumpets and celebrates the purely musical aspects of his own rap melodies as well.

Rap's Texture-Orchestration Relationship

Whether from Jay-Z, Jean Grae, or Notorious B.I.G., all of the songs considered so far have done an excellent job of manifesting the privileged connection that texture and orchestration in rap share. This connection is embodied in the fact that, at a certain point, a rapper's control over the number of voices in a musical texture, as well as each voice's respective function within their polyphonic community, is oftentimes very limited. This is because, typically, the means by which heterophonic or polyphonic elements could be introduced into a rap song texture, such as by a backing performance ensemble, are restricted to being within the hands of only a song's producer. Consequently, a rapper's main level of textural control remains only at what their own texturally-dominant, single melodic voice is doing at any given moment. Indeed, a rapper might elaborate a single, main melodic line with backing vocals, but such lines usually constitute no more than restatements or elaborations of rhythms that were already present in the foregrounded part of the texture. What this means is that texture and orchestration are tied together in a special way in rap, and that such texture-orchestrations are almost always of a homophonic nature.

Take, for instance, the following example from a different type of music, which will outline the uniqueness of rap. Hypothetically, any part of the classical orchestra and the instruments therein can be used to play the role of any voice in any texture. The violin section, for example, could be the supporting accompanimental voice in a homophonic texture, or a leading melodic voice in a monophonic texture. No classical composer would hesitate to consider such a possibility, even if they might not work to bring those specific relationships to fruition within a particular piece of music. However, it is just these types of possibilities that are often precluded in rap a priori, because of the division of responsibility between production and rapping that was described in the above.

The rapping voice will rarely take on a strictly accompanimental role within a homophonic texture, wherein an instrumental voice might have the role of lead melody, except through a strong reversal of generic norms, as well as acoustic perception. Because of all this, a description of rap textures must take as its foundation a departure point that is quite different from one that might be equally helpful for more instrumentally-focused genres, like jazz or classical. The following systemic categorization accordingly places special emphasis not on what just any voice is doing at any given moment in a composition in relationship to the other musical ideas therein, as might be done in analyzing a specific orchestral piece from the Western art music tradition. Instead, it begins by asking what just *one* voice is doing at any given moment in a composition in relationship to the other musical ideas therein, and that voice is the rapping voice.

Monophonic Rap Recordings

So far, only rap recordings with multiple musical ideas playing simultaneously have been examined. This designation covers every single example in this book up until now, from the very first bar of Eminem's "Rap God," all the way down to what was just heard on Jean Grae's "Excuse Me Sir." Although the voices within each song may have had different hierarchical relationships to each other in each song, there was still always more than one. However, this is not necessarily a requirement in the rap genre. In fact, there is a select handful of recorded rap songs where the rapping voice performs completely alone, without a backing accompaniment.

A first example comes from The Roots and their 2008 song "@ 15." Although their production team is both critically and popular acclaimed, having earned both Grammys and certified record sales, the members of this large Hip Hop collective step into the background here and allow their lyricist, Black Thought, to occupy the listener's attention alone. Judging from the title, this song captures the thoughts of a young Black Thought, back from when he was a 15-year old rapper taking music lessons at The Philadelphia High School for Creative and Performing Arts in Philadelphia, Pennsylvania. No matter its inceptive background, the quality of this track is extremely raw, and not just because the recording quality is understandably quite rough. To be sure, Black Thought's rapping voice is the only source of musical sound over the entire course of this admittedly short track.

Black Thought, in fact, takes full artistic advantage of his lack of a recording studio on "@ 15." For example, he periodically employs a tempo rubato style, as well as other methods of expressive microtiming, in order to bolster the delivery of his boasts and punch lines. It's essential to note that such extreme microtiming would largely be prohibited by the quantized nature of digitally-created musical accompaniments and their theoretical reliance on the square, symmetrical rhythmic philosophy of studio sequencers. Furthermore, Black Thought also allows the strong prosodic accents of his text to set the music's meter by particularly emphasizing the most important syllable–notes and melodic phrases. Even without a musical accompaniment behind him in this genre's semi-ubiquitous 4/4 meter, Black Thought's own rhythms on this track can be easily fit into symmetrical lengths of four equal beats.

Another gripping backstory behind a monophonic rap comes from OutKast's 1998 album *Aquemini*. To be sure, "Nathaniel" the only track from this album on which neither André 3000 nor Big Boi appear. A close OutKast associate by the name of Supa Nat performs on a grainy recording whose monophonic texture is closely akin to Black Thought's own. Supa Nate's use of uneven ritardando and extended, fermata-like pauses at the end of his melodic phrases at 0:53 and 1:06 reinforces his text's angry impatience with the chaotic forces that control his life with little regard for his own welfare or well-being. These poetic sentiments are further underscored by his fragmentation of phrasal structure towards the end of the track, when he unexpectedly blurs the line between music and non-music as he switches from rapping to sprechstimme, with no preparation, after a long, cadential rhythmic pause.

The single, unaccompanied melody of Mobb Deep's "(Just Step Prelude)" is also predominantly concerned with the destructive effects of jail, but from the other side of a cell's walls this time. Again, it's not an official member of the headlining group, Mobb Deep, who takes center stage, but a close associate. Rather than Havoc or Prodigy, it is Big Noyd who starts off his monophonic rap from 1995 by lamenting the societal paradox within which he is somehow supposed to live his life as if nothing is wrong. He must earn money in dangerous ways to survive, but those stressful actions only make his life more hectic and uncontrollable, which in turn make him even more desperate. Right afterwards, Prodigy, who is himself actually an official part of the Mobb Deep crew, likewise picks up on the same themes.

These three aforementioned monophonic songs altogether manipulate certain technical aspects of music that would not be easily changeable by a rapper who opts for the supportive uniformity of a digital studio workstation. In a certain way, the removal of what is, in most cases, essential parts of a studio-recorded song now actually works to make the music of these three rappers' melodies more texturized than usual. This is a result of the fact that the entire burden for the genesis of innate musical structure, such as by means of the positioning and grouping of pulse durations, is now the responsibility of the melody writer, and not the backing musical accompaniment. Consequently, the monophonic rapping voice is left on its own to create this form and structure for itself. This leads to very complex rhythms in not just terms of subdivisions, but in large-scale groupings of meters as well, as was seen in the case of Supa Nate and Black Thought.

This can be seen in the structure of Big Noyd's melody on "(Just Step Prelude)." Here, without a backing beat, Big Noyd's own melody constitutes the only metric information in the texture, and so it is his accented syllables and rhythms that drive his flexible time signature—sometimes 2/4, sometimes 4/4, sometimes a combination of the two—further forward over time. Because his timing is irregular and freer to an extent that is nearly impossible for a producer to replicate in a studio with a quantized, symmetrical sequencer, Big Noyd is able to stretch and compress the repeating pulse behind him to a degree that is much greater than what is usually found on most accompanied rap tracks.

Not only is Noyd deciding how his syllables are to be grouped together inside of a bar, but he's also deciding how long those bars are to be as well, since there is no repeating musical loop behind him to decree, through loud dynamics and sharp timbres, where a bar "should" start and stop. For example: when he raps his particular melodic phrase at 0:34, about what his friends should do if he dies, the phrase lasts for only three beats, instead of four, as had been happening before this point in time. Since this is a monophonic texture, this truncation of the normal phrasing pattern does not mean that the melody ended on the third beat of a 4/4 measure. Instead, Noyd has composed a bar with a new, different time signature of 3/4, since he is the only source of musical information for metric accent and repeating pulse.

Monophonic rap also allows more micro-temporal variation within a single performance. In addition to consisting of only homophonic musical textures, all of the songs before this chapter that have been considered also stuck to only a single tempo throughout the entire song. But when a voice is unaccompanied and unencumbered, it is easier for it to execute subtle shifts of accelerando or ritardando. At 0:37 on "(Just Step Prelude)," Big Noyd's melody executes just this temporal trick, when its tempo slows down ever so slightly in a circuitous ritardando. In a regular rap song, this might be interpreted as being simply rhythmic values that are increasing in length. But in a monophonic texture, it instead comes to be heard as an expressive manipulation of the song's underlying tempo.

Live Monophonic Raps

Monophonic textures, as the nature of this previous survey might have broadcasted, are somewhat rare in official rap recordings. In the context of live concert recordings, however, monophonic textures are much more common in rap than might be thought. Indeed, they frequently occur in the form of the rap battle, where two rappers trade rhymes back and forth in front of a crowd and, possibly, judges, who thereafter determine who won the verbal fight. The most masterful battle rappers, indeed, are very often those who are best able to take full advantage of the blank sonic canvas that an unaccompanied rapping voice is gifted with.

Instead of being restricted to ciphers on street corners, these rhyme battles can now be seen and appreciated across the whole Internet, where the dozens of leagues that host such competitions can post streamed videos of performances. One of the battle rappers who occupies a top position in many of those leagues is a lyricist by the name of Rone, from Philadelphia, Pennsylvania. For a battle rapper like Rone, whose acclaimed status relies on an objective record of wins and losses, it is often his poetry, working in tandem with his musical rhythms, that results in victory. In addition to clever puns and rhymes, Rone's battle rap techniques include a consistent achievement of the rhythmic freedom that a voice rapping with no musical accompaniment behind it can feel entitled to.

Rone's ascent to be champion of the "King of the Dot" battle league was originally jumpstarted by a trio of opening and unanimous decisions in his favor. However, it might counter-intuitively be the very first rap competition that Rone lost where his exploration of rhythmic freedom in terms of tempo reached its highest degree of refinement. This occurred when he lost a split decision to the New York lyricist D.N.A in 2009.[1]

Rone's poetry displays many of the expected aspects of the expertly technical rapper, such as long, multisyllabic rhymes. But what gives such poetry its full impact comes, in large part, from the persona of swagger and confidence with which Rone imbues those long rhymes. That swagger, in turn, is largely due to how the audience hears and feels the compositional techniques of Rone's rhythms. Those rhythms are typically ultra-independent from the regulation of any repeated rhythmic pulse or meter. Consequently, Rone's rhythms are interpreted by his audience as being appropriately presumptive in their annexation of both physical and musical space, which befits a musical competition very well. As a foray into the emotive interpretation of a musician's live performance, this current discussion might a little afield of this book's subject matter up to this point. But because battle rap constitutes such a perfectly distilled and controlled environment in which a composition's technical aspects is immediately and qualitatively interpreted by a live audience—without any confounding musical accompaniment, without a refractive studio lens, without any qualifying artistic collaborators present—it does, perhaps, warrant further discussion.

In this live setting, Rone consistently walks the line between a quasi-improvisational performance on the one hand, and a standard concert that he has practiced and rehearsed for months or weeks beforehand. If the crowd interrupts his previous flow with a raucous outburst after one of his puns, he'll bring his melody to a temporary, premature close, as if to let the audience's applause and acclamation take center-stage in the musical texture for a time. If the dynamics of one of his lines are overwhelmed by the audience's applauding interruptions, he'll re-rap it, so that the audience can then recognize that they should make their dynamics more pianissimo, because he has even more rap melody to unfurl thereafter.

As a starting departure point, it can be said that Rone very often organizes the rhythms of his raps in a tempo rubato style. Tempo rubato, being a rhythmic style in which a performer constant manipulates their tempo, alternately slowing down or speeding up as their own radical tastes might freely dictate, is thus, unmistakably, the optimal technical tool for a rapper engaged in a verbal contest. This is because such a rapper must display to a crowd not just that he is the most talented rapper, but, simultaneously, that he is unfailingly trusting in his own, personal belief in himself as being the most talented rapper ever. Unless a rapper believes that they are the best rapper to ever perform in front of a microphone, no other listener will believe likewise—such are this subgenre's historical origins.[2]

Because it is a musical technique wherein a performer is freely enabled to make the most diverse rhythmic decisions that they care to, tempo rubato perfectly fulfills this functional need of rappers within their culture. Rone's utilization of tempo rubato is by no means unprecedented within rap, but the extent to which he deploys it certainly does mark his style as unique.

For example, when Rone feels that the energy of the crowd is ready

5. Texture and Orchestration   153

to burst, he often accordingly speeds up the musical tempo of his rap, which is exactly what happens in the latter half of his final regular-time verse from the D.N.A. battle, around video time stamp 9:29. After such a moment—once he feels, perhaps, that the crowd must be prepared by him and his rhythms for the next musical climax—he'll lower the musical tempo of his rap, by bringing it back down and not just rapping larger subdivisions of the beat, but expanding the distances between the repeating pulses that govern those subdivisions as well. These designations can be applied to Rone's wrap-up of the second part of his battle against D.N.A., the overtime round, at 4:31.[3] There, in the more staid overtime round that is being conducted just for the fun of it, as the battle has already been settled in D.N.A.'s favor, Rone takes on a noticeably more subdued tenor. At 4:31, he keeps his final lines on the more piano side of the dynamic spectrum, delivering them flippantly and carelessly in a drawn-out, tongue-in-cheek delivery. This offhand manner seems to communicate that Rone is so far from holding the thought that D.N.A. might ever be his rap superior that the judge's controversial decision, delivered just minutes ago, will never faze him, even for a second. In contradistinction to those purposeful, expressive lulls, Rone usually ends his rounds on a high note, so to speak, so that he can leave the audience with a final jolting feel as they prepare to listen to his adversary. His growling, louder dynamic at 3:50 from the same fight is just such an example.

An identification of musical technique with emotive evocations is necessarily a minefield fraught with pitfalls, but here, many of the confounding factors in such a tit-for-tat translation have been controlled for. In response to some of the major obstacles to analysis that are identified by Kivy in *The Corded Shell*, the composer and performer in this instance are in the first place the same person; secondly, there is only a single source of emotive sound in this texture; thirdly, the music is sung; and fourthly, the music has text. As Kivy writes, "Surely Tovey could not intend these descriptions to apply to the music. Only sentient beings can have emotions.... In other words, talk about emotions in music always seem to come down to talk about emotions in composers or listeners."[4] To be sure, Kivy could never have foreseen the coming of a musical subgenre where the composer would be doing nothing but displaying emotion, through musical *and* bodily gestures working in tandem, to achieve an objective goal within the context of a live performance. In this manner, many of the obstacles to the assignation of emotive capabilities in music are overcome. Battle rappers, like the composer-performer Rone, are obviously sentient beings whose musical interpretations can constantly be understood by, evaluated through, and judged against their physical gestures. This consideration is not incidental to emotive interpretations of the coming music, but integral to it, as Kivy describes: "The feeling of love may not only be described as 'soft,' but 'softens' our countenance; anger is not only violent in feeling, but violent in music ... and music, [Daniel] Webb wants to say, reflects all of this in some way...."[5] For all of these reasons, then, battle rap makes for an excellent study of the emotive capabilities of music.

To return to the specifics of this discussion: the acceleration or deceleration of Rone's emotive tempo rubato over time actually follows a discernible pattern across the entire three-round format of the first battle league that this lyricist joined, called Grind Time. His tempos usually begin at a very even, moderate level for the start of his battles, around 81 BPM, which is the exact BPM of the first bar that he delivers against D.N.A. This is done in order to set the interpretive stage for his coming, faster BPMs, like the several bars of 130-BPM material that immediately follow that opening.

In fact, over the first and second rounds of his battles, Rone then usually goes on to vary his BPM rate up and down, never reaching his highest absolute BPM, and never falling too far below his original BPM. These subsequent tempos might range anywhere from adagio to moderato. By the end of the battle, however, Rone usually concludes his melody in the realm of allegro, at his highest BPM yet. This musical journey from lowest BPM, to temporal digressions, to highest BPM, are perfectly manifest in a previous battle against a rapper by the name of Prophit, which analytical dissection will be saved for a following chapter. For now, it'd do well to note the beginning tempos for each of his three rounds in that fight, which are 85 BPM (at 2:31), 132 BPM (at 5:15), and 156 BPM (at 7:43), respectively.[6]

This basic temporal plan is essential in fulfilling many of Rone's practical objectives when engaging in these kinds of verbal battles. He must convince the crowd that he is the best rapper, by giving them something not just creative, but a creative-something that they have never heard before; he must convince the crowd that he himself believes he is the best rapper, by showing that he is independent and unafraid to perform daredevil acts in his rhythm; and, perhaps most importantly, he must send the judges off to their resultant decision with his strongest impression on them yet, or else run the risk of communicating that he is only a good rapper in short spans, but not a great rapper over time. Because this slow-to-fast temporal arc is enabled by the vehicle of tempo rubato, it is an approach to rhythm that can expertly fulfill all of the generic goals that Rone has in battling.

In addition to tempo rubato, Rone also frequently utilizes the concept of the dramatic musical caesura as he goes about projecting an appropriate musical persona. Rone will take an extended pause, almost a performance breath, in between his delivery of different phrases of his rap, as he does at 2:43 of his Prophit fight. This is yet another acknowledgment on his part of how rhythmically free he knows he can be without a dictatorial musical accompaniment deciding such matters in advance for him. His use of the caesura is another recurring musical characteristic of Rone's that projects confidence and swagger through strictly musical aspects of his live performance. As it were, an audience member gets the feeling that Rone likes to leisurely take his time during these caesural pauses for a chance to stop and smell the roses, as he draws out the precious enjoyable moments wherein he verbally bests whatever dope was unlucky enough to show up in front of his hundreds of fans. When these caesuras are combined with his tempo rubato, it makes for a panoply of unique technical aspects that all work towards the single goal of securing victory from an audience who can be persuaded through both conscious appeals to a mental parsing of his poetic abilities, as well as subconscious musical appeals to the effect that his melody has on the emotions of onlookers.

Homophonic Raps

The studio monophonic texture and the live monophonic texture can now be seen in context of the texture in rap that is most prevalent: the homophonic texture. An example of a fairly standard homophonic texture comes from one of the artists who has already been considered, the lyricist Black Thought of The Roots. In contrast to the monophony of "@ 15," a particularly excellent example of homophony comes on The Roots song called "Don't Say Nuthin." This track was one of The Roots' singles from their 2004 album *The Tipping Point.*

On this third track from that album, Black Thought's rap is supplied to the listener in a manner that is much more regular and standardized than what is heard on "@ 15." On "Don't Say Nuthin," the two musical elements necessary for the creation of a homophonic texture are both present: a single leading melodic voice (Black Thought as he raps), and a backing musical accompaniment (which takes the form of guitars, drums, and bass synths).

The most important feature here of "Don't Say Nuthin'" isn't just that the music is homophonic. In truth, the most important feature of this recording is just how homophonic the music actually turns out to be. The alignment here between the technical aspects of the music, and the effect on the listener's emotions from hearing that music, is just as close as the intimate relationship was between those two complementary artistic interpretations in the battle rap melodies of Rone. That is, the straightforward, brutal duplet rhythms and restricted registers of Black Thought's melodic range work on the listener's emotions in a manner that's both subtly standoffish and severely confrontational.

This unvarnished, raw musical approach is further underscored by the musical texture, in addition to the specific features of Black Thought's melody just described. The musical texture supports the gratuitous, graphic themes of Black Thought's melody and poetry in three main ways. First, Thought's voice is almost always mixed in the stereo environment to the front, center panning position, at a very loud dynamic, and with almost no reverb echo; second, Black Thought's voice is almost never doubled with a studio chorus effect, or manipulated in other ways that would be impossible outside of a studio environment, which might in turn undermine the specific expressive context that Black Thought has worked so hard to create for his listeners; and, third, Black Thought's own melody constitutes the only human voice that is ever heard over the course of this entire track. Even when this dynamic seems to be subverted—such as when Black Thought raps at an almost unintelligible dynamic level and delivery during the chorus—it actually only serves to re-enforce, through antithesis, his main poetic theme. Any straightforward or affirmative answers to questions of melodic, accompanimental, poetic, or stereophonic organization would strongly undermine the ominous poetic messages of Black Thought on "Don't Say Nuthin," and so the artists here work hard to avoid any such indications of positive justification.

As for how the homophonic texture functions on this song specifically, Black Thought's rap takes the lead in the musical texture, as it contains the most complex rhythmic and melodic action in its own line. His radical departures of non-scalar pitch intonation and non-duplet, expressively microtimed rhythms are in turn supported by the snare drums and bass kick, both of which count off the music's meter in a much more regular way behind him. In this manner, Black Thought's voice constitutes an unconventional melody within an unconventional musical accompaniment that nevertheless remains strongly within the realm of the homophonic texture as it has existed for centuries in the Western art music tradition.

Polyphonic Raps

As it turns out, however, rap as a genre or art form does not restrict itself to homophonic or monophonic textures, wherein the number of independent, fully functional voices is never more than one. Such a texture that has at least two voices that both carry equal melodic weight constitutes an instance of textural polyphony, and there are several instances within rap of this multilayered kind of texture. To start with, a strong example of a polyphonic texture can be seen on the 1999 Dr. Dre song "Ackrite." Rather than focusing on the raps of the album's headliner, Dr. Dre, it is his former protégé, named Hittman, whose dual raps on this particular track set up the manifold musical space that ends up comprising a polyphonic rap canon.

On "Ackrite," Hittman keeps the structures of his melodic phrasing rather regular and standard, as almost all of his phrases start or end where the 4/4 bar lines divide up the music, and almost all of them last either two, four, six, or eight beats. In de-emphasizing some aspects of his melody, however, Hittman allows himself musical room to bring other potential relations situated within it to the forefront. Specifically, Hittman foregrounds the relationship of his own main melody to the musical ideas that exist right alongside it, in equal hierarchical importance. The musical gesture in question here is a second melody that is also rapped by Hittman, which is allowed by this artist's utilization of the technical capabilities of the modern studio recording environment. By means of that digital workstation, Hittman actually introduces two simultaneous, but separate, melodies on this track's chorus.

Backing vocals have for a long time been utilized in rap. Often, however, they are not utilized for structural purposes, but for a doubling or choir effect that is more orchestrational, or coloristic, than structural or textural. Such examples include everything from Lauryn Hill's "Lost Ones," to the 2009 Drake song "Best I Ever Had." Even Hittman's producer, Dr. Dre himself, has used this arranging technique elsewhere, such as on the 2006 Game song "How We Do." But on "Ackrite," Hittman and his producers, Dr. Dre and Mel-Man, use two instances of Hittman's voice to not just increase the instrumental strength or impact of the rapper's musical line, but to also create a polyphonic, imitative texture.

In specific terms, Dr. Dre and Mel-Man use that aforementioned studio environment to allow Hittman to record two primary melodic line. Although they start out in an uneven relationship, where one is more important than the other, their equal sharing of melodic responsibilities is made clear by the end of the chorus section.

This multi-layered textural dynamic initially plays itself out at the 1:01 mark of the song, when the first chorus begins. At this point, Hittman begins to deliver those symmetrical melodic blocks that were described previously. However, he also adds a second voice behind his main melody, largely independent and individuated from the first, that adds shades of rhythmic variation and registral contrast to the texture of the music.

The producers and rappers work in tandem on "Ackrite" in order to supplement and support this desired textural effect. In the first place, this second melodic line is placed further back in the mix, in terms of both reverb and dynamic level, so that it almost seems to whisper behind the back of the first Hittman, even while it remains clearly audible. At the same time, the second melodic line that is delivered by Hittman stands out from the foregrounded one due to the former's large amount of rhythmic and melodic deviation from its temporary leader.

In technical terms, this foreground–background dynamic in this song's melody can be described like so. At the end of almost every melodic phrase on the chorus, such as at 1:03 or 1:05, Hittman repeats the final note of the lead canonic line's phrase, but with an expressive rhythmic delay added on to it. In actuality, this secondary melodic voice does very closely echo the first melodic voice's poetic line in both rhythm and pitch. Specifically, Hittman performs the same rhythms and melodic contour in this second voice, but in a different register, with a different delivery style of coloristic whispering, and with a greater amount of rhythmic trailing behind the beat. However, at the end of each melodic line on the chorus, this secondary melodic line of Hittman's furthermore tacks on an added, extra 8th note. As a result, this second melody extends noticeably past the point at which the lead canonic line has stopped rapping the corresponding ending note.

It is also important to note that this was not the work of the producers, who might have simply taken the same exact vocals from Hittman, doubled them, and then separated them up so that it merely appeared as if Hittman had rapped the same words twice, but not actually done so. Such a misinterpretation would credit these developed techniques to the wrong musicians: the producers, not the rappers. This is all self-evident because, if one pays very careful attention to the secondary Hittman,

5. Texture and Orchestration   159

they'll notice that his voice moves up and down, in terms of its pitch, in ways that are different from those of the lead melodic voice. While the lead voice mostly gravitates a single pitch, and barely varies from its close orbit around it, the second voice sounds more thoughtful and pensive. The pitch space over which it ranges is far more extensive, with a higher high note, as well as a lower low note. It's almost as if the second voice is asking us to consider the implications of what the first voice is saying, both in lyrical terms, rhythmic terms, and harmonic terms. Once again, we see a close interplay between the technical aspects of a rap, and the qualitative interpretation of what the semantic content of those technical aspects actually might be.

The final piece that will complete this polyphonic puzzle, however, has not yet been supplied. This comes in the final bar of every chorus, wherein the previously-secondary melody now steps forward and assumes center stage in the texture. Here, while the other melodic line becomes quieter and less rhythmically active, the Hittman voice that was previously whispering now assumes a head voice, and delivers a menacingly-intricate rendition of this song's title. As a result, it can be truthfully said that the chorus of "Ackrite" contains two polyphonic rapping voices that both carry equal weight in the musical texture. It might further be denoted as constituting a canon, since the relationship of those two equally-independent voices remains somewhat similar over the course of its chorus.

Harmony in Rap Textures

Being the first in-depth instance described in this book of two rap notes being sounded at the same time, Hittman's "Ackrite" affords the analyst an opportunity to describe the ways in which rap engages and interacts with harmony. The reader might have noticed that there is, in fact, no section of this book specifically dedicated to harmony, one of the indisputably pre-eminent aspects of music.

This is not to say, however, that rap doesn't have harmony, nor is it meant to call for a project that would dubiously expand the definitions of rap or harmony so that it would eventually reach the point where those two musical concepts have lost all explanatory meaning. Instead, it is meant to communicate the need for a stricter application of non–Western ideas of harmony, possibly timbral ones, to what is a vocal idiom that counter-intuitively first came of age in a Western nation.

To put these ideas to the test: the harmony of Hittman on "Ackrite" differs from the functional tonality of common practice period composers like Bach, Mozart, or Beethoven, because the pitches of the notes that Hittman is rapping on "Ackrite" do not fit into any easily-defined scale. The notes in his scale are not related to each other in nice, round integer fractions, in the same way that the C major scale is built out of 5/4, or 9/8, mathematical proportions between the frequencies of vertical or horizontal sonorities. However, since Hittman is rapping two voices at the same time, his music is still, in some sense, harmonic, even if its harmonic concerns cannot be easily explained by the traditional Western analytical harmonic frameworks of tonality, key, dominant relationships, functional substitutions, etc.

Indeed, it is possible that rapping musicians like Hittman do not possess the knowledge that would allow them to compose harmonic cadences, such as a traditional resolution of a dominant seventh chord to its tonic key's home chord. However, it seems as if artists like Hittman have internalized the qualitative effects of those quantitative musical events. For example, his melody's simultaneous increase in the pitch level of both voices on "Ackrite" increases the harmonic tension of his musical texture, and the lowering of those pitches in this multivocal texture likewise lowers the harmonic tension of the song. Therefore, the introduction of a higher harmonic range by means of a second melodic voice on the chorus of "Ackrite" logically works to craft an engaging narrative arc by associating heightened drama with the musical section that will be this song's final impression on this listener. To be sure, it is the chorus that's the last musical section heard by a listener on this song.

While not being directly equivalent, this treatment of harmonic density and tension might be analogous to the functional resolution of a leading tone from a dominant chord up to the tonic note at the conclusion of a movement's final resolving cadence in an extremely thick orchestration. Hittman, subconsciously or otherwise, similarly understands that the unexpected introduction of a new voice into a musical texture can increase the drama of a piece of music. This is indicated by the fact that the polyphonic, three-dimensional texture of "Ackrite" is reserved only for the chorus of this song, and so works to help the chorus achieve its functional, foundational goal of being memorable.[7] Indeed, musicologists actually can find examples of rappers, such as MF DOOM, who gravitate around structural harmonic pitches, like the subdominant or tonic, in their melodies. But in his own right, perhaps Hittman has here contributed just one more voice to the debate of how harmony can function in a more global, universalist sense.

5. Texture and Orchestration 161

In the end, all of these explicitly musical considerations of Hittman's carefully-crafted chorus on "Ackrite" should lead us describe this music as being a type of musical canon. Even though it is more rhythmically complex, Hittman's own take on the musical technique of a canon is not as harmonically complex, from a traditional viewpoint, as the chordal canons of Western classical music that have just been referenced. But in the end, almost all of the technical details of a canon can still be found on "Ackrite": the multiple voices, the imitation of a line, and then the subsequent variation from that initial, ideal, archetypal melody.

Heterophonic Raps

Frequently, parodies of rap include a satirical imitation of the genre's much-maligned hype man. A hype man is a co-performer of the main rapper who emphasizes and underscores the vocal deliveries of the rapper themselves by punctuating the final words of their lines, or even preparing the first entrance of the rapper themselves by ad-libbing throughout the beginning of the song. At it turns out, the musical rhythms of the typical hype man constitute an excellent departure point for this next investigation into rap's musical textures.

One of the most famous relationships between a hype man and a rapper was the one between Sean "Diddy" Combs and Notorious B.I.G. in the early 1990s. In addition to many of the other roles that he played in B.I.G.'s career, Diddy also periodically acted as a backing musical voice on certain Notorious B.I.G. tracks, such as "Hypnotize." However, the hierarchical relationship between the two separate voices on this song is far different from the relatively egalitarian dynamic that governed relations between the two instances of Hittman's voice on "Ackrite."

Throughout the course of "Hypnotize," Diddy (formerly known as Puff Daddy) punctuates and accents Notorious B.I.G.'s musical phrasings with interjections of his own, which can range in rhythmic scale from the monosyllabic to the multi-phrasal. Such vocal backing punctuations come at points such as 0:14, 0:23, or 0:25. As a result, the music of "Hypnotize" consists of one more musical texture in rap wherein multiple voices co-exist with each other simultaneously.

The question to be answered here, then, is the following: what is the relative relationship, in terms of textural hierarchy, between the melodic voice of Notorious B.I.G. on the one hand, and the melodic voice of Diddy on the other?

To begin with, the note-to-note, syllable-to-syllable rhythms of Diddy's backing rap don't often abide by, or follow closely, where the repeated pulses within each bar are regularly falling. Diddy's melody is prone to completely ignore the organizing directives of this song's metric pulse, with the result that there is a dearth of instances wherein Diddy accents his notes so that they are "appropriately" arranged in musical time. Diddy's melody ignores metric accent to such a strong degree that can't be parsed as a case of incredibly strong syncopation, either. In this manner, his rap comes across being a musicalized case of sprechstimme, similarly to those previously examined in the melodies of rappers like MF DOOM.

On the other hand, Diddy is also not randomly placing his notes wherever he'd like. He is responding to the pulse, but in an indirect way, using Notorious B.I.G. as a transmitter for the pulse's current position. Diddy almost always waits for Notorious B.I.G. to stop rapping at least once before he himself intercedes, and at that point, Diddy is being indirectly governed by the presiding tempo and beat, through the melody of Notorious. This is because B.I.G. himself is indeed rapping in time to the song's BPM rate and meter. It's almost as if Diddy is following along to the song's main idea (the structure of its leading melodic voice's phrasing) while ignoring that main idea's details (the rhythmic arrangement of the subdivisional rhythms inside of the leading melodic voice's phrasing, as they respond to a repeating pulse).

In isolation, Diddy's vocals on "Hypnotize" recall the rhythmically-free style of spoken word artists like Gil Scott-Heron, or even more modern rappers, like the songs by Pharoahe Monch and André 3000 that have already been examined. On such spoken word tracks, the artists seem to have been guided by an extra-musical tempo, one that necessarily resides outside of timing concerns that are as strict as those of tempo, meter, and pulse. Instead, these artists are indeed guided by a repeating pulse, but one that is more malleable and shifting. Perhaps this pulse is governed by a non-musical rhythm like their own breathing rate, whose organizing directives are then applied to speed shifts that are minute but not insubstantial.

Diddy's vocal contributions to "Hypnotize" is accordingly a merger of two distinct musical traditions from the history of the rap genre. His adherence to the rapper's melodic phrasing bespeaks the influence of the hype man convention, while his purposeful ignorance of the music's repeating pulse recalls the origins of rap from the spoken word genre.

This coupling of adherence to phrasing structure with ignorance of pulse can also be used to elucidate the texture of "Hypnotize," in addition to its historical origins. Through its dualistic treatment of the organizational concepts of rhythm, Diddy's vocals seem to be a mediation between the ideals of multi-vocal textures on one hand, and the ideals of monophonic textures on the other. In specific terms, there is more than one musical voice on "Hypnotize" that is constantly performing, as would be generally characteristic of polyphony. But, simultaneously, one of those voices—Diddy's own—is not always as important as the other voice, due to its purposeful ignorance of metric pulse.

From this point of view, then, the texture of "Hypnotize" might be said to interact with the heterophonic principles of texture, even if it might not be considered a textbook example of such. In heterophony, the equal independence of multiple voices of polyphony is tempered by the fact that those multiple voices are elaborations of a single melodic line. With the addition of the stipulation that each heterophonic voice must also perform in a manner that's idiomatic to its instrumental tradition, then the case for a heterophonic classification of "Hypnotize" is even stronger. Diddy performs according to the stylistic specifications of a hype man in one part of the texture's melodic voicing, at the same time that Notorious B.I.G. performs according to the stylistic specifications of a rapper in another part of the texture's melodic voicing. Always, though, they are both working together to generate the same musical idea that occupies the focus of the musical texture, and if either of the voices were ever able to be completely removed from the texture, it would lose its substantial essence.

Call-and-Response Textures in Rap

In addition to homophonic, monophonic, and polyphonic textures, call-and-response textures are quite identifiable within the genre of rap as well.

Rappers have always made songs out of this basic musical idea, going back to Afrika Bambaataa's "Planet Rock" in 1982 and before, but the group Run-D.M.C. is notable for having made an entire career out of understanding just how novel this type of musical dialogue can be. The rappers of Run-D.M.C. are almost constantly finishing the semantic meaning of each other's melodic phrases, while still giving each other's position within the texture enough space to come to the forefront. An example of this call-and-response texture comes from the rhythmically-unstable opening to this group's 1986 song "Peter Piper," which is found on their album *Raising Hell*.

Altogether, the a cappella intro on this song lasts for a relatively brief length of just nine seconds. While Run and D.M.C. are well known for their rhythmically-quick transference of rhymes and phrases, here, they parse their shared melodic ideas right down to individual words, syllables, and notes. It is remarkable that, in actuality, Run-D.M.C. trades the melody back and forth so quickly on "Peter Piper" that barely any Internet transcription databases indicate which rapper is delivering which opening line. This might be due to the fact that these two lyricists trade the place of leading melodic line back and forth a full five times over the course of this track's opening sentence and its nine total words.

The dualistic source of this deceivingly simple melody on "Peter Piper" is further underscored by the mixing decisions of this song's producer. In addition to being delivered from the mouths of two different vocalists, the opening rap of "Peter Piper" is delivered from two separate spatial positionings within the stereophonic environment as well. That is, one rapper is panned ever so slightly to the side, while the other occupies dead center. This localizing reflection of the song's musical reality further serves to both underline and emphasize just how this tripartite rap group is conceiving of this song's performance.

This demonstrates just how flexible, deep, and renewable the call-and-response texture can be. Indeed, the two rappers Run and D.M.C. do not seem to conceive of the call-and-response as a heightened stylization of everyday speech that is still governed by the transactional norms of quotidian conversation, as another rapping duo, like Mos Def and Talib Kweli on their song "Re:DeFinition," might. Instead, Run and D.M.C. greatly extend the intricacies of this musical dialogue when they exchange not just sentences, but individual words and syllables as well.

Even many standardized rap song structures might be thought of as constituting call-and-responses that have been expanded to much larger structural proportions, wherein multiple rappers contribute their own musical takes on the same basic material or content. Such an interpretation would involve an observation of very long "sentences" that can last sixteen bars or longer in the form of verses, with interceding, punctuating choruses that come in between their exchanges. Such a song might be "Karma," from Waka Flocka Flame's 2010 *Flockaveli* album, where Waka, YG Hootie, and Papa Smurf all contribute lyrics. Although this extension of the call-and-response texture might be considered, at first, to be an unwarranted stretch of musical logic, it would certainly account for the rap genre's predilection for involved artistic collaboration. Additionally, it might also provide the background for the frequent inter-generic feuding over the alleged plagiary of characteristic melodic techniques, as well as the motivic recycling of similar expressive material in both verses and songs. That is, to rappers, these songs might not be music, but actual, semantic conversations that are no different from their everyday talking. They might also be telling their audiences who they are, and that to imitate someone else's style without attributing it properly could never lead to artistic homage, but only outright identity theft, through a co-opting of someone else's legal right to promotional presentations of their own likeness in public.

Summary

With just a small re-orientation of the definition of some very well-established musical terminology, we find that the music of rappers presents a very wide array of solutions to the problem of managing the interactions that can occur spontaneously between numerous competing voices as they appear simultaneously within a single piece of music, as well as the relative hierarchical relationships of those voices to each other.

In this way, it seems that the polyphonic legacy of the common practice period of Western music has not simply been ignored by modern American rap music. Instead, it has simply been expanded and re-worked to include a diverse spectrum of sounds that the rules of fugues, strict canons and the like might never have been able to generate previously.

6

Instrumentalism

Even though many members of the rap community might not realize it, their judgment between the skilled lyricist vs. the unskilled lyricist is often based on no more than an examination of the vocal abilities of a particular rapper, by means of the same basic rubric that's used to judge an instrumentalist of the violin, guitar, or piano. When rap fans say, "That rapper has no flow," what they often really mean is something along the lines of, "That rapper does not possess enough direct control over his voice to make it do whatever he or she wants it to do at any given moment on their recordings." Such criticisms might be more specifically manifest in the fact that that particular rapper has no articulation, and so listeners can't understand what they're saying as clearly an audience needs to. Alternately, they might be proffering a negative criticism of a certain rapper because that rapper simply does not take long enough breaths of air in between their melodic phrases, which would then allow them to make their voices more audible. All of these specific concerns can be examined under the heading of instrumental ability, or instrumentalism. Instrumentalism, in short, is defined here as the study of the ability of an instrumentalist, such as a rapper, to perform their music in a clear, articulate manner.

Unfortunately, rap's lack of a standardized educational path, which is elsewhere the source of such creativity, is here an un-ignorable obstacle to analysis. There is no school for rappers to attend, and any individual teachers who offer publicly-documented lessons for pay are. Because of this, there is a noticeable dearth of pedagogical materials that could now be quoted in order to serve as direct evidence of the thinking of rappers on instrumentalism.

Compare the case presently at hand to that of any other instrument that has existed for centuries, such as the piano or guitar. One can receive a degree in guitar performance, and there is a multitude of personal teachers one could patronize in order to learn how to play that instrument. These guitar instructors would begin by teaching the basics, such as positions for different scales, the placement of fingers on the fingerboard, or the reading of music Western music notation. However, rappers don't make music with scales, they don't play chords, and they don't need to read music. So what, exactly, are they doing when they are improving their instrumentalist rapping abilities?

In order to answer that question, one can start by defining the phrases "instrumentalism" or "instrumental ability" a bit further. Instrumental ability, in a very wide definition that will soon be applied more specifically, is the ability to not just play an instrument, but to play that instrument *well*. Although the importance of being able to play an instrument well might be obvious, the important differences between a good player and a bad player are not always apparent to musical laypeople. That's because one of the greatest indicators to some people of musical skill, the ability to play fast, can actually turn out to sometimes be little more than superficial fireworks, rather than a foundation on which a musician can build good technique. It is, in truth, much easier to play quickly than is thought by many. It is much more difficult to play fast, while making each phrase stand out clearly with good breath around it, while bringing the most important notes to the forefront with the proper dynamic level, while leaving the less important notes in the background through solid articulation. In a nutshell, these are the all-important talents that rappers with good instrumental ability possess.

Scholars might be able to start understanding the necessary technical skills it takes to rap well if the rapping voice is first compared to more traditional instruments, like electric guitarists. Much of what makes a good performer on a traditional instrument is also necessary for the making of a good rapper.

Instrumentalism in Chordophones and Singing

To begin with, one can consider guitarist Jimmy Page's performance with Led Zeppelin at the Earls Court Exhibition Centre in London in May 1975as comprising an instructive example for what instrumentalist stamina means.

This particular Led Zeppelin concert clocks in at a total length of almost three-and-a-half hours. While much of that time is spent in between the playing of songs, much of it also has Jimmy Page playing along with his band. For instance, when they perform "In My Time of Dying," the song lasts for over 11 minutes. That might not song like a lot of time in chronological terms, but in musical terms, on a song with a BPM of around 111, that can add up to over 300 bars of music. Thus, Page is obviously an instrumentalist with great stamina and endurance who can play his instrument for long periods of time at a single stretch. But it's not just about how long Page plays for here; it's also about how well he still manages to play. Page even manages to carry the texture successfully when all the focus is on him during his guitar solo, wherein any wrong note would sorely stand out.

An instrumentalist with good articulation is someone whose notes can always be clearly picked out by their listeners' ears. They don't blend one into the next, and the dynamics of the notes aren't constantly changing in unpredictable, meaningless ways that would undermine interpretation of musical structure. Jimmy Page manages to maintain excellent articulation all throughout Led Zeppelin's performance in London in 1975, just as he did in other concerts as well. One of the biggest problems with amateur instrumentalists, such as those on chordophones like the guitar, is that they don't respect the articulative tone of their instrument. They may be able to hit all of the notes, but they can't do so in a very articulate manner, or in a way that places each individual note in its proper position within the musical line.

Indeed, traditional vocalists need to have good stamina as well in order to sing everything that's demanded of them. One of the benchmarks for separating the truly great operatic singers from the average vocalist is the Wagnerian cycle of operas *Der Ring des Nibelungen*. The shortest and first opera, *Das Rheingold*, is typically performed so that it lasts two-and-a-half hours. The final opera, *Götterdämmerung*, can take up to five hours. Now, again, no single vocalist sings for every minute of those five hours, or even for a majority of them. But the sopranos, tenors, and other singers must always be ready and in singing mode, so to speak, for such an extended time. Rappers, in fact, must possess this same kind of vocal stamina if they wish to make their mark in the genre, through either critical or popular acclamation.

In general, the rap genre has not figured out a very good way to seamlessly translate its finely-delineated musical experience from the studio to the stage.[1] A hype man, pre-recorded lyrics, and a rapper standing isolated do not make for a very engaging or overpowering experience for an audience. However, the live stage does delineate between good rappers and bad rappers in a live performance, since there is a smaller amount of digital

6. Instrumentalism 169

fixes that a rapper can rely on there in order to improve their performance. This has direct consequences for an audience's evaluation of the instrumentalist categories that have been discussed so far, like stamina, articulation, and breath control. Most important, rappers *can't* do multiple takes when performing live, which might otherwise allow them to take the necessary breaths in between lines. Based on just how fast he can perform his raps, someone who has apparently mastered his body's conscious control over his breath is Chicago lyricist Twista.

Twista's Stamina, Articulation and Breath Control

In fact, the importance of articulation in rap is underscored by the rap world's fascination with battles over the title for faster rapper in *The Guinness Book of World Records*. Variously held by Twista, then Rebel XD, it is, in fact, now held by a Seattle rapper named NoClue, who earned the title by rapping 723 syllables in 51.27 seconds. When one hears NoClue rap so quickly, the fact that a listener can't understand what he's saying is only the first problem. That alone might be enough to disqualify this particular rapper from being included within the genre's listing of all-time greats, since this hyper-fast style obfuscates rap's original historical purpose to act a vehicle for political struggle and resistance.

But rapping so quickly also actually strangles the palette of rhythms that are available to a rapper who chooses to rap in such a manner. If one listens to NoClue's rhythms on other very quick songs, there is no special differentiation between melodic rhythms and the song's metric subdivisions. There, in short, no rhythmic variation, but only an endless stream of incoherent musical information. As a result, the listener is never brought along for an engaging musical journey. As a result, such hyper-quick melodies seem to march in lockstep, rather than unfurling with the flow that even the rap community's own preferred term for melody connotes.

Whenever Twista's own "flow" has received the most acclaim, the praise has almost always come for one of his performances alongside a rapper who is able balance out his more hectic style.[2] This includes Cam'ron's slower, longer rhythms and sentences on his 2004 song "Adrenaline Rush," or Kanye West's 2004 recording "Slow Jamz."[3]

At first look, Twista's place on a song entitled "Slow Jamz" might seem to be completely out of place. But such is Kanye West's mastery over production that even the style of a technical rapper like Twista could fit onto a song whose overriding poetic tone is a relaxing one. Kanye West, deploying Twista's technical breath control like a fine instrument, inserts him into the song for its musical climax at 2:58. To be sure, Twista nearly bursts into the texture at this point, with a series of blazing rhythms at bar 45. Comparing them at the rhythmic subdivision level, Twista is sometimes fitting as many as three or four syllables in the same amount of musical space, whereas Kanye was fitting only one or two. Even from the first two bars, this difference is apparent: Kanye has 29 notes in his opening couplet, while Twista has an amount that's exactly twice as many (58).

This variety in artistic expression that is displayed by Twista does not just happen alongside his instrumental ability, but is founded upon it. This is because Twista could not rap in his favored, hyper-triplet style without being able to control his breath in such an evenhanded manner. Even as Twista delivers such speedy rhythms, he still articulates them in a manner that allows his listeners to understand the sonic (if not semantic) meaning of every single syllable he pronounces. Moreover, Twista's tight breath control is confirmed in live performances of this song, where he still manages to rap the rhythms in perfect time with the meter of the backing track behind him.[4]

Besides articulation and breath control, though, what other elements of instrumental ability must a rapper master? The next example comes from Kendrick Lamar, who demonstrates just how essential it is for a rapper to be able to quickly move their own voice over a wide range of pitches.

Kendrick Lamar's Tessitura and Passaggio

Another element of a good vocalist that is recognized by many is the ability to vocalize beautifully over a wide range of pitches. Legends like Freddie Mercury, for instance, can sing over the length of almost four octaves, while Paul McCartney himself can sing over a full four octaves. How does an artist like Kendrick Lamar and his rapping, then, compare to those two pioneers in his own command of vocal range?

The song "Backseat Freestyle," from his 2012 album *good kid, m.A.A.d city*, acts as an excellent showcase for Kendrick's most expressive, widest leaps in melodic pitch. The instrumentalist climax arrives during this song's bridge, at 2:13. It is here that Kendrick reaches his highest identifiable performing note on this song, a D#3, at 2:28. It is not, of course, simply enough to just be able to sing (or rap) very high and low notes. One must also be able to also move over this large range with alluringly deceptive ease, and this bridge acts as a perfect display of that special vocal flexibility that Kendrick possesses as well.

Indeed, Kendrick negotiates these frequent melodic jumps in bars 34 and 38 of his rap so expertly that it almost sounds as if Kendrick is rapping two different melodic lines. He performs this psychoacoustic trick by greatly contrasting where each of those quasi-contrapuntal lines falls in the overall range of pitch: one is very high up, and the other is rather lower. After Kendrick has repeated his insults in the higher range around D#3, his melody then goes on to, conversely, fall very far down in terms of its pitch. In fact, he drops all the way from D#3 to the pitch E2, around 2:27. As this four bar grouping is repeated twice, Kendrick also executes this extreme melodic leap at 2:39 and 2:40, when he leaps all the way down from a note on C3 to a note on C#2 in an amount of musical space that lasts only a fraction of a second. In this manner, Kendrick displays an adroit melodic passaggio, which is a term used to describe the ability of a vocalist to shift between registers while maintaining their tone.

If "Backseat Freestyle" is a showcase for Kendrick to expertly navigate the top end of his range, then "Swimming Pools (Drank)" is the place where Kendrick lets the lower range of his voice dominate his melody. Most of his rap verses fall around the range of the note D2, but at certain points—0:46, 1:45, and 1:50—he lets his melody fall all the way down to Bb1.

All of this means that Kendrick's tessitura—the pitch range where his voice most comfortably resides—seems to be from Bb1 to B2. This is where most of the rap from his verses on "Backseat Freestyle," "The City," "Swimming Pools (Drank)," and "Bitch Don't Kill My Vibe" falls. In traditional musical terminology, Kendrick clearly possesses some kind of bass voice range, which is traditionally defined as stretching from E2 to E4. Kendrick also probably has the further distinction of being what is called a basso profondo, the "profondo" designation referring to a particularly low bass. As a final note, and in contrast to the coming analysis of Eminem's own vocal weight, Kendrick's voice could probably be designated as possessing a "dramatic" heaviness to it.

Of course, it is not a wide vocal range alone that denotes a skilled vocalist. Such a vocalist must also be able to negotiate that wide range with agility. Indeed, it is to Kendrick's credit that his transitions through his vocal passaggi are so smooth that they are often repurposed for the goal of expressive timbral contrast. This is exactly what happens on the bridge for "Backseat Freestyle," as described in the following section.

Kendrick Lamar's Timbral Flexibility

A single vocal quality is often associated with many of the most famous rappers: for Eminem, it might be his faux childish, mocking tone of voice, of "My Name Is" and elsewhere; for Mos Def, it could be his honeyed, mellow delivery, such as on DJ Honda's "Travellin' Man." But all of these rappers, of course, have more than one approach to their music, and that's what makes them all so widely heralded. For good articulation, a rapper needs breath control; for range, a rapper need good articulation; but what all of these aspects of instrumental ability really add up to is a certain level of control over their voice's timbre, or sound quality.

As was mentioned before, articulation and breath control are really important insofar as they impact the production of new, successive timbres. As an example, Kendrick has good range and articulation, and he uses this to make his voice have many different kinds of qualities, whether those are heard as being emotively intimidating, revealing, angry, violent, etc. The most widely-acclaimed rappers can use their technical abilities to conjure the impression of an entire orchestra being housed within the confines of a single human voice.

This tight command of his voice over a wide range in pitch, along with good articulation and breath control, allows Kendrick to subsequently vary the timbre of his voice. For the bridge of his 2012 song "Backseat Freestyle," Kendrick's voice sounds incredibly primal and intimidating. There are many ways to up tension in a rap melody, such as by increasing the number of accents, or by rapping more quickly. Here, though, Kendrick upends the relative calm of his previous head voice register by shifting into a nasty, guttural growl, low in the bass range, and imbued with his chest voice timbre.

However, Kendrick also has his lighter, softer moments, such as on "Sing About Me, I'm Dying of Thirst." On this track, Kendrick's voice, softer and more vulnerable now, comes across as confessional and wounded, based as it is in a higher range of pitch. But while all pianists mostly play the same set of piano sounds, all rapper's have their own unique instrumental timbre: their own voices. A rapper's timbre, then, is probably the ineffable quality of a certain musical artist's work that we characterize as being expressive of their personality. Because Kendrick's voice can sound as menacing as a threatening animal who might attack us, and because Kendrick is both the composer, songwriter, and performer of the melody on "Backseat Freestyle," his audience is apt to think that he has a rather unforgiving side to his personality. The totality of Kendrick's diverse timbres communicates in miniature the importance of instrumental control in contributing to an audience's interpretation of rappers' melodies.

Due to the ubiquitous presence of compressors in music studios, some of the capabilities that a rapper's control over their voice's instrumentalist parameters allows them to possess, such as a manipulation of the loudness of their voice, have recently taken on a more minor position. Plug-ins like compressors can take an audio signal and normalize, or level out, the signal's overly high peaks and overly low valleys. Because of this, a producer is largely able to fix any irregularities or deficiencies in a rapper's voice in a studio recording. However, the situation is very different for rappers in live contexts like rap battles.

Rone's Dynamic Control

In live performances, a rapper is robbed of the potential aid of compressors and other would-be artistic crutches of the recording studio. As a result, the live rap battle makes an excellent setting for evaluating the abilities of certain rappers to finely control the high or low dynamic levels of their voices.

A rapper's instrumental ability clearly plays a large part contributing to his defeat or victory in rap battles. Within the context of any musical performance that carries the title of "battle," it is, perhaps, to be expected if the standard dynamic level of instrumentalists is at a rather loud, forte level. But the place from which this louder level of dynamics draws its strength is actually those parts of a battle rapper's melody that are delivered at quieter volumes, and an expert battle rapper will use both in order to win over the crowd.

This dynamic can be played out in any number of scenarios, but a particularly consequential one can be observed in the rapper Rone's battle with New York lyricist Prophit. In the second verbal contest during his ascent to champion of King of the Dot, Rone actually begins his raps at a very even, calm dynamic level. This is a signature musical approach of some expert battle rappers: to fool their opponents and crowd with an everyman demeanor, and to then pull the musical rug out from underneath his onlookers once he's lulled them into a false sense of security.

Indeed, in contrast to his opening verse at time stamp 2:31, Rone is actually almost yelling at the top of his lungs by the time his third verse is ending, at 8:30.[5] Neither does he dull the ear's perceptiveness by utilizing only these forte, subito forte, and fortissimo dynamic levels.

Instead, Rone alternates them with more piano dynamics, in order to imbue his sonic events with structure by means of contrast. The causal effect of this initial musical event is not only sonic, but physical: during moments of quieter dynamics, the crowd must strain harder in order to hear Rone's melody. With this trap having been cleverly set, Rone next surprisingly lowers his dynamic level greatly, in order to catch the audience off-guard once more. When Rone ends his raps at 8:40 by momentously belittling his opponent's supposed profession at an extremely reserved, quiet level of volume, the emotive effect is devastating, as demonstrated by the crowds whoops and jeers. It's as if the audience has just been left floored by a lyricist who is so confident in his rapping abilities that he doesn't even care whether he's rapping too quietly for you to hear him or not. Rone, then, is a rapper who displays an extremely fine type of instrumental control, just like other musical instrumentalists that use dynamics to give a proper shape to their melodic phrases.

Eminem's Spinto Vocal Weight

Simply put, a rapper's vocal weight is just how "heavy" their words sound to a listener. This qualitative designation can be quantitatively defined by conducting a spectral analysis of a certain rapper's typical mode of vocalizing, which would find the ranges along the frequency spectrum where a rapper's voice is at its highest decibel level and present them in the form of a spectrogram. Because of the two concepts' obvious similarities, the concept of vocal weight is closely akin to the rap community's somewhat ambiguous idea of delivery. In fact, a rapper's delivery is also a candidate for constituting the hallmark of the highest instrumentalism. This distinction between good vocal weight and poor vocal weight can be seen concretely in the differences between Eminem's own delivery at different points in his career. A comparison of Eminem's vocal weight on his early song "Foolish Pride" with his vocal weight in his 1999 song "Bad Meets Evil" will bear this out, and will, accordingly, remove any possible confounding factors that might be introduced by comparing two different rappers' vocal weights.

"Foolish Pride" was a song Eminem recorded very early on in his career, when he was still a teenager. Qualitatively, Eminem here sounds very unsure of himself as he delivers his rhymes, as well as very unconfident. Musically, it can be said that his voice lacks a sufficient amount of vocal weight or support. This might be anathema to members of the rap community, which has been built on strong, assertive passions for some time, as communicated by the feuds that have erupted between 2Pac and Notorious B.I.G., Game and 50 Cent, or Jay-Z and Nas.

On his 1999 track "Bad Meets Evil," from about seven years later, Eminem's vocal weight is instead full, aggressive, and underpinned heavily. By means of this spinto level of vocal weight, Eminem is able to communicate a deep self-belief and confidence. Lying somewhere between a lighter lyric weight and the deeper dramatic weight of traditional vocal designations, this spinto vocal weight means that the spectral force of Eminem's voice is of a moderate kind.

By hearing just how different the very same person's voice can sound over the span of just a few years—unconvincing in the younger context, confident in the more mature context—one can see just how important vocal weight is to rap, and just what large a space it occupies in any rapper's compositional toolbox. Eminem never changed his voice between 1993 and 1999. However, he certainly changed the way he used that same voice over the course of decades of practice, to the excitement and delight of rap fans all over the world, who were able to enjoy what he had to say only once he was able to deliver his words with the full vocal weight that they demanded.

Summary

Rappers have an almost obsessive fascination with the ways in which the human voice can be modulated. A rapper that does not have absolute control over their voice so that it does exactly what the rap performer wants it to at all times is a rapper that readers have simply never heard of. In the same way that the fundamentals of piano-playing can be found in the repetition of scalar and chordal exercises, rappers are always practicing in order to improve their stamina, breath control, articulation, tessitura, passaggio, dynamic control, timbral flexibility, and vocal weight. As a result, it will often by the rap genre that is looked too for ideas of innovations in musical vocalizations, as displayed by the recent collaboration between Pulitzer Prize winner Caroline Shaw and rapper Kanye West on the latter's 2016 album *The Life of Pablo*.

7

Masters of the Form

What follows is a list of the 56 rappers who have been mentioned by name and individually analyzed across 135 separate songs so far:

Eminem, Drake, Talib Kweli, Mos Def, Kendrick Lamar, MF DOOM, André 3000, Busta Rhymes, 50 Cent, Run, D.M.C., Game, AZ, Slimkid3, Black Thought, Afrika Bambaataa, Waka Flocka Flame, Killer Mike, Jonny 5, El-P, Captain Murphy, Lin-Manuel Miranda, Big Sean, Pharoahe Monch, Kanye West, Eve, Big Daddy Kane, Wu-Tang Clan, T-Pain, Twista, DMX, Dr. Dre, B-Lo, Lil Wayne, Big Boi, Wyclef Jean, Havoc, Prodigy, Ludacris, Daz Dillinger, Kurupt, Notorious B.I.G., Diddy, Nas, Elzhi, Souls of Mischief, Tribe Called Quest, Lauryn Hill, The Sugarhill Gang, Jay-Z, Jean Grae, Supa Nate, Big Noyd, Rone, and Hittman.

This chapter was originally meant to act as a summarizing capstone to this book by supplying factual musings on how a selecting of the greatest rappers of all time might be conducted. But, as the length of that above list shows, that might not be possible, without addressing at least each of those 56 rappers individually, as well as many others besides. Instead, it's a summary of the wide extent to which diverse interpretations of rhythm, melody, motivic development, structure, performance practice, texture, orchestration, and instrumentalism have proliferated throughout the modern rapping idiom, delivered in individual sections on the rappers who have already appeared multiple times through this book.

When rappers who all perform within artistic contexts and performance venues that are as varied as musical theatres, battle rap rings, huge stadiums, and underground dives can all be gathered together in one place in an examination of rap vocalizations as pure music, than that might be the greatest proof possible for the existence of extremely complex musical mechanisms found in rap. This generalized finding might, in turn, overwhelm the force of any of the localized findings contained therein. As a result, it would be unfair to focus on only the five best rappers, or even the ten best rappers, in trying to determine who most amply makes use of the musical materials that rap supplies to its performance. Consequently, the selection of rappers that follows, rather than constituting a definitive list of the greatest rappers ever, is more of a wide-ranging meditation and empirical reflection on who the greatest rapping-musicians might be.

This list is thus a very specific one. Rather than detailing who is the single greatest rapper ever, or who has the best rhymes, the best poetry, or the best stories, parodies, satires, jokes, puns, punch lines, double entendres, battle tracks, styles, beats, or delivery, this list is looking to add up all of the quantitative findings of this title's previous chapter six into a series of condensed recapitulations. For these reasons, certain rappers are not covered at all, or do not receive as high marks as they might elsewhere. For example, it isn't necessarily true that 2Pac is less than the greatest rapper of all-time, although he very may well be. It's just that his particular style of rapping isn't as melodious as it could be.

It might do well to then use some of the most popular rappers as example test cases here, as it were, so that the reader might be reminded of some of the recurring principles that were taken away from this rather-extended investigation, and how they might behave in a discussion of this nature.

Kanye West

The rap of Kanye West is like a prism through which the work of others can be understood. In short, he is good at rap in just about every way that this book is not focused on, and for this reason, he makes an excellent first study. He is probably the best comedian to ever record raps in the studio booth; his puns, double-entendres, and jokes are raucously funny, and yet still clever and subtle. His jokes about the American Express Black card on "Last Call," or his comparison between mayonnaise and top notch cars on the same track, would be just as funny in a televised sketch comedy ski.

Kanye's arduous saga to fame and fortune, as he relates it, is engaging, intensely personal, and very relatable. His origin story—akin to those told in comic books, as they are for all rappers, Jean Grae or otherwise—as told through "Through the Wire," "Jesus Walks," and "Family Business," measures up to the legendary tales of any rap griot, including Slick Rick's

"Children's Story" or 2pac's "Brenda's Got a Baby." What's more, is that all of those Kanye songs all appear on his first debut album. When his successive achievements are piled on top of those, such as "Hey Mama" (from *Late Registration*), "Blame Game" (*My Beautiful Dark Twisted Fantasy*) or "Everything I Am" (*Graduation*), then his corpus becomes even more impossible to ignore.

Kanye can even combine his gags and epics with some real musical trickery at times. This element of Kanye's rap is often overlooked in favor of his peerless production and ear for the perfect soul sample. On a pre–College Dropout mixtape track called "Overreact," Kanye drops a long, extended rhyme chain of multiple syllables that could be found in the work of even the most complicated rappers in the genre.

So far, we've identified a few elements of Kanye's rapping style: humor, storytelling, and rhyming, to a certain extent. Unfortunately, they also have little to do with what this whole book has been establishing as constituting a fundamental aspects of the rapping idiom's identity. Those three aspects of rap just listed, even if they're as impressive as could possibly be, simply have little to do with the strictly musical aspects of rapping. Long rhymes matter in this book, but only insofar as they inform the musical rhythms of the rapper's melody.

When the rap is judged on its musical aspects—his manipulation of pitch, his shaping of melodic contour, his rap's interaction with the harmony behind him, how much groove the vocals have, how well he plays with the listener's expectation—then Kanye's melodies turn out to be of a very standard nature. Most of his melodic phrases last for an even number of beats, and most of them start and end exactly where the bar lines behind him start and end. Furthermore, most of his songs are in an extremely straightforward verse-chorus form. After his early career, he seems to largely resist free-structures, although his work on *My Beautiful Dark Twisted Fantasy* is an exception. Even there, though, the extended structures, which last for at least six minutes on average during each track, are simply caused by the accompaniment, and not by the rap. That is, they might be made of extended instrumental solos, rather than an integration of the freestyle and verse-chorus form.

After the wonderful creativity and innovation that's found on his early mixtape series, such as his false entrance at 2:11 from the same "Overreact" song, most of his song structures fit into a predictable mould. Contrast this with the artistic explorations of a fellow rapper-producer, Wyclef Jean, who has been analyzed and discussed within this current work.

It must be said: despite these prior conclusions, Kanye West is, nevertheless, one of the most talented, greatest, and important rap artists of all time, if only for the effect he had on the business side of the industry. Many of his musical arrangements would themselves take up most of the spots available on any corresponding top-ten, or even top-twenty, list. However, his artistic innovations remain restricted to those production considerations, and not his melodic creations.

Kendrick Lamar

Kendrick Lamar's inclusion here might be greeted with skepticism by some. This is not due to any disbelief on detractors part, but simply because, comparatively, Kendrick Lamar has simply not released as much material as the other rappers included herein by the time of this book's writing. Black Thought has released eleven albums with The Roots. Eminem himself has eight studio albums. André 3000 has six albums with OutKast; Nas has a full ten studio albums; 2pac has eleven studio albums. Thus, it seems that it would have to take a prodigious talent to make this list having released only one or two major albums. Kendrick Lamar now, and, later on, Notorious B.I.G., are just those types of talents.

Kendrick Lamar's critical acclamation could have been established by only four songs: "m.A.A.d city," "Backseat Freestyle," "Rigamortus," and "King Kunta." As has already been detailed in this book, each one of this song's documents Kendrick Lamar's methodical exploration of a separate musical aspect. "m.A.A.d city" displays Kendrick's ability to link fractured, complex subdivisions together inside of a single melody that's been prepared by an unexpectedly-delayed appearance. "Backseat Freestyle" is a showcase for Kendrick's timbral flexibility and manipulation of the listener's perception of melody, as well as elided song structures. "Rigamortus" is proof of his heightened instrumentalism, as he delivers a large number of notes within very small musical windows. It equally shines a spotlight on his ability to develop a theme through variation, preparation, repetition, and an augmentation of thematic density. "King Kunta" is evidence for his ability to unbalance his melodic phrasing structure in the shape of intricate structures that are as unexpected as they are tantalizing.

Kendrick, to his credit, makes use of all of these musical techniques, which are so essential in updating and renewing musical material and songs for a listener, play after play. Because of this, despite his comparatively small output, Kendrick deserves a prominent place in the structure of this chapter.

André 3000

All of these rappers are, of course, highly skilled. However, the amount to which they are enjoyed by individual fans is bound, of course, to change, based on personal and individual preferences. Because of the inaccessibility of his complex syntax, as well as his wonderfully stubborn refusal to bow to generic norms, André 3000's oeuvre might constitute some of the most impenetrable work that is widely consumed in rap.

For example, he frequently inverts the normal subject-verb order of spoken English, and invents new words that have no identifiable meaning outside of their own local situation. He is given to stream-of-consciousness arrangements of grammar, and does not think it inartistic or unseemly to combine grotesquely juxtaposed metaphors and references, such as. Moreover, his vocabulary is highly dense, and frequently requires the use of a dictionary or, at the very least, a parsing of context. None of these are, at all, drawbacks in his rap. Instead, they all add up to a wonderfully unique type of rap that is still fairly accessible, if one is willing to make an effort in exploration and, thus, to get more enjoyment out of it than they would otherwise.

In fact, it is he who most closely approaches Notorious B.I.G.'s easy dexterity in either poetic line or musical line. However, 3000's style is most digestible when in the context of the more easily intelligible poetry of his partner in crime Big Boi, as on the entire album *Aquemini*. André 3000's rap also contains many examples of the two obvious benchmarks for inclusion as a technically complex rapper: the ability to extend their melodic phrases in intricate ways across the bar line, as well as the use of metric transference.

More than any other rapper here, with the possible exception of Pharoahe Monch, 3000's rhythms come across as particularly angular. His respect for the rules of syntax and grammar, as on the song "Aquemini," is oftentimes mere vocal lip service, as was mentioned before. From one point of view, this bespeaks a delightful lack of respect for the allegedly inarguable boundaries of an art form. From others, this is the essence of innovation: an ability to hit an artistic target that no one else even sees. Recognizing this difference in tastes, he should still easily make the list of any top-ten compilation of rappers.

Pharoahe Monch

Because of the two's similarity in their united variety, complex technique, and purposeful inaccessibility, Pharoahe Monch is of a pair with

André 3000. This vocalist's jazz influences, however, are even stronger and more radical than André 3000's ear. On any given Pharoahe Monch song, the listener is likely to be treated to something that, quite simply, they have never heard before. This is true of songs like "Intro," or even "Body Baby," where Monch simultaneously combines a timbral imitation of Elvis Presley, a structural fadeout, a 12/8 meter, and a splitting of the traditional jazz shuffle feel into noctuplets, rather triplets. Pharoahe Monch's extended tracks, such as "Trilogy" and its tripartite A-B-C structure, always manage to carry along the listener's interest, even across its seven minutes of length. Just like many of the other rappers here, such as Talib Kweli or Jean Grae, the rap genre as a whole can contribute more towards listener's enjoyment if more of the music of Pharoahe Monch becomes more widely known.

Because of all this, Pharoahe Monch's place within rap should be quite secure. Just like Lauryn Hill, a strictly-musical rendering of his voice would lose none of its appeal, although what would be lost is his incisive musical commentary. Due to his penchant for thinking on grand scales, just like Eminem, in his own concept albums, Pharoahe Monch has a musicianship in rap that is equaled by few others.

Black Thought

Even though he is the lead vocalist for the house band of one of the most popular television shows in the world, Black Thought continues to be underrated and underappreciated. Someone of his talent is always likely to be. This might be the result of the fact that the rap aspects he possesses such a knack for are not always immediately apparent on first listen.

It is quite easy to pay attention to, and appreciate, a finely-told rap story, or a well-delivered rap joke. This is due to the fact that semantic information is communicated and proliferated more widely in a manner that is much more fluid than the manner in which musical or rhythmic information is communicated and proliferated. To an extent that is not always true for other rappers, a listener might almost have to be an educated musician in order to appreciate the depth of the musical thinking behind Black Thought's melodies.

In the first place, Black Thought is incredibly versatile, as this book's rhythm chapter detailed. As on "Boom!" or the song "Here I Come," Thought is able to rap in a wide range of subdivisions, over a wide range of tempos, over a wide range of timbres and generic feels. This necessitates that listeners know almost his entire body of work, before they truly begin to understand his work.

Notorious B.I.G.

Notorious' specific musical expertise is somewhat ineffable. It might be able to be objectively established, but might still rely on qualitative statements of hyperbole and embellishment. Like nowhere else, exaggeration might actually be perfectly accurate in this case.

Mos Def has referred to Notorious B.I.G. as the "mathematician of flow," and this particular honorific, with its connotations of symmetry, balance, proportion, and geometry, could not be more fitting. The second verse of "Kick in the Door" deserves special mention, but his "Hypnotize" is the rare song that is as much a masterpiece as it is a smash hit. Biggie's skillful subversion of prosodic accent, which he uses to craft heretofore unheard-of rhythmic phrases, allows him to shift the boundaries of music in ways that many listeners aren't even aware of. The ingenuity of his musical phrasings would be right at home in any instrumental jazz horn solo.

The important difference between André 3000 and Notorious B.I.G. is that the former ignores the conventions of the human speaking voice when he raps, such as when he takes unnaturally long breaks between sentences. There is none of these kinds of unnatural lapses when Notorious B.I.G. flows. It is not that one is better than the other; it is just that the two approaches to rupture and disruption in melody have as their departure points two quite different assumptions.

In his own right, Notorious B.I.G. knows how to place accents in a sentence so that disruptive changes in intonation, such as a definitive downturn when a sentence hasn't ended, doesn't occur. When combined his rich, deep, bass vocal register, B.I.G.'s melodies, whether on "Hypnotize" or "Mo' Money Mo' Problems," are almost impossibly lyrical and smooth. For being the first to introduce into rap melodies many of the forthcoming norms, such as unbalanced melodic structures that do not align with metric structure, Notorious B.I.G.'s position within the genre is not only justified, but unquestionable.

Eminem

Similar to Kanye West, most of the public attention and acclaim for the rap of Eminem falls on his rhyming or poetic abilities. However, his strictly musical capabilities are no less impressive. In the large group of twenty-two songs he's made in this book that have been mentioned so far, he has included an example of many different kinds of melodic and rhythmic phenomena. "Guilty Conscience" and "Beautiful" were both noted for the ways they subvert and extend the typical pop song form. His multiple "Paul" skits were all remarked upon for creating a skit that spans not just albums, but years.

In the domain of rhythm, Eminem is no less varied and diverse. In his presto rhythms from "Rap God," or his through-composed verses from "Encore (Curtains Down)," Eminem is always marrying an adroit poetic technique with musical thinking that is no less texturized.

Those same presto rhythms also displayed Eminem's highly-developed rap instrumentalism. Only someone with good breath control, stamina, and articulation could fire off those incredibly fast raps at the end of "Rap God." In this way, Eminem's treatment of rap tends to be thorough and encyclopedic. In contrast to other rappers, he is not only interested in defining a unique, identifiable style on which he can build. Instead, he is mainly focused on pushing rap to its breaking limits, whether that's testing the physiological limits of quick vocal articulation, or expanding its sound world to encompass different genres, like country. Consequently, Eminem might not just be the best rapper ever; he might also be its best artistic ambassador.

Jean Grae

While the poetic capabilities of Kanye West or 2Pac might overwhelm.

What is most titillating about this fact is that Jean Grae herself, whether in interviews or rap melodies, actually refers to the technical details of her melodic structures. She refers to through-composition, triplets, pedal point pitches, and more in her lyrics. Just like with Lauryn Hill, we see not only artistic, but logistical, evidence for this kind of highly-developed musicianship. Both of Jean Grae's parents were well-known South African jazz performers who made sure that their children were deeply educated in all kinds of music, and not just Jean Grae's desired rap idiom.

Perhaps as a result of this cosmopolitan exposure to the entire musical world at a young age, Jean Grae is aware of the musical approaches available to rappers, to an extent not often reflected or recognized in the work of others. Even when Jean Grae is quiet does it speak volumes; her lack of sprechstimme ad libs on her song "Style Wars" is a perfect, eerie support for the broken grammatical syntax and inhumanly long pauses that dominate her melodic delivery on this minor-key song. On another song, she semantically acknowledges in her rap, rather than musically, that she prefers through-composed phrases, rather than repeated motives or gestures.

In addition to always beginning many of her raps with a play on her name, she is known by her fans for her intricate and extended ad libs, which often comprise stories in themselves. She has even confirmed, in published interviews, that she might spend more time writing than her raps themselves.

In this manner, it appears that Jean Grae is so highly conscious of her available compositional tools that she has transformed her ad libs into constituting true musical topics. By normalizing their use and appearance across a body of work that spans decades, these musical phenomena can tell their own story in their arrangement and succession of ideas, just as the purely musical narratives of dance schema do in some common practice period pieces.

At the end of it all, Jean Grae's rap is some of the most melodious that has ever been composed. And, because she is very likely the artist who is least well-known in this chapter, it would most certainly behoove rap fans everywhere if her critical and popular platform were expanded.

Nas

As a rapping musician, Nas is the thinking man's technician. His tools and techniques, even when restricted to a few heightened examples like "Don't Get Carried Away," are always of a quite complicated nature. He takes unbalanced melodic phrasings and converts them into polyrhythms, and takes complex subdivisions and turns them into expressive microtimings. Similar to Eminem, Nas, at times, can seen interested in rap as a primarily musical art form. No doubt, his poetic and storytelling capabilities deserve equal recognition, such as on his song "I Can." However, without rappers like Nas and their complex compositional techniques, analytical studies on this genre's melodies would likely be shorter in length.

Much of Nas' melody display a level of detail that is almost obsessive. Just like the best work of the revered classical musical composers, not a single note of his is ever out of place, and a line or syllable is never a throwaway.

Every syllable serves a purpose—whether in speeding up the rhythmic pacing, setting up the comedic timing of a punch line's delivery, etc.—which is unfailingly delivered in the verse's final couplet.

Truly, Nas is one of the few rappers that would have flourished in any musical genre, with any musical training. His manipulation of expectation on songs like "Don't Get Carried Away," or "Represent," display such an understanding of music's dual temporal–sonic metaphysical nature that they would be right at home in jazz, blues, rock, electronica, or classical. Because of this, rap fans everywhere should be thankful that it did not take Nas long to show up on the scene with his innate artistic understandings.

Talib Kweli

More than any other rapper here, Talib Kweli is possibly the single artist who makes the widest, deepest, and most frequent use of the musical techniques that are covered herein. His raps sketch out the territory of his entire vocal idiom, from rhythm, to melody, to any of the other fundamental aspects of music that headline this title's chapters. One almost sees the gears in his musical mind churning and turning on songs like "Joy," "Re:DeFinition," or "Twice Inna Lifetime." He handles the rap line with such care that every bar is always imbued with an object of focus that is thoroughly gripping. It could be his penchant to purposefully get ahead of the beat by cramming lots of syllables into an impossibly small amount of musical space, or it could be his penchant for catching the listener equally off-guard by suddenly returning to the more standardized 1-bar, even-numbered-beat flow of the genre.

In any event, the evidence is clear that Kweli is always interested in moving the genre forward. This occurs not only through his incorporation of complex musical techniques, but through his expansions of the palette of sound qualities and timbres that can be comfortably assimilated into rap songs as well. When coupled his support and grooming of the younger generation of rappers, such as The Underachievers or NIKO IS, Talib Kweli turns out to be a true rap statesman.

MF DOOM

MF DOOM constitutes yet another singular example within the rap genre. This is because he takes as his starting point an assumption that few other rappers, with the possible exception of Aesop Rock, ever come close to: the assumption that his rap must make grammatical, but never semantic, meaning. That is, he will not break the hierarchical rules of language; his subjects will have predicates, his pronouns will have antecedents, and so on. However, those subjects, predicates, pronouns, and antecedents will rarely, if ever, unfurl a succession of ideas in the manner of a straightforward story or narrative.

In this way, his rap is rather akin to the surreal movie of artists like Luis Bunuel in the early 1900s. The sequence of events make sense in themselves, but are in no way dramatically connected to each other through their characters or action, as in "The Andalusian Dog" of 1929, by Bunuel and Salvador Dali. The unfortunate thing, though, is that MF DOOM seems to have taken this artistic leap of faith, and then left it at that. For example, he seems not to have realized that an avoidance of overbearing dictates of semantic meaning in art can free him up to whole new palettes of subdivisional rhythms, or even tempos.

In any event, most listeners, on first listen, will be floored by MF DOOM's spastic explosion of logorrhea and dense verbiage. After this bump has worn off, though, what remains is still very similar to that which can be hear din other rappers: long rhymes, square melodic structures, and verse–form choruses. The result is that, although he is often hailed as being one of the greatest rappers ever, the truth might be better reached when he is called one of the most unique rappers instead. In this way, he is almost like a rap philosopher, similar to the role John Cage played in experimental music of the 20th century. Many of Cage's works, such as his prepared piano, or years-long pieces, were important not in themselves, but for what they lead to. They challenged long-held assumptions about what art could be; they charted the way, without ever getting there.

In a similar way, it might be left to future generations of rappers in order to make good on the promises that MF DOOM has made, but has yet to keep.

Mos Def

Mos Def, just like Kanye West or 2Pac, is likewise a rapper who is listened to more for his poetic abilities, rather than his musical abilities. That is not to say that the latter is of an inferior type; it is just that the former is of such a superior kind. Whether it was the decrying of petty feuds on "What's Beef," or the social commentary of "Mathematics," Mos

Def is a rapper who can always be counted on to write songs that matter, and to write songs that deliver messages which listeners need to hear. For all of these reasons, the presence of Mos Def in any kind of discussion on rap should never be lamented or regretted; he makes any conversation much more serious, and that is a good thing, which cannot be said of a majority of rappers.

Mos Def's utilization of a generically standard melody belies his truly mellifluous timbre, which might be the most recognizable within the whole genre. That is saying something, for a genre within which popularity is handed out based on, pretty much, who has the most pleasant voice. As a result of his combination of generic standards with widespread critical and popular acclaim, Mos Def is proof of the ultimate dominance of timbre in the reception of rappers. That is, it must be noted that, even though a full 56 rappers have been examined within this book, they still only represent an exclusive brotherhood and sisterhood. Most rappers do not have a single song that is neither a freestyle, nor a verse–chorus form, for example. What with its global popularity, and its overriding generic standards, an explanation for rap's ubiquity must then be supplied. This can be found in the form of detailed, texturized, versatile, and varied vocal timbres within the genre.

In classical music, the ideal vocal delivery is communally and universally honed towards the achievement of an optimized, single aesthetic. In rap, this focus on a standardized tone does not exist. Instead, each rapper is praised for the uniqueness of their voice, and few people's voices are as unique as Mos Def. Because of this, Mos Def is indirectly proof for the fact that, in rap at least, an ability to deliver a minimum of rhymes in time to a beat, coupled with a pleasing vocal timbre, is all the criteria sufficiently required for popularity, if not, necessarily, artistic greatness.

2Pac

Much like Kanye West, the focus in 2Pac's rap is pre-eminently on the storytelling and the poetry. His standard melody does not often shift far beyond the generic norms of melody either, although his frantic triplets and careful rhythmic pacing on "Hail Mary" are an exception to this. This is not to say that 2Pac is a worse rapper than the other ones included herein who are receiving more attention for their melodic natures. It is simply to say that his best skills are on full display in another aspects of rap, just like Kanye West.

Those other aspects, however, are not, by any stretch, of no consequence in the rap genre. It is often helpful to parse that larger conversation about the greatest rapper ever, no matter their particular focus, into three separate discussions of their storytelling abilities, their comedic abilities, and their musical abilities. An exemplar of storytelling prowess would be someone like 2Pac, while exemplars of the comedic and musical expertise would be Kanye West and Eminem, respectively. With these three working together in tandem, most roles and responsibilities of the typical rapper can thus be covered in-depth. With designations in those three areas having been assigned, the discussions can then more empirically be combined to come to a larger decision.

In the storytelling arena, 2Pac's presence is likely to dominate. A starter list for the greatest stories ever told within the genre of rap would very likely have to account for these seven 2Pac songs, at least: "Brenda's Got a Baby," "Changes," "How Long Will They Mourn Me," "Unconditional Love," "Dear Mama," "Hit 'Em Up," "Life Goes On." Similar to the citations Bob Dylan received from the Nobel committee for his award, 2Pac's stories are timeless and universal. Whether it is the deep personal loss in "Brenda's Got a Baby," or a discussion of the death wish in "Dear Mama," or a confrontation with mortality in "How Long Will They Mourn Me," 2Pac's stories can be understood by anyone, from any period of time. They are direct, and are not heard by his listener's ears, but heard by his listener's hearts.

For all this, then, as well as what his raps would eventually inspire in the work of Kendrick Lamar and others, 2Pac's position on a list of the greatest rappers ever, no matter the rubric or standards, is very likely to be quite assured.

Lil Wayne

For all of the recent bewailing over his supposed decline in quality, it cannot be denied that Lil Wayne has left his fans an early body of work that is deep, varied, and engaging. Whether it's by means of his through-composed, call-and-response dialogue on "Ridin'," or his intricate rhyme-chaining across phrases on "Walk In," it cannot be denied that Lil Wayne understands rap.

That song "Ridin'" could, in itself, be a full chapter within a book. In a manner reminiscent of Wyclef Jean's own subversion of the verse–chorus structure that was detailed in this book's section on "80 Bars," "Ridin'" subverts the typical structure of a rap song's chorus. In this Hot Boys' song from 1999, Lil Wayne combines with fellow Southern rapper Juvenile to craft a series of choruses that are all subtly differentiated from each other. Lil Wayne accomplishes this through musical imitation, echoing, and canon.

Even his own idiosyncratic performance practices arguably had an effect on this genre's commercial, professional, and artistic behavior. As Shea Serrano wrote in his 2016 title "The Rap Yearbook," Lil Wayne's 2008 track "A Milli" showed that writing the type of free and radical melody typically heard on a rap mixtape could pay off with equal dividends on an album. The rhythms of Lil Wayne on "A Milli" are positively uncontrollable, and this melodic anarchy and independence would go on to filter down over the years to the artists he would influence.

Based on all of these positive contributions, perhaps observers should be thankful for what they have gotten from Lil Wayne, rather than pining after that which he never promised them.

Wyclef Jean

Wyclef Jean has had seven different songs mentioned and analyzed by name within this book. The series of song's in this book's chapter on structure and performance practice, including "Oh What a Night," "Trying to Stay Alive," and "No Woman No Cry" catalogued his ability to seamlessly blend timbres that are traditionally unrelated into rap, such as those of disco, or folk's acoustic instrumentation. Coupled with this was his adept ear for integration the generic traditions of the freestyle and the verse-chorus form into each other.

As a result, Wyclef Jean's position among the true greats of the rap genre is due, in large part, to his refusal to separate the responsibilities and musical jobs of the producer from the responsibilities and musical jobs of the rapper. Many other artists, because they either only rap or only produce, but never fulfill both functions, do not have this luxury. To be sure, there is a long and strong tradition of rapper-producers in the genre, such as Dr. Dre, Evidence, and Kanye West. However, such artists do not typically receive equal popular and critical acclaim for both their rap and their production. For example, Dr. Dre has been giving his rap composition duties to ghostwriters since his 1999 album *2001*, while Evidence's reach with his excellent group Dilated Peoples is more modest than Wyclef's own.

As a result, Wyclef is in an enviable position, of his own making, to survey and chart out new artistic territories in rap. Although many people know his name, that recognition might be the result of endeavors outside of rap, such as his public romantic relationship with Lauryn Hill, his run for the presidency of Haiti, his samba collaboration with Shakira called "Hips Don't Lie," his charitable foundation Yélé, or his public endorsement deals, such as one with Pepsi. Accordingly, the analysis of his seven different songs might not make this rapper-producer more well-known, but only better known. As long as more artistic praise keeps coming to him, as in the form of Young Thug's dedication of a song from his 2016 album *No My Name Is Jeffrey* to his "idol," then it is likely guaranteed that Wyclef Jean's inclusion in a discussion of the greatest rappers will one day no longer seem abnormal to some. Wyclef Jean's structural innovations, when taken together with his timbral expansion, surely demands this.

Lauryn Hill

Lauryn Hill is another rapper included in this chapter who might not show up on a great number of lists of the best rappers ever. Although she also has an amount of published rapping that is more comparable to Kendrick Lamar's own smaller amount than the lengthy corpus of someone like 2Pac, she has not, for whatever reason, received the same amount of attention and acclaim. This might have something to do with her having recently turned to a style that incorporates more pure singing lately, as on *Lauryn Hill Unplugged*, or in her comeback *Khulami Phase* album. Additionally, the parts that misogyny and sexual objectification play in the modern rap industry can also not be ignored in her failure to receive all of the acclaim she is due, which is a great deal. However, rather than focus on the negative results of these obstacles to her reception, it would do well to take these findings as a message to keep fighting for recognition of musical greatness, wherever it is found.

Whether it is on her 1999 solo album *The Miseducation of Lauryn Hill*, or either of the albums she released with certain songs by some of the artists in this chapter fall flat, either because they are bereft of interesting melody, or focus too much on a non-musical aspect of rap, like comedy. However, all of Lauryn Hill's raps are always completely perfect, in musical terms. This could, perhaps, be a result of her dual training as both a singer and a rapper. Whatever the reason, however, it always has the consequence of engaging raps that are continuously manipulating expectation, incorporating complex compositional techniques, and keeping the listener's ears floored.

On "How Many Mics," she is the first rapper to ever truly merge equal parts singing with equal parts rapping together into a single, balanced style, that did not focus on one style while merely incorporating the other. On that second track from the Fugees' *The Score* album, she actually harmonizes her non-scalar melody in thirds at the end of every line. Some singer-rappers, such as Drake, either do one or the other at any given moment; other singer-rappers, like Young Thug, clearly focus on rapping more than singing; and still others, such as Frank Ocean, are clearly singers first. Even rappers like Lil Wayne or T-Pain, who arguably helped make singing a standard in rap songs nowadays, relied on AutoTune in order to support their pitch melodies.

None of this is true for Lauryn, who is both fully a singer and fully a rapper, at all times on her tracks. On "Ready or Not," from the same album as "How Many Mics," she does more than carry the chorus with her divine singing. She also lays down a rap that is blissful in its consistent inconsistency, particularly in how she is always varying just how far behind the metric pulse she is placing her microtimed accents. On "Desperadoes," she even displays a fine timbral flexibility, when she modulates her rich contralto to emulate the lower, harsher delivery of her rapping partner Rah Digga.

Some rappers start off with lots of potential, and never make good on it. Lauryn Hill is not such a case. In fact, she is the complete opposite. If anything, she is the one who has composed the rap that is the most musical and melodic. This is so to the point that, if her raps were ever isolated and performed freely in an instrumental, nonverbal context, their emotive impact would not have weakened, even by a bit.

Busta Rhymes

Along with Wyclef Jean and some other rappers in this chapter, the reputation of Busta Rhymes likewise needs to be rethought in the current climate of rap. In his early work with A Tribe Called Quest, Busta Rhymes was clearly in the forefront of innovation in the genre. He accomplished this by always treating his rap as a musical phenomenon first, and a poetic phenomenon second.

His verse on 1991's "Scenario," with A Tribe Called Quest, is well-known, both inside and outside the rap community. However, it has no long rhymes, it did not become super popular at the time of its release, and it does not tell a heart-wrenching poetic story. When all of the usual means by which a rap is judged are seen to not apply in the case of Busta's verse on "Scenario," then the question is about what makes this verse so great.

To be sure, that problem can be resolved by considering Busta's rap on this song as a purely musical phenomenon. Obviously, rap had always been music, and rappers had focused on its musical nature to greater and lesser degrees for centuries. Even the call-and-response dialogues of Run-D.M.C. predate the lyricist at hand now, having appeared at their apex on 1986's *Raisin' Hell*.

However, Busta's music moved to a place that Run-D.M.C.'s didn't when he created enough interest in his rap melody on his own, without the help of a partner to add timbral and rhythmic diversity to the mix by their very presence. On "Scenario," Busta Rhymes constantly repeats his own words, and his words rely heavily on onomatopoeia. Furthermore, his poetry is made up of all brags and boasts. What this does is shift the listener's attention from his semantic meaning, to his musical meaning.

The revealed song is thus a complex web of incredibly syncopated rhythms, and cleverly-designed rhythmic lapses. Busta was acutely aware of the extent to which the rhythms of everyday speech are an a priori constraint on the palette of rhythms available to the rapper. For example, rappers are mostly prevented from using longer rhythmic durations like half notes and quarter notes, because that is not how the people whose everyday speech they must inherently emulate normally exchange information.

Busta's innovation, then, was to undermine the listener's perception of his rap as constituting little more than a heightened, stylized form of speech. He did this, paradoxically, by thus communicating a minimum of semantic information, but rather sonic and timbral information, by means of the aforementioned repetition, onomatopoeia, etc.

This highlighting of rap's musical nature is not restricted to the early part of Busta Rhymes' oeuvre, either. His songs "Holla," "Don't Get Carried Away," and "Break Ya Neck" all display the same kind of melodic concerns, in their own unique ways. As has already been detailed herein, "Don't Get Carried Away" take the repeated rhythmic gesture to intra-verse heights, while "Break Ya Neck" is a show of every kind of physiological basis for tight rap instrumentalism, such as breath control. "Holla," meanwhile, shows off Busta's ability to craft an extended rap with rhythms that are unpredictable, and yet still compelling and traceable.

For all of these reasons, Busta Rhymes should likewise be in any discussion of the greatest rapping-musicians ever. Although the place that is currently accorded to him is already quite high, it should be even higher.

Jay-Z

Jay-Z's rap is an interesting case in melodic studies, because he apparently seems to have purposefully dumbed-down his melody, in order to become more popular. At least, this is exactly what he himself declares on his 2004 song "Moment of Clarity."

When a rapper publicly proclaims that he lowered his art in order to make more money, and seems proud to have done so, then the scholar who loves that art form just as much is caught in a bit of a bind. Should they accurately report their findings, even though doing so might commodify and disrespect the art form? Or should they possibly distort the historical record, in an attempt to do what's truly best for the genre? Perhaps these choices are not as mutually exclusive as they've been presented here, but nonetheless, this still might be the catch-22 in broad, general outlines. Indeed, many classical music commentators are caught in a similar dilemma, having to make such calls on artists who frequently lived in times that were rife with anti–Semitism, homophobia, misogyny, and other societal ills.

Such a discussion must still begin the facts, as it would with any other rapper. Jay-Z, in his own right, certainly possesses a keen musical intellect. He is just as apt to manipulate the amount of rhythmic trailing behind his beats in a manner that is just as extreme as even the best ambassadors of the genre, like Lauryn Hill or Talib Kweli, who actually himself cleverly answers Jay-Z's line by quoting and reversing his forebear's conclusions. An example of that can be found his 2004 song "Dirt Off Your Shoulders." Additionally, Jay-Z also shows a predilection for unbalanced musical phrasing that crafts dramatic and structural climaxes, as on the beginning of "Jigga That Nigga."

With his musical skill having been established, the original decision now remains: what is a historical commentator to say? For now, a straightforward answer to such a question will be declined. At the moment, it might just do well to note that the same debate between good people and good artists goes on in rap, as well as other types of music. In any event, Jay-Z's recent musical work, such as on his *Kingdom Come* or *Magna Carta … Holy Grail* album, is of a lesser caliber. To this, of course, he would reply that, of course it is! He planned it out that way, so that his lowest common denominator could have the widest possible impact. To be sure, that artistic-professional plan has paid off in spades. Indeed, Jay-Z's audience is now in the million, rather than his initial thousands, and his importance for the several generations of listeners that came of age after his emergence has been established by means of collaborations with younger artists like Kanye West.

Summary

Rap's approach to greatness is a fickle one, and deserves a deeper discussion. Like most debates of this nature, it depends not on a discussion of what musician is great, but what greatness actually consists of. In this book's particular case, greatness depends on the appearance or absence of musicality, rhythm, and melody inside of a lyricist's rap.

In more general terms, though, the biggest rap fans will basically look for the rappers that they consider to be the greatness as being capable of doing many things, outside of the strictly musical realm. That is, the greatest rapper will be every to tell an engaging story; they will be able to deliver a funny joke; they will sound fully convincing; they will have a backstory or origin history that is relatable, and that gives translatable meaning to their current drama; they will never fail to miss a juicy pun or double-entendre; they will satirize the establishment as caustically as the great parodists, while retaining the gripping imagery of the Symbolists, while cataloguing history like the belles-lettrists.

Basically, the greatest rapper will be the greatest at everything. Discussions of the greatest sports stars ever might come down to gaudier stats, or a great number of championships, but in rap, the typical listener will always want the best of both worlds.

Epilogue

The main body of this book consisted of a quantitative and qualitative dissection of rap along the lines of the most fundamental, basic aspects of music, which are transferrable and identifiable in any genre. These primordial aspects of rap music, locatable in any genre and geographical tradition, consisted of rhythm, melody, motivic development, structure, performance practice, texture, orchestration, instrumentalism, and greatness. What was found is a modern vocal idiom that is developed, sophisticated, and complex in its adroit synthesis of radical departures in the most integral aspects of music from a wide variety of sources, influences, and traditions. With this corpus-based, empirical survey having been undertaken and affirmatively terminated, the question is what should be done with that information.

As was outlined in the introduction, the hope is certainly that this purposeful identification of rap with other musics in the generalities, if not the specifics, will lead to a wider appreciation of this genre's artistry. As was also elucidated previous, this is no low-stakes battle for scholarly recognition, or generic bragging rights. Due to the rap genre's close identification with the minority community of America in both its audience and creators, widespread opinions on rap are never relegated or confined to the level of pure music itself, even if such genres can be constructively examined as such in the first place.

Instead, scholarly consensus, whose conclusions underpin many issues in the ongoing culture wars, is always used, tacitly or not, for the purposes of endorsing or refuting counterculture or African–American art forms. As a result, the next thing to be done is to keep this conversation going. Indeed, multiple musical scholars were contacted during the course of this book's writing for the purposes of penning a rebuttal to be included herein, but, unfortunately, could not be included. The ability of musics like rap to improve the world is not aided by agreeing with itself. Instead, it must continue to be challenged from the outside. This must be done so that the genre can evolve and transform in a manner that will help it overcome the real, actual problems that this author believes continue to plague his most beloved art form.

While lamentations of rap music's lack of musicality, musicianship, or melodiousness were found to have been made in earnest error, this does not mean that rap is perfect. Indeed, despite an increasing amount of recognition of the existence of misogyny or homophobia within rap, these issues still have yet to be confronted head on by rap fans and rap artists themselves. Despite the release of accepting songs like "Same Love" by Macklemore in 2012, and the justified backlash against a Rick Ross lyric from his verse on a 2013 track "U.O.E.N.O." that seemed to revel in date rape, rap music still has much work to do. The hope here, then, is that authors like this one can stop spending their time and energy in refuting straw man arguments, and turn their attention to the truly important problems.

More must be written, and more rap must be made. To do otherwise would be a dereliction of civic duty on the part of this genre's fans and investigators. Due to its presence in Carnegie Hall and the other most hallowed grounds of the musical kingdom that were documented in this book's introductory chapter, rap might be the most important genre in the world today. It is the single type of music that is most often heard by humans. This is a blessing and an achievement, yes, but also a responsibility to the world. Just as it has in the past—whether in defending the rights of free speech, or organizing activists for demonstrations against police brutality,[1] or calling out the federal government for ignoring the concerns of its minority communities—rap is bound to make good on that promise, and to continue to be our society's musical guardian angel.

Afterword
by Ilan Zechory

I've been a rap fanatic since I was 10 years old. Before then I listened to the music my parents played for me, mostly classic rock and folk. As I came of age, Biggie, Tupac, and Nas were each putting out the records that made them famous. My friends introduced me to rap, and I was galvanized by the instant classics of the moment.

From middle school onward, rap was ubiquitous in my life, as it is for so many kids. It was the pop music of my peers, and it was the soundtrack of my social life, of driving around. The more bars you had memorized, the more juice you had amongst your friends. Rap knowledge was social currency, but it was a fairly basic kind of knowledge that we valued; which album is better, which artist is better, what's the newest thing, do you have this CD, and so on.

When I arrived in college, everyone was sizing each other up, asking what we liked and who we liked, and more than before, perhaps owing to the "college atmosphere," I was asked *why* I liked it. I found myself surrounded by fans who, like me, had grown up memorizing the lyrics to Tupac songs, but people also had a lot to say about the music itself, and the poetry. For the first time, the idea of critically thinking about rap became part of the culture around me.

Get Rich or Die Tryin' came out early in my freshman year of college. It was this new, strange, unplaceable sound that came from New York but sounded like the South, and everyone became obsessed with talking about it and trying to understand what made it so great. There was an unspoken desire to use the same tools we were learning in school to talk about something we actually liked; we were critiquing the album in the manner of literary analysis. It was a constant dialogue about the beats, the lyrics, and the strange sound that made the album irresistible.

Afterword by Ilan Zechory

A ton of incredible rap albums came out during the period when I was in college. It was the height of the OutKast era, the beginning of Kanye, *The Black Album*, *Drop It Like It's Hot*. The first Grammy for Best Rap Song was given during my sophomore year. There was a real zeitgeist, a shifting tide toward the acceptance of rap music in popular culture. I never questioned whether rap was music, but I watched people stop asking that question.

As the story goes, Rap Genius was born in the East Village apartment I shared with my co-founder Tom. He was one of these new rap converts, having his mind blown by *Purple Haze*, but having no point of entry to understand what the album was about, or the history of the music that led Cam'ron to make it.

It's exciting to share something you love and care about with people who want to learn. It's so beautiful to me that I've been a part of creating a space for people who love something to share it with each other and to grow and learn together. My hope is that your experience with this book is similar to Tom's experience working his way through the rap canon, and that you come out on the other side with a much greater appreciation and understanding of this art form.

I know Martin because he's been an active member of the Rap Genius community since the earliest days. He saw what we were doing way before it was at the level it is now and recognized why it was important, and took the initiative to become a part of it. We all have our own reasons when we pass a pair of headphones or plug an aux cable into our phone and say, "Listen to how cool this is," but we're all motivated by the same thing, the spark of sharing something we love—"You have to hear this!"

Martin's spark is particularly exciting because, unlike me and most of my friends, he's a musician and an actual scholar. We all stand to benefit from familiarizing ourselves with Martin's method; the closer you get to art, the more angles you can appreciate it from, the deeper your love for it can be.

Ilan Zechory is the co-founder and president of the Genius project, the Internet's largest collection of song lyrics and crowdsourced musical knowledge. It began with Rap Genius, annotating hip-hop lyrics, and expanded to all genres. Genius has been profiled in The New York Times, The Wall Street Journal, The Washington Post, *and* Fast Company.

Appendix
Songs Analyzed

Afrika Bambaataa
"Planet Rock"
"Zulu Nation Throwdown"

Akon
"Holla Holla" (feat. T-Pain)

AZ and Nas and Foxy Brown
"Firm Fiasco"

Big Daddy Kane
"Wrath of Kane"

Busta Rhymes
"Break Ya Neck"
"Don't Get Carried Away"
"Match the Name with the Voice" (feat. Flipmode Squad)

Captain Murphy
"Gone Fishing" (feat. Jeremiah Jae)

Consequence
"03 Til Infinity"

DJ Honda
"Travellin' Man" (feat. Mos Def)

DMX
"Who We Be"

Dr. Dre
"Ackrite" (feat. Hittman)
"Some L.A. Niggaz" (feat. Hittman, Ms. Roq, Knoc-Turn'al, Time Bomb, Koka Kambon, Defari, MC Ren and Xzibit)

Drake
"Best I Ever Had"

El-P
"Dear Sirs"

Elzhi
"Detroit State of Mind"
"Represent"

Eminem
"Bad Guy"
"Beautiful"
"Bitch Please II" (feat. Dr. Dre, Snoop Dogg, Xzibit and Nate Dogg)
"Business"
"Encore (Curtains Down)" (feat. Dr. Dre and 50 Cent)
"Foolish Pride"
"Guilty Conscience" (feat. Dr. Dre)
"Kim"
"My Name Is"
"Never Enough" (feat. 50 Cent and Nate Dogg)
"Paul Rosenberg"
"Rap God"
"Role Model"

"The Way I Am"
"White America"
"Wicked Ways"
"Without Me"

Eminem and Paul Rosenberg
"Paul"

Eminem and Royce
"Bad Meets Evil"

Eve
"What"

50 Cent
"If I Can't"

Flobots
"Jet Pack"

The Fugees
"Fugees on the Mic (Remix)"
"Killing Me Softly"

The Game
"The City" (feat. Kendrick Lamar)
"How We Do" (feat. 50 Cent)

Hamilton
"Meet Me Inside"

Jay-Z
"Excuse Me Miss"
"U Don't Know"

Jean Grae
"A Little Story"
"Breathe Easy"
"Excuse Me Sir"
"High"
"You Don't Know"
"You Don't Want It"

Kanye West
"Black Skinhead"
"Get Em High" (feat. Talib Kweli)
"Jesus Walks"
"U Know" (feat. B-Lo, Whiteboy and John Legend)
"Who Will Survive in America"

Kendrick Lamar
"Backseat Freestyle"
"Bitch, Don't Kill My Vibe"
"Look Out for Detox"
"m.A.A.d. city" (feat. MC Eiht)
"Poetic Justice" (feat. Drake)
"Sherane A.K.A. Master Splinter's Daughter"
"Sing About Me, I'm Dying of Thirst"
"Swimming Pools (Drank)"

Kurupt
"Who Ride Wit Us"

Lauryn Hill
"Lost Ones"

Lil Wayne
"Got Money" (feat. T-Pain)

Ludacris
"Rob Quarters"

MF DOOM
"Vomitspit"

Mike Posner
"Cooler Than Me" (feat. Big Sean)

Mobb Deep
"(Just Step Prelude)"
"Shook Ones, Pt. II"

Mos Def and Talib Kweli
"Re:DeFinition"

Nas
"N.Y. State of Mind"
"Represent"

Notorious B.I.G.
"Big Poppa"
"Hypnotize"
"Kick in the Door"
"Who Shot Ya?"

OutKast
"Aquemini"
"Nathaniel"

"Return of the 'G'"
"Skew It on the Bar-B" (feat. Raekwon)
"The Whole World"(feat. Killer Mike)

Pharoahe Monch
"Intro"
"Simon Says"

The Roots
"@ 15"
"Ain't Sayin Nothin' New"
"Boom!"
"Don't Say Nuthin'"
"Here I Come"
"The Seed/Melting Pot/The Web"
"The Session (Longest Posse Cut in History)"
"Stay Cool"
"What They Do"
"Without a Doubt"

Run-D.M.C.
"Peter Piper"

Slimkid3 and DJ Nu-Mark
"Bom Bom Fiya"

Souls of Mischief
"'93 Til Infinity"

Sugarhill Gang
"Rapper's Delight"

Talib Kweli
"Joy" (feat. Mos Def)
"Rush"

A Tribe Called Quest
"Electric Relaxation"

Twista
"Adrenaline Rush"
"Slow Jamz" (feat. Kanye West and Jamie Foxx)

Waka Flocka Flame
"Karma" (feat. YG Hootie, Popa Smurf and Slim Dunkin)

Wu-Tang Clan
"Can It Be All So Simple"

Wyclef Jean
"80 Bars"
"Guantanamera" (feat. Refugee Allstars)
"Kenny Rogers—Pharoahe Monch Dub Plate"
"Knockin' on Heaven's Door"
"No Woman No Cry"
"Oh What a Night"
"Pussycat" (feat. Tom Jones)
"We Trying to Stay Alive" (feat. Refugee Allstars)
"Wish You Were Here"

Chapter Notes

Introduction

1. To see the transcription corpus in whole, see www.RapAnalysis.com. There, readers are also invited to reach out to the author with any comments, criticisms, or questions, who himself can be found at martinedwardconnor@gmail.com. Through that email address, I can also supply uncut versions of these chapters, updates on forthcoming work, and, additionally, a version of these ideas that can be consumed by those among us who cannot read music notation as well.

2. "Instrumentalism" is the term I will use to refer to the study of an individual musician's performance abilities and technique on their own specific instrument.

3. Adam Krims, *Rap Music and the Poetics of Identity* (Cambridge: Cambridge University Press, 2000), 121.

4. James Lincoln Collier, *The Reception of Jazz in America: A New View* (Brooklyn, NY: Institute for Studies in American Music, Conservatory of Music, Brooklyn College of the City University of New York, 1988), 2, 127, 3.

5. In 1989, Milt Ahlerich, an assistant deputy at the federal agency, penned a letter to N.W.A. that decried their recordings' encouragement of "violence against and disrespect for the law enforcement officer." Meanwhile, no such public outcry was nationally evinced by artistic demonstrations from white musicians that likewise question the effectiveness of police authorities, such as The Clash's 1980 "Police On My Back," or Bruce Springsteen's 1982 song "Highway Patrolman." For more information on the F.B.I. letter to N.W.A, see Suebsaeng, 2014.

6. For more, see Jeff Chang, *Can't Stop, Won't Stop: A History of the Hip-Hop Generation* (New York: St. Martin's, 2005), 22; or Bradley, DuBois, et al., *The Anthology of Rap* (New Haven: Yale University Press, 2010).

7. As the namesake of my current graduate school and first Jewish Supreme Court Justice, Louis Brandeis, wrote in 1914, "Publicity is justly commended as a remedy for social and industrial diseases. Sunlight is said to be the best of disinfectants."

8. Akeem Sule and Becky Inkster, "A Hip-hop State of Mind," *The Lancet Psychiatry* 1, no. 7 (2014): 494.

9. Christopher Hooten, "Hip-hop is the Most Listened to Genre in the World," *The Independent* (London), July 14, 2015. http://www.independent.co.uk/arts-entertainment/music/news/hip-hop-is-the-most-listened-to-genre-in-the-world-according-to-spotify-analysis-of-20-billion-10388091.html.

Chapter 1

1. Scott F. Parker, *Eminem and Rap, Poetry, Race: Essays* (Jefferson, NC: McFarland, 2014), 89–109.

2. Kyle Adams, "On The Metrical Techniques Of Flow In Rap Music," *Music Theory Online: A Journal of the Society for Music Theory*, (Oct. 2009): 120–121, accessed 2011, http://www.mtosmt.org/issues/mto.09.15.5/mto.09.15.5.adams.html.

3. Adams, in Williams, *The Cambridge Companion to Hip-Hop* (Cambridge University Press, 2015),132.
4. Indeed, even the developer of this legally-protected transcription system cannot help but eschew the periodic burdensomeness of transcribing microtimed rhythms herein, as in the section on Killer Mike.
5. Stuart Paul Duncan, "The Concept of New Complexity: Notation, Interpretation, And Analysis," *Empirical Musicology Review*, (2016): 28, accessed December 1, 2016, http://emusicology.org/article/view/4961/4496.
6. Jeff Chang, *Can't Stop, Won't Stop: A History of the Hip-Hop Generation* (New York: St. Martin's,2005), 22.
7. Ibid., 249.

Chapter 2

1. Arnold Schoenberg, *Pierrot Lunaire*, trans. Otto Erich Hartleben and Stanley Applebaum (1912), 2.
2. Boulez, 330–335. Pierre Boulez and Jean Nattiez Jacques, *Orientations* (Cambridge, MA: Harvard University Press, 1986), 330–335.
3. Philip Larkin, *All What Jazz: A Record Diary 1961–1971* (New York: Farrar, Straus, Giroux, 1985), 151.
4. The design of this chart is largely indebted to List, 9.
5. Anthony Kelley, "A Melody? Word," *The Duke Chronicle* (Durham, NC), Apr. 01, 2011.
6. Adam Krims, *Rap Music and the Poetics of Identity* (Cambridge: Cambridge University Press, 2000), 1.
7. Ibid., 49.
8. Ibid., 50.
9. Ibid.
10. Ibid.
11. Ibid., 51.
12. Ibid., 50.
13. Ibid., 51.

Chapter 4

1. Williams, *The Cambridge Companion to Hip-Hop*,134.
2. Such an instance of a change in direction is apparent in the opening section of another 2016 article by Dr. Adams, entitled "Playing with Beats and Playing with Cats: Meow The Jewels, Remixes, and Re-interpretations," for Music Theory Online, where he writes: "In a 2008 article, I gave rappers exclusive credit for any musical correspondences between beat and flow. The article painted a picture in which the beat is presented in finished form to the rapper...Although these statements may represent hip-hop practice some of the time, both Justin Williams and Noriko Manabe correctly pointed out that my conception was incomplete."
3. Possible exceptions to this uneven relationship, where the musical accompaniment instead overwhelms the rapping melody through louder dynamics, faster rhythms, etc. (or is, at the very least, just as important,) might be said to be found in the short, free interludes of The Roots, such as on 2008's "Becoming Unwritten," or 1993's "The Roots Is Comin,'" as well as the coda section of Talib Kweli's 2002 song "Joy" with Mos Def and the coda section of Kanye West's "Two Words" (featuring Mos Def.)
4. Adam Bradley, *Book of Rhymes: The Poetics of Hip Hop* (New York: Basic Civitas, 2009), 7.
5. The most immediately comparable structures within the repertoire are the thirty-two bars of Eminem's extended opening verse on his own song, called "Never Enough."
6. Robert Schumann, "Hats Off, Gentlemen, a Genius," *Piano Street*, last modified 2010, http://www.pianostreet.com/blog/files/schumann-article-on-chopin-opus-2.pdf.
7. Joel Zimmerman, "We All Hit Play," United We Fail, *Tumblr*, (June 2012).
8. Ibid.

Chapter 5

1. Available online at https://www.youtube.com/watch?v=_BrxemL1CT0.
2. Bradley, DuBois, et al, *The Anthology of Rap* (New Haven: Yale University Press, 2010), xxiii (in a foreword by Henry Louis Gates, Kr.:) "[S]ubgenres emerged out of the African American rhetorical practice of signifying...These oral poets practiced

their arts in ritual settings...sometimes engaging in verbal duels with contenders like a linguistic boxing match. These recitations were a form of artistic practice and honing, but they were also the source of great entertainment displayed before an audience with a most sophisticated ear."

3. Available at https://www.youtube.com/watch?v=4pPFt1-d9Wo.

4. Peter Kivy, *The Corded Shell: Reflections on Musical Expression* (Princeton: Princeton University Press, 1980), 6.

5. Ibid., 36. Although Kivy is here positing the ideas I'd like to cite as being those of Webb, the fact that he himself holds these ideas, if not their evidential foundation, to at least some degree is clear in the writing that follows the above: "We can, of course, reconstruct Webb's theory accordingly, to meet our needs. In fact, there is no need to do so. Such a theory already existed in Webb's own time, propounded some thirty years before by the composer and highly influential musical theory, Johann Mattheson. As I have already observed, Mattheson is generally taken to be offering nothing more than the usual arousal theory. I shall argue in the next chapter that this is a misreading of what he actually said. What we are disappointed not to find in Webb, we can find in his predecessor: namely, an elaborate iconography of musical expression...."

6. Footage of this contest available online at https://www.youtube.com/watch?v=xkN0U0BbZ6Q.

7. By no coincidence, choruses are usually referred to as "hooks" in rap, because they "hook" a listener in.

Chapter 6

1. A major exception is, of course, The Roots and their live instrumentation setup.

2. The use of the term "flow" is generally to be avoided in rap studies, as it is a concept that obfuscates more than it explains, combining as it does such unrelated notions of linguistics, musicology, physiology, emotion, and physics, all of which confuse interpretations of each other when combined so unhelpfully.

3. Twista received a Grammy nomination for "Slow Jamz" in 2005, in the category of "Best Rap/Sung Performance."

4. As can be heard at 1:46 of the video at https://www.youtube.com/watch?v=I_RBD05krfg, or at 1:38 of the video at https://www.youtube.com/watch?v=mPEwQaabo3Q.

5. Footage of this contest available online at https://www.youtube.com/watch?v=xkN0U0BbZ6Q.

Epilogue

1. In 2015, it was observed that Black Lives Matters demonstrators were observed frequently chanting lines from Kendrick Lamar's 2015 song "Alright." See Tate, 2015.

Bibliography

Adams, Kyle. "On the Metrical Techniques of Flow in Rap Music." *Music Theory Online: A Journal of the Society for Music Theory*, Oct. 2009, http://www.mtosmt.org/issues/mto.09.15.5/mto.09.15.5.adams.html. Accessed 2011.

———. "People's Instinctive Assumptions and the Paths of Narrative: A Response to Justin Williams." *Music Theory Online: A Journal of the Society for Music Theory*, June 2009, http://www.mtosmt.org/issues/mto.09.15.2/mto.09.15.2.adams.html. Accessed 2011.

———. "Playing with Beats and Playing with Cats: Meow the Jewels, Remixes, and Reinterpretations." *Music Theory Online: A Journal of the Society for Music Theory*, Sept. 2016, Accessed 2016.

Balliett, Whitney. *American Musicians: Fifty-six Portraits in Jazz*. New York: Oxford University Press, 1986.

Boulez, Pierre, and Jean Nattiez Jacques. *Orientations*. Cambridge, MA: Harvard University Press, 1986.

Bradley, Adam. *Book of Rhymes: The Poetics of Hip Hop*. New York: Basic Civitas, 2009.

———, Andrew Dubois, Henry Louis Gates, D Chuck, and Common. *The Anthology of Rap*. New Haven: Yale University Press, 2010.

Brandeis, Louis. *Other People's Money: And How the Bankers Use It*. New York: Harper's Weekly, 1914.

Chang, Jeff. *Can't Stop, Won't Stop: A History of the Hip-Hop Generation*. New York: St. Martin's, 2005.

Collier, James Lincoln. *The Reception of Jazz in America: A New View*. Brooklyn, NY: Institute for Studies in American Music, Conservatory of Music, Brooklyn College of the City University of New York, 1988.

Condit-Schultz, Nathaniel. "McFlow: A Digital Corpus of Rap Transcriptions." *Empirical Musicology Review*. 2016. http://emusicology.org/article/view/4961/4496. Accessed 1 Dec. 2016.

Day, Aidan. *Jokerman: Reading the Lyrics of Bob Dylan*. Oxford, UK: B. Blackwell, 1988.

Duncan, Stuart Paul. "The Concept of New Complexity: Notation, Interpretation, and Analysis." Diss. Cornell, 2010.

Dyson, Michael Eric. *The Michael Eric Dyson Reader*. New York: Basic Civitas, 2004.

Edwards, Paul. *How to Rap: The Art and Science of the Hip-Hop MC*. Chicago: Chicago Review, 2009.

Eliot, T. S. *The Sacred Wood: Essays on Poetry and Criticism*. London: Methuen, 1960.

Eminem, and Sacha Jenkins. *The Way I Am*. New York: Dutton, 2008.

Fausset, Richard. "Lil Boosie Murder Trial: Did His Lyrics Show an Intent to Kill?" *Los Angeles Times*. 10 May 2012, http://articles.latimes.com/2012/may/10/nation/la-na-nn-rap-lyrics-at-heart-of-murder-trial-20120510. Accessed Feb. 2014.

Finkelstein, Sidney. *Jazz: A People's Music*. New York: Citadel, 1948.
Hooten, Christopher. "Hip-hop Is the Most Listened to Genre in the World." *The Independent*. 14 July 2015. http://www.independent.co.uk/arts-entertainment/music/news/hip-hop-is-the-most-listened-to-genre-in-the-world-according-to-spotify-analysis-of-20-billion-10388091.html.
Goldstein, Joseph, and J. David Goodman. "Seeking Clues to Gangs and Crime, Detectives Monitor Internet Rap Videos." *New York Times*. 7 Jan. 2014. https://www.nytimes.com/2014/01/08/nyregion/seeking-clues-to-gangs-and-crime-detectives-monitor-internet-rap-videos.html. Accessed Feb. 2014.
Kelley, Anthony. "A Melody? Word." *The Duke Chronicle*. 01 Apr. 2011. Accessed 02 Apr. 2011.
Kivy, Peter. *The Corded Shell: Reflections on Musical Expression*. Princeton: Princeton University Press, 1980.
Krims, Adam. *Rap Music and the Poetics of Identity*. Cambridge: Cambridge University Press, 2000.
Larkin, Philip. *All What Jazz: A Record Diary 1961–1971*. New York: Farrar, Straus, Giroux, 1985.
Leonard, Neil. *Jazz and the White Americans: The Acceptance of a New Art Form*. Chicago: University of Chicago Press, 1962.
List, George. "The Boundaries of Speech and Song." *Ethnomusicology*. vol. 7, no. 1, 1963, pp. 1–16. www.jstor.org/stable/924141.
Manabe, Noriko. "The Role of the Producer in Hip-Hop: An Ethnographic and Analytical Study of Remixes." Noriko Manabe, Oxford-Princeton Conference in Music Theory, 18 Mar. 2011, http://www.norikomanabe.com/the-role-of-the-producer-in-hip-hop-an-ethnographic-and-analytical-study-of-remixes. Accessed Nov. 2016.
"Michelle Obama Hosting Vile Rapper at White House?" Fox Nation. 09 May, 2011. http://nation.foxnews.com/common/2011/05/09/michelle-obama-hosting-vile-rapper-white-house. Accessed Feb. 2014.
Nielson, Erik, and Charis E. Kubrin. "Rap Lyrics on Trial." *New York Times*. New York, 13 Jan. 2014. https://www.nytimes.com/2014/01/14/opinion/rap-lyrics-on-trial.html. Accessed on Feb. 2014.
Ohriner, Mitchell. "Metric Ambiguity and Flow in Rap Music: A Corpus-Assisted Study of Outkast's 'Mainstream' (1996)." *Empirical Musicology Review*. vol. 11, no. 2, 2016. http://emusicology.org/article/view/4896/4498. Accessed 7 Jan. 2016.
Parker, Scott F. *Eminem and Rap, Poetry, Race: Essays*. Jefferson, NC: McFarland, 2014.
Ramsey, Guthrie P. *Race Music: Black Cultures from Bebop to Hip-Hop*. Berkeley: University of California, 2003.
"Rap Genius." Genius. https://genius.com/. Accessed 2016.
Russell, Bertrand. *History of Western Philosophy*. London: Routledge, 2004.
Schoenberg, Arnold. *Pierrot Lunaire*. Translated by Otto Erich Hartleben and Stanley Applebaum, 1912.
Schumann, Robert. "Hats Off, Gentlemen, a Genius." *Piano Street*. 2010. https://www.pianostreet.com/blog/files/schumann-article-on-chopin-opus-2.pdf. Accessed 1 Jan. 2014.
Serrano, Shea, Arturo Torres, and Ice-T. *The Rap Year Book*. New York: Abrams Image, 2015.
Suebsaeng, Asawin. "The FBI Agent Who Hunted N.W.A." *The Daily Beast*. The Daily Beast Company, 14 Aug. 2015. https://www.thedailybeast.com/the-fbi-agent-who-hunted-nwa.
Sule, Akeem, and Becky Inkster. "A Hip-Hop State of Mind." The Lancet Psychiatry 1.7 (2014): 494. Web. Oct. 2016.
Tate, Greg. "How #BlackLivesMatter Changed Hip-Hop and R&B in 2015." *Rolling Stone*. Rolling Stone, 16 Dec. 2015. http://www.rollingstone.com/music/news/how-black-livesmatter-changed-hip-hop-and-r-b-in-2015-20151216?page=2. Accessed 2017.

Tommasini, Anthony. "The Greatest." *New York Times*. New York: New York Times, 22 Jan. 2011. http://www.nytimes.com/2011/01/23/arts/music/23composers.html?pagewanted=all. Accessed 1 Jan. 2015.

Wheeldon, Marianne. *Debussy's Late Style*. Bloomington: Indiana University Press, 2009.

Williams, Juan. "Songs of the Summer of 1963 ... and 2013." *Wall Street Journal* [New York City] 26 Aug. 2013. https://www.wsj.com/articles/songs-of-the-summer-of-1963-and-2013-1377559164. Accessed 23 Apr. 2014.

Williams, Justin. "Beats and Flows: A Response to Kyle Adams, 'Aspects of the Music/Text Relationship in Rap.'" Music Theory Online: A Journal of the Society for Music Theory, 2009. http://www.mtosmt.org/issues/mto.09.15.2/mto.09.15.2.williams.html. Accessed 2011.

_____. *The Cambridge Companion to Hip-Hop.* Cambridge, United Kingdom: Cambridge University Press, 2015.

Yauch, Adam. "100 Greatest Artists." *Rolling Stone*. 2 Dec. 2010. http://www.rollingstone.com/music/lists/100-greatest-artists-of-all-time-19691231/public-enemy-20110420. Accessed 2014.

Zimmerman, Joel. "We All Hit Play." United We Fail. Tumblr, June 2012. Accessed 2016.

Index

"A Milli" (Lil Wayne song) 189
accelerando 18, 115, 150, 154
accompaniment 37, 50, 52, 56–61, 78–79, 86–87, 89–95, 99, 106, 109–115, 118–119, 122, 129, 131–132, 134, 137, 139, 144–145, 148–152, 155–156, 178
"Ackrite" (Dr. Dre and Hittman song) 157–161
"Act Won (Things Fall Apart)" (The Roots song) 6
activism in rap 196
ad libs 116, 128, 161, 184
Adams, Kyle 1–5, 8, 18, 20–21
additive rhythm 59–63
"Adrenaline Rush" (Cam'ron and Twista song) 74, 169
Aesop Rock (rapper) 186
aesthetics 63, 106, 136, 140, 187
African American community and rap 5, 7, 11, 195
Afrika Bambaataa 42, 163
"Ain't Sayin Nothin' New" (The Roots song) 41
alignment: emotive and structural 156; metrical and phrasal 52, 62, 118–119; prosodic and metrical 74
Allen, Harry 6
André 3000 18, 50–59, 64, 149, 162, 180–182
Anthony Kelley 71, 74
Aquemini (OutKast album) 18, 149, 180
"Aquemini" (OutKast song) 18
aria (form) 14
arrangement 91, 110, 112, 114–116, 118, 120, 140, 142, 144–146, 157, 162, 179–180, 184
articulation 1, 20, 22, 87, 115, 166–172, 175, 183; articulation (instrumental-ism) 169–170; legato (articulation) 20; staccato (articulation) 87
As Nasty as They Wanna Be (2 Live Crew) 6
"@ 15" (The Roots song) 46, 148, 155
atonality 66, 69–70, 76
augmentation (rhythmic) 103–107, 179
authenticity 134, 141
authority 131–140
AutoTune 70–71, 191
AZ 37–39, 74–75

B-Lo (rapper) 78, 99–106
Bach, Johann Sebastian 107, 133, 160
backbeat 85–92, 98, 113, 118, 137
"Backseat Freestyle" (Kendrick Lamar song) 68, 170–172, 179
"Bad Guy" (Eminem song) 121
"Bad Meets Evil" (Eminem song) 174–175
balance (musical) 83, 98, 102, 118–119, 124, 134, 169, 182
ballad (pop song form) 71, 132
Barber, Samuel 8
Bartók, Béla 8
bass kicks 85, 113, 115, 136, 156
basso (vocal range) 171
battles 151–155, 173–174
The Beatles 65, 68–70, 72, 75, 131–132, 145
"Beautiful" (Eminem song) 128
Bee Gees (musical group) 136
Beethoven, Ludwig van 106–107, 132–133, 138–139, 160
Besides (Fugees mixtape) 136
"Best I Ever Had" (Drake song) 17, 157
Big Boi 50, 110, 149, 180
Big Daddy Kane 21, 61–63

209

Index

Big Noyd 149–150
"Big Poppa" (Notorious B.I.G. song) 146
Big Sean 53–56, 161
"Bitch, Don't Kill My Vibe" (Kendrick Lamar song) 50, 171
"Bitch Please II" (Dr. Dre and Eminem song) 127
Black Hippie (rap group) 111
"Black Skinhead" (Kanye West song) 47–50, 53–54
Black Thought 39–46, 110, 121, 148–150, 156, 181
"Blame Game" (Kanye West song) 178
Blueprint 2 (Jay-Z album) 145
blues (musical genre) 11, 56, 59, 136, 185
boasting 149, 192
Bob Dylan 65–75, 136–137, 188
Bob Marley 136
"Body Baby" (Pharoahe Monch song) 181
"Bom Bom Fiya" (Slimkid3 and DJ Nu-Mark song) 38
Boogie Down Productions 56
"Boom!" (The Roots song) 40, 181
Bootleg of the Bootleg (Jean Grae album) 145–146
Boulez, Pierre 66
Brahms, Johannes 133
"Break Ya Neck" (Busta Rhymes song) 29–30, 35, 119, 192
breath control 169–170
"Breathe Easy" (Jean Grae song) 146
"Brenda's Got a Baby" (2Pac song) 178, 188
bridge sections 108, 121, 142, 170
Britten, Benjamin 8
Broadway 52
Buñuel, Luis 186
"Business" (Eminem and Dr. Dre song) 27–30, 141
Busta Rhymes 29–31, 35–36, 38–39, 119, 122, 191–192
Byrd, Donald 129

cadence 16, 65, 72, 83–84, 149, 160
cadenza 22, 30, 57
caesura 94, 56, 155
Cage, John 106, 186
call and response 163–165
"Can It Be All So Simple" (Wu-Tang Clan song) 122
canon (musical form) 157–161, 165, 189, 198
"Can't Hold Us" (Macklemore song) 40

Can't Stop Won't Stop (Jeff Chang book) 56
a cappella 37, 46, 112–113, 115, 136, 164
Captain Murphy 51–52
Carnegie Hall 8
The Carnival (Wyclef Jean album) 136
Carter, Elliott 8
Cassidy, Aaron 22
censorship of rap 6, 9
Chambers, Joe 129
Chang, Jeff 56
"Changes" (2Pac song) 17, 188
The Chic 136
Chicken-n-Beer (Ludacris album) 122
"Children's Story" (Slick Rick song) 178
Chopin, Frédéric 138
chordophones 167, 168
chords 5, 72, 132, 136–137, 160–161, 167, 175
chorus (song section) 23, 38, 46, 69, 108, 111, 114–121, 123–128, 130, 142, 156–161
Chuck Berry 132
"The City" (Game and Kendrick Lamar song) 171
classical music 3, 8, 11–12, 14, 56, 65, 75, 79, 85, 138–140, 147–148, 161
coda (song section) 108, 121
Coleman, Ornette 8
collaborations 74, 98, 106, 111, 152, 164, 175, 190, 194
Coltrane, John 133
comedy 59, 125–126, 177, 185, 188, 190
commercialism 6, 51, 138–139, 189
commodification 193
Common (rapper) 8
community 5–6, 8, 11, 22, 49, 107, 134, 145, 147, 166, 169, 174–175, 191, 195, 198
compositional transmission 17
conjunction in structure 118
consonance 118
contour (of melody) 16, 158, 178
contralto (vocal range) 191
convention 52–53
"Cooler Than Me" (Mike Posner song) 53–56
Copland, Aaron 8
The Corded Shell (Peter Kivy book) 153
counterpoint 56 118, 171
country music 137, 183
couplet 73, 162, 185
covers (song form) 129, 131–135, 137, 140, 148

Index

Crosby, Bing 133
Crumb, George 8
Crutch of Memory (Aaron Cassidy composition) 22
culture 5, 7, 31, 54, 71, 107, 117, 127, 139, 152, 195, 197–198

dancehall music 56–57, 59
Das Racist (rap group) 109
Day, Aidan 66, 70
Daz Dillinger (Tha Dogg Pound Member) 126
"Dead Presidents" (Nas song) 135
deadmau5 (Joel Zimmerman, house producer) 141
"Dear Mama" (2Pac song) 188
"Dear Sirs" (El-P song) 51–52
"December, 1963 (Oh What a Night)" (The Four Seasons song) 137
decibels 174
declamatory speech 75
Defari (rapper) 78
delivery 19, 36, 70, 84, 93, 126, 149, 153–158, 161, 172, 174, 177, 184–185, 187, 191
Denver, John 137
"Desperadoes" (The Fugees song) 191
Detox (Dr. Dre album) 17
"Detroit State of Mind" (Elzhi song) 129–130
development (music section) 8, 14, 21, 25, 78–79, 81 83, 85, 87, 89, 91, 93, 95, 97, 99, 101, 103, 105, 107
"Devil in Her Heart" (The Beatles song) 132
Diddy (rap artist) 161–163
Dilated Peoples 189
"Dirt Off Your Shoulder" (Jay-Z song) 17, 193
disco 189
disjunction 38, 50, 90, 112, 115, 118
DJ 38, 40, 56, 129
DJ Nu-Mark 38
DJ Premier 129
DMX 78–85, 98–101, 106
D.N.A. (battle rapper) 151, 153, 154
Do You Want More?!!!??! (The Roots album) 40
Dr. Dre 35, 41, 82, 85–86, 93, 98–99, 106, 109, 119–123, 141, 157–158
The Documentary (Game album) 33
dominant chord 15, 118, 160
Don Giovanni (The Mozart opera) 138–139

"Don't Get Carried Away" (Busta Rhymes song) 30–31, 185, 192
"Don't Say Nuthin'" (The Roots song) 155–156
doubling (vocals) 156–158
downbeat 29, 36, 63, 82, 84, 96, 100–104, 112, 122–123
Drake 17, 109, 157
drama (in rap music) 90, 160, 194
drums 15, 84–85, 92, 115, 118, 137, 155–156
duodecaphony 14
duos 50, 109, 118, 164
duplet rhythms 18, 49–50, 54–55, 101–102, 156
duration 19–21, 28, 38, 58–60, 100, 105, 113
Dvořák, Antonín 8
dynamics 152–153, 173–174; dynamic control 173–174

The Ecleftic: 2 Sides II a Book (Wyclef Jean album) 137–138
"80 Bars" (Wyclef Jean song) 115–117
elaboration 146–147
Electric Light Orchestra 132
"Electric Relaxation" (A Tribe Called Quest song) 134
electronic music 131–135, 138–141, 185
Elmatic (Elzhi album) 129–130, 133, 137
Elvis Presley 181
Elzhi 128–133, 137
Eminem 11–39, 46, 60, 110–111, 119–128, 142, 145, 148, 171–184
emotion in rap music 7, 41, 110–111, 137, 141, 152–156, 172, 174, 191
emphasis (verbal) 11, 32, 66, 90, 92, 102, 148
"Encore (Curtains Down)" (Eminem song) 23–24, 26, 183
Encore (Eminem album) 23–26, 33
ensemble 53, 147
entrances (in melody) 19, 38, 118
Eric B. and Rakim 109
etymology 32, 65
Eve 59–61
Evidence (rap artist) 189
"Excuse Me Miss" (Jay-Z song) 145–146
"Excuse Me Sir" (Jean Grae song) 145–146
experimental music 45, 124, 186
exposition (song section) 36–38, 114, 117
expressionism 11, 17–19, 24–25, 47, 51,

Index

63, 74, 84, 100, 149, 151, 153, 156, 158, 165, 170–172, 184

"Family Business" (Kanye West song) 177
50 Cent (rapper) 31–39
"Firm Fiasco" (The Firm song) 37, 74
The Firm (rap group) 37, 74
"Flight Time" (Donald Byrd song) 129
Flobots 50–52
Flockaveli (Waka Flocka Flame album) 43, 164
flow 2, 4, 11, 18, 49, 54–55, 111, 121, 136, 152, 166, 169, 182, 185
folk music 189, 197
"Foolish Pride" (Eminem song) 174
"Forgot About Dre" (Dr. Dre and Eminem song) 119
form 5–6, 12–14, 20–22, 33, 50, 53, 55, 57, 63, 71, 75, 77, 79, 84, 98–99, 101–102, 110–111, 115–117, 121, 123–128, 131–132, 136, 138, 144, 150–151, 155, 157, 164, 174, 178, 180, 183–184, 186–187, 189–190, 192–193, 196, 198
The Four Seasons 136
fragmentation 74, 115, 149
Frank Ocean 191
Freddie Gibbs 109
Freddie Mercury 170
freestyle (song form) 111, 115–117, 121–125, 145, 178
The Fugees 136–137, 191
"Fugees on the Mic (Remix)" (Fugees song) 136
fugue form 165
function 15, 25, 115–116, 120, 123–124, 126–127, 135–136, 145, 147, 160
funk (musc genre) 98, 136
Fuzzy Jones 56

"The Gambler" (Kenny Rogers song) 137
Game (rapper) 33, 35, 40, 83, 157
Game Theory (The Roots album) 40
Gershwin (George and Ira) 133
"Get Em High" (Kanye West song) 110
Get Rich or Die Tryin' (50 Cent album) 197
ghostwriting 17, 189
Glass, Philip 106
"Gone Fishing" (Captain Murphy song) 51–52
good kid, m.A.A.d city (Kendrick Lamar album) 36, 170
"Got Money" (Lil Wayne song) 110

Götterdämmerung (The Wagner opera) 168
*Graduation (*Kanye West opera) 178
Grammy Awards 148, 198
Grand Wizzard Theodore 129
Grandmaster Flash and the Furious Five 73
Greenwood, Johnny 131
Grind Time (rap battle league) 154
groove 132, 136, 178
growl (vocal delivery) 153, 172
"Guantanamera" (Wyclef Jean song) 137
Guilty Conscience (Eminem song) 121–126, 183
Guinness Book of World Records 169

"Hail Mary" (2Pac song) 187
Hamilton (hip hop musical) 8, 52–53
Harburg and Arlen 71
harmony 4, 11, 71, 118, 132–139, 159–160, 178
Havoc (Mobb Deep member) 109, 117–119, 149
"Here I Come" (The Roots song) 40, 181
heterophony 147, 161–163
"Hey Mama" (Kanye West song) 178
"High" (Jean Grae song) 146
Highway 61 Revisited (Bob Dylan album) 66
"Hips Don't Lie" (Wyclef Jean and Shakira song) 190
history (musical) 8, 19, 50, 125, 129–131, 133–135, 141, 144, 162, 194, 198
"Hit 'Em Up" (2Pac song) 188
Hittman 78, 81, 92–100, 106, 157–161
"Holla" (Busta Rhymes song) 72–73, 75, 192
"Holla Holla" (T-Pain song) 72, 73, 75
homophobia 193, 196
homophony 4, 144, 147–148, 150, 155–157, 163
hook (song section) 46, 116, 115, 143, 145; false hooks (Eminem) 119–120
Hot Boys (rap group) 189
house music 141
How I Got Over (The Roots album) 40
"How Long Will They Mourn Me" (2Pac song) 188
"How Many Mics" (Fugees song) 191
"How We Do" (Game and 50 Cent song) 34–35
hypermeter 35–39, 112–124; tripartite hypermeter 38–39

Index

"Hypnotize" (Notorious B.I.G. song) 58, 161–163, 182

I Have a Dream (Dr. Martin Luther King, Jr., speech) 7
idiom 3, 6, 19, 57, 63, 69–70, 73, 75–76, 133, 137, 159, 163, 176, 178, 183, 185, 195
"If I Can't" (50 Cent song) 32–34
Illadelph Halflife (The Roots album) 6, 40
Illmatic (Nas album) 129–130
imitation (rhythmic) 63, 87, 90–91, 112, 114, 119–120, 129–130, 136, 139–140, 146, 157, 161, 165, 181, 189
improvisation 116
The Infamous (Mobb Deep album) 118
Infinite (Eminem album) 126
influences 54, 56, 59, 120, 129, 135, 138, 162, 181, 189, 195
instrumental (type of beat) 37, 116
instrumentalism (musical skill set) 166–175
instrumentation (also orchestration) 119, 144–145, 189
instruments 16, 137–138, 147, 167
intercantuality (musical intertextuality) 31–35
interludes (song form) 120–125; arrhythmic interludes 32, 120–125, 127
Internal Affairs (Pharoahe Monch album) 58
Internet 7, 151, 164, 198
interpolation 130–131, 140
intertexuality (musical) 32–35, 85
intonation 3, 14–16, 65, 67, 69–70, 73, 75, 156, 182
intro (song section) 112, 115, 122, 164
"Intro" (Pharoahe Monch song) 57–58, 181
Ives, Charles 8

Jackson, Michael 129
Jamaica 56
Jay-Z 7–8, 17, 135, 145–147, 175, 193–194
jazz 5, 11–13, 46, 53–56, 59, 96, 129–130, 132–136, 138–139, 148, 181–183
Jean Grae 144–148, 181, 183–184
Jesus Walks (Kanye West) 49, 177
"Jetpack" (Flobots song) 51
"Jigga That Nigga" (Jay-Z song) 193
Jonny 5 (Flobots rapper) 51–52
"Joy" (Talib Kweli song) 185

"(Just Step Prelude)" (Mobb Deep) 149–150
Juvenile (rapper) 189
juxtaposition 98, 180

Kanye West 3, 8, 17, 46–49, 53–56, 74, 99–100, 106, 110, 134–135, 169–170, 175–178, 182–183, 186–189, 194
"Karma" (Waka Flocka Flame song) 112–115, 164
Kendrick Lamar 4, 17, 35–37, 39, 50, 53, 67–68, 70, 72, 75, 170–172, 179, 188, 190
Kenny Rogers 136–137
"Kenny Rogers–Pharoahe Monch Dub Plate" (Wyclef Jean song) 137
key (harmonic key) 55, 69–72, 75, 84, 99, 110, 130, 160, 184
Khulami Phase (Lauryn Hill album) 190
"Kick in the Door" (Notorious B.I.G. song) 182
Killer Mike 49–50, 53–54
"Killing Me Softly" (Fugees song) 136
"Kim" (Eminem song) 128
"King Kunta" (Kendrick Lamar song) 179
King Tee 81, 90–93, 99–100
Kingdom Come (Jay-Z album) 193
Kivy 153–154
"Knockin' on Heaven's Door" (Wyclef Jean song) 137
Kool Herc 56
Krims, Adam 3–4, 72–75
kung-fu films 63
Kurupt (Tha Dogg Pound member) 126

Large Professor 129
Larkin, Philip 66
Late Registration (Kanye West album) 178
Lauryn Hill 136, 157, 181, 183, 190–193
Lauryn Hill Unplugged (Lauryn Hill album) 190
layering 21, 109, 158
leap (melody) 15, 72, 170–171, 186
"Leaving on a Jetplane" (John Denver song) 137
Led Zeppelin 167–168
"The Lesson" (The Roots song) 121
"Let It Be" (The Beatles song) 69
Lex Luger (rap producer) 112–114
The Life of Pablo (Kanye West album) 8, 175
Lifted (rap producer) 56

Index

"Like a Rolling Stone" (Bob Dylan song) 66–69
Lil Boosie 8
Lil Wayne 70, 110, 188–189, 191
linguistics 4, 72
"A Little Story" (Jean Grae song) 146
"Look Out for Detox" (Kendrick Lamar song) 17
loops 38–39, 114, 118–119, 120, 129, 150
"Lost Ones" (Lauryn Hill song) 157
Ludacris 122

"m.A.A.d city" (Kendrick Lamar song) 35–36, 170, 179
MacArthur Genius Award 8
Machaut 107
Macklemore 40, 196
The Magic Flute (Mozart opera) 139
Magna Carta ... Holy Grail (Jay-Z album) 193
mainstream and rap 5, 32, 127, 136
major keys 9, 15, 36, 42, 72, 79, 107, 114, 153, 160, 179
manufacture (of rap songs) 108, 111, 144
Marriage of Figaro (Mozart opera) 139
Marshall Mathers LP (Eminem album) 121
Marshall Mathers LP 2 (Eminem album) 126
Martinez, Josh 109
The Masquerade (Wyclef Jean album) 137
"Match the Name with the Voice" (Busta Rhymes song) 122
"Mathematics" (Mos Def song) 186
medley (song form) 46
"Meet Me Inside" (*Hamilton* song) 52–53
Mel-Man 157–158
melody 64–77; melodic entrances 35–37
"Mercy" (G.O.O.D. Music song) 56
metaphor 137, 180
metaphysics 12, 185
meter 46–56; complex meters (Flobots) 50–52; complex meters (*Hamilton*) 52–53; complex meters (Waka Flocka Flame) 112–115; compound meter 47–48, 50; Kanye West's meters 46–49; Kendrick Lamar's triplet meters 50; Killer Mike's triplet meters 49–50; iambic meter 86; *see also* time signatures
methodology 2, 4, 21, 72

metric transference 25, 60, 104, 164, 180
M.F. DOOM 18, 69–72, 75, 160, 162, 185–186
MIDI 141
Mike Posner 53–54
"A Milli" (Lil Wayne song) 189
"Mind Rain" (Joe Chambers song) 129
minor keys 15, 138, 173, 184
"Minority Report" (Jay-Z song) 7
Miranda, Lin-Manuel 8
Miseducation of Lauryn Hill (Lauryn Hill album) 190
misogyny 190, 193, 196
mixtapes 54, 99, 134, 145, 178, 189
"Mo' Money Mo' Problems" (Notorious B.I.G. song) 192
Mobb Deep 109, 117–120, 149
modulation 4, 9, 115, 129, 175, 191
"Moment of Clarity" (Jay-Z song) 193
"Momma" (Kendrick Lamar song) 4
"Money (That's What I Want)" (The Beatles song) 132
monophony 46, 113, 144, 147–151, 155, 157, 161, 163; live monophony 151–155
Mos Def 17–18, 117, 129, 134, 164, 172, 182, 186–187
motivic development 78–107; cyclical motives 78–85; linear motives 85–99; organic motives 99–107
Mozart, Wolfgang Amadeus 14, 75, 138–139, 160
musical accent 18, 20, 29, 33, 36–37, 58–62, 73–74, 79, 82, 84, 89–106, 111, 113–114, 146, 149, 150, 162, 172, 182, 191
musicianship 181, 183, 196
My Beautiful Dark Twisted Fantasy (Kanye West album) 178
"My Name Is" (Eminem song) 145, 172

Nas 74, 129–130, 135, 142, 146, 175, 179, 184–185, 197
"Nathaniel" (OutKast song) 149
The Neptunes 145
"Never Enough" (Eminem song) 33–35, 128
NIKO IS (rapper) 185
"93 'Til Infinity" (Souls of Mischief song) 134
No My Name Is Jeffrey (Young Thug album) 190
"No Woman No Cry" (Bob Marley song) 136

Index

"No Woman No Cry" (Fugees song) 136, 189
Noah "40" Shebib (rap producer) 109
NoClue (rapper) 169
notation 1, 4, 11–31, 38, 48, 51, 54–55, 57–58, 62, 73, 83, 100, 102–103, 105, 164; accuracy in notation 13–21, 73, 107, 182; ambiguity in notation 17, 22; archival notation 12–21, 73; compositional 16–19; orthographic notations 18, 21, 33; slurs (notation) 20, 105; typographical notation 20, 21, 38, 116, 124
Notorious B.I.G. 58, 129, 134, 146–147, 161–163, 175, 179–180, 182
N.W.A. 6
"N.Y. State of Mind" (Nas song) 129–130

Obama, Barack 8
objectification 190
octave 15, 170
"Octopus' Garden" (The Beatles song) 69
Odd Future (rap collective) 111
offbeat rhythms 63, 103
"Oh What a Night" (Wyclef Jean song) 137, 189
onomatopoeia 112, 192
opera 65, 75, 77, 138–139, 168
oral cultures 17, 19, 130
orchestration 120, 129, 136, 144–165, 176; borrowed orchestration (Jean Grae) 144–146
Organix (The Roots album) 40
OutKast 18, 49–50, 57, 149, 179, 198
outro (song section) 116, 122, 126, 128
"Over the Rainbow" (Harburg and Arlen song) 71
"Overreact" (Kanye West song) 178

Page, Jimmy (Led Zeppelin guitarist) 167–168
Papa Smurf (rapper) 164
parody 125, 161, 177, 194
Pärt, Arvo 106
"Party Up (Up in Here)" (DMX song) 83
passaggio 170–171, 175
"Paul" (series of Eminem songs) 126–128
Paul McCartney 170
"Paul Rosenberg" (Eminem and Paul Rosenberg song) 127
percussion 12–16, 73

performance practice 108–143
persona 147, 151, 155
Pete Rock 129
"Peter Piper" (Run-D.M.C. song) 32–33, 163–164
Pharoahe Monch 52, 56–59, 137, 162, 180–181
Phrenology (The Roots album) 40
piano 20, 118–119, 129, 153, 166, 172, 174–175, 186
Pierrot Lunaire (Arnold Schoenberg piece) 65–66
Pink Floyd 136, 138
pitch 5, 12, 14–16, 22, 33, 64–67, 69–71, 73–77, 79, 99, 146, 156, 158–160, 170–172, 178, 191
"Planet Rock" (Afrika Bambaataa song) 42, 163
"Please Mister Postman" (The Beatles song) 132
"Poetic Justice" (Kendrick Lamar song) 36–37
poetry 32, 115, 126, 145, 147, 151, 156, 177, 180, 187, 192, 197
polyphony 11, 12, 120, 147, 157–161
polyrhythms 4, 12, 73–74, 184
pop (music genre) 4, 71, 73, 129, 145, 183
portamento 69
Porter, Cole 133
Pras (Fugees rapper) 136
Prodigy (Mobb Deep member) 109, 117–119, 149
producer 35, 37–38, 53, 86, 109–112, 141–142, 147, 150, 157, 164, 173, 178, 189–190; rapper-producer relationships 108–112
production 108–110, 115, 140, 144, 147–148, 169, 172, 178–179, 189
Prophit (battle rapper) 154–155, 173
prosody 11, 20, 32–33, 57–59, 66–70, 72–75, 90, 92, 96, 102, 105, 111, 149–152, 154, 173, 182
psychedelic (music genre) 136, 138
Public Enemy 56
Pulitzer Prize 8, 175
punch line 59, 93, 110, 149, 177, 185
puns 98, 110, 151–152, 177, 194
Purple Haze (Cam'ron album) 198
"Pussycat" (Wyclef Jean song) 138

Q-Tip (A Tribe Called Quest member) 129
quantization 47, 149–150
quotation (musical) 33, 65, 137–140

Das Racist (rap group) 109
Radiohead (rock group) 131
raga 60
Rah Digga 191
Raisin' Hell (Run-D.M.C. album) 163, 192
Rakim 109
Ramsey, Guthrie 3
"Rap God" (Eminem song) 13, 16, 22–30, 148, 183
Rappa Ternt Sanga (T-Pain album) 71
"Rapper's Delight" (Sugarhill Gang song) 136
"A Rat's Nest" (Thom Yorke song) 131
"Ready or Not" (Fugees song) 191
Rebel XD 169
recitative (vocal style) 64, 68, 75–77
"Re:DeFinition" (Mos Def and Talib Kweli song) 164, 185
referentiality 33–35
refrain (song section) 127
Reich, Steve 8
Relapse: Refill (Eminem album) 127
remakes (song form) 128–143; Wyclef Jean's remakes 135–138
remix (song form) 4, 53, 130–140
repertoire 130, 135, 139
"Represent" (Elzhi song) 130, 185
"Represent" (Nas song) 130, 185
"Return of the 'G'" (OutKast song) 57–58
Das Rheingold (Wagner opera) 168
rhymes 29–31, 36, 39, 73, 111, 119, 122, 129, 151, 164, 174, 177–178, 182, 186–187
rhythm 11–64; constrained rhythms 24–26; flam (drum rhythm) 79, 84; microtiming 47, 51, 100, 149, 156, 184, 181; noctuplets 1, 13–19, 30, 57, 181; non-subdivisional rhythms 23–24; presto rhythms 22–23; quintuplet rhythms 18; shuffle rhythm 53–55, 101, 181; sextuplet rhythms 9, 48–49; strophic rhythms 27–29, 30–31; swing rhythms 53–56; trochaic rhythms 37
"Ridin'" (Hot Boys song) 188
"Rigamortus" (Kendrick Lamar song) 179
Der Ring des Nibelungen (Wagner opera) 168
Rising Down (The Roots album) 40
ritardando 149–150
"Rob Quaters" (Ludacris skit) 122
rock (music genre) 7, 11, 42, 73, 129, 131–140, 163

"Role Model" (Eminem song) 145
"Roll Over Beethoven" (Chuck Berry song) 132
"Roll Over Beethoven" (The Beatles song) 132
Romanticism 13, 15, 138–139, 146, 190
rondo form 4, 124–125
Rone 151–156, 173–174
The Roots 6, 40, 45–46, 121, 148, 155, 179
Rosenberg, Paul 126–127
Run-D.M.C. 32–33, 163–164
"Rush" (Talib Kweli song) 17
RZA 109

Salvador Dalí 186
samba 190
sampling 21, 27, 38, 56, 70, 129–142, 146, 178
satire 125, 161, 177, 194
Saul Williams 57
scale (musical) 13–16, 42, 64, 67, 71, 75–77, 88, 150, 156, 160–161, 167, 175, 181, 191
"Scenario" (A Tribe Called Quest song) 191–192
Schoenberg, Arnold 3, 8, 59, 65–66, 69–70, 75–76, 107
Schubert, Franz 14
Schumann, Robert 138
Score (The Fugees album) 136, 191
Scott-Heron, Gil 56–57, 162
"The Seed/Melting Pot/Web" (The Roots song) 46
semantics 19, 23, 32, 159, 163, 165, 170, 181, 184, 186, 192
sequencer 149–150
serialism 25
Serrano, Shea 189
"The Session (Longest Posse Cut in History)" (The Roots song) 46
Shakira 190
Shaw, Caroline 8, 175
"Sherane a.k.a. Master's Splinter Daughter" (The Kendrick Lamar song) 36
shibboleths in genres 107, 130
"Shook Ones Pt. II" (Mobb Deep song) 117–119
"Simon Says" (Pharoahe Monch song) 137
Sinatra, Frank 132–133
"Sing About Me, I'm Dying of Thirst" (Kendrick Lamar song) 172
singing (vocal style) 65–72

Index

"Skew It on the Bar-B" (OutKast song) 110
skits (song form) 111, 121–123, 125–128, 142, 183; skits (Eminem) 125–128
Slick Rick 177
Slimkid3 38–39
Slim Shady LP (Eminem album) 126–127, 129, 145
"Slow Jamz" (Kanye West song) 74, 169
Smokey Robinson 132
snare drum 15–16, 43, 85–86, 110, 115, 118, 129, 136, 156
Snoop Dogg 98, 109
"Some L.A. Niggaz" (Dr. Dre song) 82–99
"Someone To Watch Over Me" (Gershwin song) 133
sonata form 110–111
soprano (vocal range) 168
The Soul Children 129
soul (musical genre) 129, 136, 178
Souls of Mischief 134–135
spinto (vocal weight) 174–175
sprechstimme 56–59, 65–72, 76, 149, 162, 184
stamina 167–169, 175, 183
standard deviation 44–45, 158
standards (jazz form) 132–133
statistical frequency 39–44
statistics 40, 42–46
"Stay Cool" (The Roots song) 41
stereophonic sound 69, 118, 128, 134–135, 141–142, 156, 164
Steve Miller Band 129
storytelling 178, 184, 187–188
strophic form 25, 28, 29, 31, 35
structural elision 104–105, 107, 125–126, 179
structural truncation 128, 130, 150
structure (musical) 108–143; innovations in structure 115–117, 128; outliers in structure 46; track length and structure 45–46
studio 42, 70, 126, 129, 134, 137, 140–141, 148–150, 152, 155–158, 168, 173, 177, 179
style (musical) 3, 19, 30, 39, 57, 63, 65, 68, 70, 73–74, 136–137, 146, 149, 152, 158, 162, 165, 169–170, 177–178, 180, 183, 190–191
"Style Wars" (Jean Grae song) 184
subdominant chords 160
Sugarhill Gang 136
Supa Nat 149–150

"Swimming Pools (Drank)" (Kendrick Lamar song) 36, 171
syllables 15, 20, 51, 80, 83, 150, 164, 169–170, 178, 185
Symbolists (school of poets) 194
symmetry 37, 52, 119–120, 149–150, 158, 182
symphony 78, 85, 106, 138
syncopation 25–30, 34–35, 49, 53, 60, 62, 85, 99, 103, 111, 162 192
syntax and melodic phrasing 19–20, 73–74, 81, 180, 184, 186
synthesizers 115, 144, 145, 155

T-Pain 68–75, 88, 191
"Takeover" (Jay-Z song) 135
Talib Kweli 17–18, 164, 181, 185, 193
taxonomies (of rap flow) 70–75
techniques (of rhythm) 18, 35–36, 45, 60, 65, 73, 76, 121, 123, 129, 152–153, 157, 161, 167, 180, 183
technology in rap 140–141
tempo 18, 22–23, 25, 39–48, 52, 59, 83, 101, 115, 122, 148, 150–155, 162
tempo range 39–45; Black Thought's 39–42; Rap's variation in tempo range 44–45; Waka Flocka Flame's 42–44
tempo rubato 149, 152–155
tenor (vocal range) 153, 168
tension 15, 72, 81, 83, 96, 110, 118, 160, 172
tessitura 170–175
text-setting (syllabic) 19, 72
texture (music) 8, 35–37, 46, 52, 57, 86, 88, 90, 96, 100, 110–112, 114–115, 118–120, 122–124, 144, 147–153, 155–164, 168, 170, 176, 195; background 39, 52, 75, 83, 92, 139–140, 148, 158, 164, 167; foreground, 92, 98, 111, 138–140, 158
themes 15, 38, 78–85, 88–89, 94–106, 115, 119, 127, 136–139, 149, 156, 179
Things Fall Apart (The Roots album) 6, 40
31 Minutes to Takeoff (Miker Posner album) 53
Thomson, Virgil 8
"'03 Electric Relaxation" (Kanye West song) 134
"03 Til Infinity" (Consequence song) 134
through-composition 29–30, 37, 107, 115–117, 120, 130, 150, 183–184, 188
"Through the Wire" (Kanye West song) 177

"Til' I Collapse" (Eminem song) 119
"Till There Was You" (Meredith Wilson song) 132
"Till There Was You" (The Beatles song) 132
timbre 15, 150, 159, 171–175, 179, 181, 185, 187, 189–192; timbral flexibility 172–173, 179, 191
Time Bomb (rapper) 85–99
time signatures 9, 16, 37, 47–52, 61, 65, 86, 92, 113, 143, 150, 173; *see also* meters
Tipping Point (The Roots album) 40, 155
toasting in Jamaican music 56
Tom Jones 138
tonality in rap 15, 66–71, 75, 160
"Torture" (Wu-Tang song) 125
trailing (rhythmic technique) 12, 17–18, 47, 51, 74, 100, 158, 193; *see also* microtiming
Traktor 40, 43
transcription *see* notation
"Travellin' Man" (DJ Honda song) 172
Trenchtown, Jamaica 56
A Tribe Called Quest 134–135
Triple F Life: Friends, Fans, and Family (Waka Flocka Flame album) 43
triplet rhythms 4, 9, 47–50, 53–55, 100–102, 105, 170, 181, 183, 187
Twista 74–75, 169–170
2Pac 17, 175, 177, 183, 186–188, 190, 197
2 Live Crew 6

"U Don't Know" (Jay-Z song) 145–146
"U Know" (Kanye West song) 47–50, 99–100, 105–106; ultra-delayed entrances 37–38
"Unconditional Love" (2Pac song) 188
The Underachievers 185

variations on a theme 80, 138–140
verse (song section) 14, 17–18, 27–28, 30–31, 33, 35–36, 38, 46, 53–54, 57–58, 60–63, 74, 80–81, 86, 88–90, 94, 99, 103–104, 106, 111, 116–121, 124–127, 130, 153, 173, 178, 182, 185–189, 191–192
vocables 112, 114
vocal range 170–171
vocal register 66, 83, 118, 129, 156–158, 171–172, 182
voices 4, 35–36, 46, 56, 64–66, 70–71, 87, 110, 112, 114, 118–122, 125, 127, 136, 144, 147–148, 150–151, 155–163, 166–167, 170–175, 181–182, 187
"Vomitspit" (M.F. DOOM song) 18, 69
Vonte Skinner 8

Wagner, Richard 168
Waka Flocka Flame 42–46, 112–115, 164
"Walk In" (Lil Wayne song) 188
Washington, Ned 133
Watts Prophets 56
"The Way I Am" (Eminem song) 24–25, 29, 127
"We Trying to Stay Alive" (Wyclef Jean song) 136, 189
Webb, Daniel 154
Western music 6, 11–14, 16–17, 21–22, 32, 53, 61, 71, 73, 85, 106–107, 145, 148, 157, 159–161, 165, 167
"What" (Eve song) 60–61
"What They Do" (The Roots song) 41
"What's Beef" (Mos Def song) 117, 186
"What's New Pussycat" (Tom Jones song) 138
"White America" (Eminem song) 127
"Who Ride wit Us" (Kurupt song) 126
"Who Shot Ya" (Notorious B.I.G. song) 129, 134
"Who Will Survive in America" (Kanye West song) 56
"The Whole World" (OutKast and Killer Mike song) 49–50, 53–54
"Why Shouldn't I" (Cole Porter song) 133
"Wicked Ways" (Eminem song) 128
Williams, Juan 7, 32, 74
Williams, Justin 109
Wilson, Meredith 132
"Wish You Were Here" (Pink Floyd song) 138
"Wish You Were Here" (Wyclef Jean song) 138
With the Beatles (The Beatles album) 132
"Without a Doubt" (The Roots song) 110
"Without Me" (Eminem song) 28–29
workstation (digital audio) 149, 157
"The World Is Yours" (Tip Mix) (Nas song) 135
"Wrath of Kane" (Big Daddy Kane song) 61–63
Wu-Tang Clan 63, 109, 111, 122, 125, 201
Wyclef Jean 115–119, 135–138, 142, 178, 188–191

Index

Xzibit 78

YG Hootie 164
Yorke, Thom 131
"You Don't Know" (Jean Grae song) 145–146
"You Don't Want It" (Jean Grae) 145–146
"You Really Got a Hold on Me" (Smokey Robinson) 132
"You Really Got a Hold on Me" (The Beatles song) 132
Young, Victor 133
Young Thug 70, 190–191

Zimmerman, Joel 141
Zorn, John 8
"Zulu Nation Throwdown" (Afrika Bambaataa song) 42, 63

www.ingramcontent.com/pod-product-compliance
Ingram Content Group UK Ltd.
Pitfield, Milton Keynes, MK11 3LW, UK
UKHW041954140426
5217IPUK00015B/796